AS CONSCIOUSNESS

IS HARNESSED TO FLESH

AS CONSCIOUSNESS

IS HARNESSED TO FLESH

·

Journals and Notebooks

1964–1980

Susan Sontag

EDITED BY DAVID RIEFF

Farrar Straus Giroux

New York

Farrar, Straus and Giroux
18 West 18th Street, New York 10011

Copyright © 2012 by David Rieff
Preface copyright © 2012 by David Rieff
All rights reserved
Distributed in Canada by D&M Publishers, Inc.
Printed in the United States of America
First edition, 2012

Grateful acknowledgment is made to David Goldstein and Penguin Classics for permission to reprint "Man runs towards the grave," by Samuel ha-Nagid, published in The Jewish Poets of Spain; and to John Scagliotti, administrator, the Kopkind Colony, for permission to reprint Andrew Kopkind's notes.

Library of Congress Cataloging-in-Publication Data
Sontag, Susan, 1933–2004.
As consciousness is harnessed to flesh : journals and notebooks, 1964–1980 / Susan Sontag ; edited by David Rieff. — 1st ed.
    p.   cm.
ISBN 978-0-374-10076-6 (alk. paper)
    1. Sontag, Susan, 1933–2004—Notebooks, sketchbooks, etc.
2. Authors, American—20th century—Diaries.
I. Rieff, David.   II. Title.

PS3569.O6547 Z46 2012
818'.5409—dc23
[B]

                                        2011041210

www.fsgbooks.com

1   3   5   7   9   10   8   6   4   2

Slips of the pen and other tiny errors have been silently corrected in the interest of clarity.

Contents

Preface

In the first years of the 1990s, my mother toyed desultorily with the idea of writing an autobiography. Since she was someone who had always preferred to write as little as possible about herself directly, this surprised me. "To write mainly about myself," she once told an interviewer in *The Boston Review*, "seems to me a rather indirect route to what I want to write about . . . I have never been convinced that my tastes, my fortunes and misfortunes have any particularly exemplary character."

My mother said this in 1975, when she was still in the midst of undergoing a cruelly severe regimen of chemotherapy that the doctors hoped would, but, as at least one of them told me at the time, did not really expect to, grant her a long remission, let alone cure, the metastatic, stage-4 breast cancer she had been diagnosed with the previous year (this was still the era when the family members of ill people were told more than the patients themselves). Characteristically, once she was able to write again, she chose to write the series of essays for *The New York Review of Books* that would later be published in book form as *On Photography*. Not only is she all but wholly absent in any autobiographical sense from that work, she barely appears even in *Illness as Metaphor*, a book she would certainly never have written had it not been for her experience of the stigmatization that came with cancer in those days and, while it has lessened, still exists today, usually in the form of self-stigmatization.

I can think of only four occasions when she was straight-forwardly autobiographical as a writer. The first is her short story "Project for a Trip to China," published in 1973 on the eve of her first visit there. In large measure, the piece is a meditation on her own childhood and on her father, a busi-nessman who spent most of his woefully short adult life in China, and who died there when my mother (who never ac-companied her parents to the British concession in what is now called Tianjin, instead being looked after in New York and New Jersey by relatives and her nanny) was four. The second is the short story "Unguided Tour," published in *The New Yorker* in 1977. The third is "Pilgrimage," published in 1987, also in *The New Yorker*. It is a memoir of a visit she'd paid as an adolescent in Los Angeles in 1947 to Thomas Mann, then living in exile in Pacific Palisades. But "Pilgrimage" is first and foremost an exercise in admiration for the writer my mother had then admired above all others; characteristically, the self-portrait comes in a distant second. It was an encounter, as she wrote, of "an embarrassed, fervid, literature-intoxicated child and a god in exile." Lastly, there are the autobiographical passages at the end of my mother's third novel, *The Volcano Lover*, published in 1992, where she speaks directly, and in a way she never did either in her published work or even in inter-views, about being a woman, and a few glancing childhood reminiscences in her last novel, *In America*, published in 2000.

"My life is my capital, the capital of my imagination," she told that same *Boston Review* interviewer, adding that she liked to "colonize" it. It was a curious, and uncharacteristic, turn of phrase for my mother, who was profoundly uninter-ested in money, and whom I can never remember ever using a financial metaphor in private conversation. And yet it also seems to me an entirely accurate description of her way of being a writer. It was also why I was so surprised that she would even consider writing an autobiography, which, for her, to continue the capitalist analogies, would have been not to live off the fruits, the proceeds of one's capital, but rather to dip into it—the height of unreason, be the capital in question money or material for novels, stories, and essays.

In the end, nothing came of the idea. My mother wrote *The Volcano Lover*, and, in doing so, felt she had made the return to being a novelist that had been her ambition even when she was writing her best essays. The success of the book gave her a confidence she herself conceded she had lacked since her second novel, *Death Kit*, had been published in 1967 to very mixed reviews that had bitterly disappointed her. And after *The Volcano Lover* came my mother's long engagement with Bosnia and with besieged Sarajevo—eventually an all-consuming passion for her. After that, she returned to fiction, with no further mention, as far as I am aware, anyway, of a memoir.

In my more extravagant moments, I sometimes think that my mother's journals, of which this is the second of three volumes, are not just the autobiography she never got around to writing (had she done so, I imagine something highly literary and episodic, a cousin to John Updike's *Self-Consciousness*, which was a book she admired greatly), but the great autobiographical novel she never cared to write. To pursue the conceit along its conventional trajectory, the first volume of the journals, *Reborn*, would be the bildungsroman, the education novel—her *Buddenbrooks*, to cite Mann's great achievement, or, on a lesser literary plane, her *Martin Eden*, a novel by Jack London that my mother read as an adolescent and spoke of with fondness until the end of her life. This current volume, which I have chosen to call *As Consciousness Is Harnessed to Flesh*, a line plucked from one of the journal entries contained within it, would be the novel of vigorous, successful adult-hood. About the third and final volume, I will not speak for now.

The problem with this account is that my mother, by her own proud and fervent admission, was a student her entire life. Of course, in *Reborn*, the very young Susan Sontag was quite consciously creating, or, rather, re-creating herself as, the person she wanted to be, far from the world in which she was born and in which she grew up. This volume does not involve the physical leaving of the southern Arizona and Los Angeles of her childhood for the University of Chicago, Paris, New York, and fulfillment (emphatically not happiness, which is something altogether different and, I fear, was not a well from which my mother ever was able to drink deeply). But the great success as a writer that my mother chronicles in this volume, the company of writers, artists, and intellectuals of every cast and persuasion—from Lionel Trilling to Paul Bowles, Jasper Johns to Joseph Brodsky, and Peter Brook to György Konrád—and the ability to travel anywhere, virtually at will, which had been her most cherished dream as a child, did not make her less of a student. If anything, it made her more of one.

For me, one of the most striking things about this volume is the way in which my mother moves between different worlds. Some of this had to do with her deep ambivalence, and with contradictions in her thought that, to me, far from diminishing it, in fact makes it deeper, more interesting, and, in an ultimate sense, quite resistant to . . . well, to interpreta-tion. But a more important element, I think, is that while my mother was not exactly known for suffering fools gladly (and her definition of fool was, to say the least, ecumenical), with people she genuinely admired she became not the teacher she liked to be so much of the time but rather the student. That is why for me the strongest parts of *As Consciousness Is Harnessed to Flesh* are its exercises in admiration—of many people, but perhaps most poignantly, and in their very different ways, of Jasper Johns and of Joseph Brodsky. To read these passages is, indeed, to better understand those of my mother's essays—I think particularly of those on Walter Benjamin, on Roland Barthes, and on Elias Canetti—that were themselves first and foremost acts of homage.

I like to think that this volume can also be fairly called a political bildungsroman, precisely in the sense of a person's education, her coming to maturity. In the early parts of the book, my mother is at once angry and overwhelmed by the follies of the American war in Vietnam, against which she became a prominent activist. I think even she, in retrospect, would have winced at some of the things she said during her visits to Hanoi under U.S. bombardment. I have included them without hesitation, though, just as I have included many other entries on diverse subjects that either worry me for her sake or cause me pain of my own. Where Vietnam is concerned, I will only add that the horrors of war that made her go off to an extreme were anything but figments of her imagination. She may have been unwise, but the war was still the unspeakable monstrosity she thought it was at the time.

My mother never recanted her opposition to the war. But she did come to regret, and, unlike so many of her peers (I will be discreet here, but the discerning reader will know the American writers of my mother's generation to whom I refer), to publicly recant, her faith in the emancipatory possibilities of Communism, not just in its Soviet, Chinese, or Cuban incarnations, but as a system. I cannot say for certain whether she would have had this change of both heart and mind had it not been for her profound relationship with Joseph Brodsky—perhaps the only sentimental relation of equals that she had in her entire life. Brodsky's importance to her, despite their estrangement during the last period of his life, cannot be overstated, whether aesthetically, politically, or humanly.

On her deathbed in Memorial Hospital in New York, on the penultimate day of her life, as she gasped for air, for life, and the headlines were full of Asian tsunamis, she spoke of only two people—her mother and Joseph Brodsky. To paraphrase Byron, his heart was her tribunal.

Her heart was one often broken, and much of this volume is the elaboration of romantic loss. In a sense, that means it gives a false impression of my mother's life in that she tended to write more in her journals when she was unhappy, most when she was bitterly unhappy, and least when she was all right. But while the proportions may not be quite right, I think her unhappiness in love was as much a part of her as was the profound sense of fulfillment she derived from her writing, and the passion she brought, particularly when she was not writing something, to her life as a perpetual student, as a kind of ideal reader of great literature, and ideal appreciator of great art, an ideal spectator of great theater, film, and music. And so, true to herself, that is, to her life as she lived it, the journals move from loss to erudition, and then back again. That it was not the life I would have wished for her is neither here nor there.

My edit of this volume of my mother's journals has been immensely improved by Robert Walsh's generous willingness to review the final manuscript. In doing so, he caught a large number of errors and lacunae in the draft.

Responsibility for remaining mistakes is, of course, mine and mine alone.

AS CONSCIOUSNESS

IS HARNESSED TO FLESH

1964

5/5/64

The right hand = the hand that is aggressive, the hand that masturbates. Therefore, to prefer the left hand! . . . To romanticize it, to sentimentalize it!

·

I am Irene's [*the Cuban-American playwright María Irene Fornés—SS's lover for a time in Paris in 1957 and then her partner in New York between 1959 and 1963*] Maginot Line.

Her very "life" depends on rejecting me, on holding the line against me.

Everything has been deposited on me. I am the scapegoat.

[*This entry is emphasized by a vertical line in the margin:*] As long as she is occupied in warding me off, she doesn't have to face herself, her own problems.

I can't convince her—persuade her—with reason—that it is otherwise.

Any more than she could convince me—when we lived to-gether—not to need her, clutch at her, depend on her.

•

There is nothing in it for me now—no joy, only sorrow. Why do I hang on?

Because I don't understand. I don't *really* accept the change in Irene. I think I can reverse it—by explaining, by demon-strating that I am good for her.

But it is as indispensable for her to reject me—as it has been indispensable for me to hold on to her.

•

"Whatever doesn't kill me, makes me stronger." [*a paraphrase of Goethe*]

There is no love, no charity, no kindness for me in Irene. For me, to me, she becomes cruel and shallow.

The symbiotic tie is broken. She cast it aside.

Now she only presents "bills." Inez, Joan, Carlos!

I have damaged her ego, she says. I and Alfred [*the American writer Alfred Chester*].

(The inflated, fragile ego.)
And no repentance, no apology for, no change from what was truly damaging in my behavior will appease her, or heal her.

Remember how she received the "revelation" at the New Yorker [*a Manhattan movie theater that showed foreign and revival films, where SS went several times a week in the 1960s*] two weeks ago!

"I am a stone wall," she says. "A rock." It's true.

There is no responsiveness, no forgiveness in her. To me, only hardness. Deafness. Silence. Even a grunt of assent "violates" her.

Rejecting me is the shell Irene constructs around herself. The protective "wall."

•

—Why I didn't nurse David:

Mother didn't nurse me. (I vindicate her by doing it to David—it's ok, I do it to my own child)

I had a difficult birth, caused M[other] a lot of pain; she didn't nurse me; she stayed in bed for a month after.

David was big (like me)—a lot of pain. I wanted to be knocked out, not to know anything; *it never occurred to me* to nurse him; I stayed in bed for a month after.

•

. . .

Loving = the sensation of being in an intense form
Like pure oxygen (as distinct from air)

•

Henry James—
All based on a particular stylization of consciousness
Self & world (money)—no body consciousness, among many
ways of being-in-the-world which he omits.

•

Edith Wharton's biography. Banal sensibility capped, periodically, by strong intelligent conclusion. But her intelligence
doesn't transform the events—i.e. disclose their complexity. It
only supervenes upon the banal telling of them.

•

. . .

8/5/64

Ontological anxiety, "Weltangst." The world blank—or
crumbling, shredding. People are wind-up dolls. I'm afraid.

"The gift" has meant to me: I wouldn't buy this for myself (it's
nice, a luxury, not necessary) but I buy it for you. Denial of self.

There are people in the world.

A constriction in the chest, tears, a scream that feels as if it
would be endless if I let it out.

I should go away for a year.

8/6/64

To say a feeling, an impression is to diminish it—expel it.

But sometimes feelings are too strong: passions, obsessions. Like romantic love. Or grief. Then one needs to speak, or one would burst.

•

The desire for reassurance. And, equally, to be reassured. (The itch to ask whether I'm still loved; and the itch to say, I love you, half-fearing that the other has forgotten, since the last time I said it.)
"Quelle connerie" [*"What idiocy"*]

•

I valued professional competence + force, think (since age four?) that that was, at least, more attainable than being lovable "just as a person."

•

I can't drive out my obsession with I[rene]—my grief, my despair, my longing—with another love. I'm not capable of loving anyone now. I'm being "loyal."

But the obsession must be drained, somehow. I must force some of that energy elsewhere.

If I could get started on another novel . . .

•

From Mother, I learned: "I love you" means "I don't love anyone else." The horrid woman was always challenging my feelings, telling me I had made her unhappy, that I was "cold."

As if children owe their parents love + gratification! They don't. Though parents owe these things to their children—exactly like physical care.

•

From Mother: "I love you. Look. I'm unhappy."

She made me feel: Happiness is disloyalty.

She hid her happiness, challenged me to make her happy—if I could.

Therapy is deconditioning [*SS's therapist at the time, Diana*] (Kemeny)

•

Mary McCarthy's grin—grey hair—low-fashion red + blue-print suit. Club woman gossip. She *is* [*her novel*] *The Group.* She's nice to her husband.

•

Fear of the other going away: fear of abandonment

Fear of *my* going away: fear of retaliation by the other (*also* abandonment—but as revenge for the rejection of going away).

8/8/64

I have a wider range as a human being than as a writer. (With some writers, it's the opposite.) Only a fraction of me is available to be turned into art.

·

A miracle is just an accident, with fancy trappings.

Change—life—comes through accidents.

·

My loyalty to the past—my most dangerous trait, the one that has cost me most.

·

Self-respect. It would make me lovable. And it's the secret of good sex.

·

The best things in SW [*the philosopher Simone Weil*] are about attention. Against both the will + the categorical imperative.

·

One can never ask anyone to change a feeling.

•

8/18/64   London

"Variety of Uniformities makes compleat Beauty."—Sir Christopher Wren

Buster Keaton: Candide with a frontal lobotomy

[*Description of the American novelist James Jones:*] Shoulders coming out of his ears

Ectoplasm is (displaced) seminal fluid—19th c. mediums are aberrant symptom of the wakening of "modern" female sexuality
cf. [Henry James's] *The Bostonians*, Padmore book

"The psychology and physiology of 'the instant'"

Mary McCarthy can do anything with her smile; she can even smile with it.

•

A brain-damaged woman who—even after she'd mostly re-covered—couldn't follow a movie.

The Beatles, their quaternity.

Damp mollusks of 12-year old girls.

Dexamyls [*a form of amphetamine on which SS became dependent for writing in the mid-1960s and which she used until the early 1980s, though in diminishing doses*] are called, in England, "Purple Hearts" (they're purple, not green [*as in the U.S.*]—kids take them 20 at a time, with Coke . . . Then (lunch hour) pop into a "cave" (nobody over 21 admitted) and [dance the] Watusi

•

Hemingway wrote a parody of Sherwood Anderson's *Winesburg, Ohio*; it's his 2nd novel, *Torrents of Spring* (1926), just before *The Sun Also Rises*.

•

Arnold Geulincx (1624–69), the Belgian philospher—follower of Descartes—[Samuel] Beckett, as a student, read him— [Geulincx] holds that a reasonable man is nowhere free, except in his own mind—doesn't waste energy trying to control his body in the external world.

•

Adjectives:

Punctuate	(Punctate?)
Simian	Vermillion
Impudent	Crafty
Whooping	Glottal
Laconic	Unnerved
Besotted	Cerulean
Gritty	Stout
Cracking	Vivid

Septic	Feckless
Ruttish	Ogival
Aporetic	
Terse	Toothy
Barmy	Streamlined

. . .

8/19/64

Story: "The infinite system of Couples"

. . .

•

Cockney slang: rhyming plus knight's move to the side
Breasts = Bristol (city > titty)
Teeth = Hampteads (heath > teeth)

Verbs:

Slash	Slip away
Flake	Barter
Judder	Tamper
Spurt	Blunt
Sprint	Bash
Jar	Whimper

. . .

•

Horrifying to feel one's integument (skin) pierced

Annealed . . .

•

[*the American writer William S.*] Burroughs:
Language = control
"Terrorist" attacks on language (cut-up method)
cf. [*The French experimental writer Raymond*] Roussel—
Comment J'ai Écrit . . .

Escape into space (sci-fi) vs. History

[*The*] *Soft Machine*
Nova Express
Naked Lunch
Dead Fingers Talk

•

"Bumtrinkets"—bits of feces stuck to hairs of anus (cf. Cicely
Bumtrinket in [*the seventeenth-century dramatist Thomas*]
Dekker's *Shoemaker's Holiday*)
Ditto for "dingleberries"

•

Nouns:

Panache	Armature
Parameter	Scuffle
Neologism	Cistern

Guts	Persiflage
Integument	Tempo
Snap brim fedora	Furore
Gruel	Imbroglio

. . .

•

"Une incertitude de jeunesse" [*"youthful uncertainty"*] (of [*Bertolt Brecht's first play*] *Baal*)

•

Sci-fi essay

1. Films better than the books—why?
2. Content

Figure of the scientist as Satanist ([Goethe's] *Faust*, Poe, [Nathaniel] Hawthorne)

- treatment of the scientist as one who releases forces which if not controlled for good could destroy man himself
- cf. old vision of scientist (Prospero, etc.) as a dotty magician only partly in control of the forces in which he dabbles.

Sci-fi as modern allegory:
Modern attitude toward madness (being "taken over")
Modern attitude toward death (incineration, extinction)

•

Rich fund of metaphors (Jonathan [*Miller, British writer and director*]) from:

1. Computers
2. Hydraulics
3. Photography; optics
4. Physiology of crustaceans
5. Architecture
6. Chess + military strategy

[*Examples of Miller's use of these metaphors:*]
"Like the kick-start on a motor-bike—now I'm going on my own."
"Yards of prose."
"Final suicidal Pickett's charge against . . ."
"Chromium-plated with charm."

•

Jonathan: the intersection between psychiatry and aesthetics

. . .

•

British pops

    Lonnie Donegan
    Chris Barber
    . . .
    Cliff Richard + his Shadows
    Cilla [Black]
    Helen Shapiro
    . . .

Mersey [*Beat*]:
Beatles
Dave Clark 5
The Rolling Stones
The Beasts
The Pretty Things
The Birds
. . .

Dusty Springfield

•

. . .

Sequence of a migraine:

Loss of perspective (flattening out) > "fortification phenomena" (white lines—zooming in from side; one-sided) > nausea and vomiting > acute hemicrania
(holding site is always part of acute pain)

•

SMELL is the largest sensory area in the brain and also the most primitive
Very powerful but not articulated—can't do anything with it
  (just *naming*)
All accent, no syntax
Smelling gives one a knowledge of sensation rinsed clean of
  thought (unlike hearing and seeing)

Osmology, as opposed to logology

•

[*The French writer Nathalie*] Sarraute—

Tropismes (first book)—something like "prose poems"—
Sarraute calls them that.
First one written in 1932.
Volume was published in 1939 (Denoël), republished by
Éditions de Minuit in 1957, with 6 more written between
1939 + 1941

This is her form!—her texture is anti-novelistic, though she's
decided to write "novels" + launched an important critique
of the novel on the basis of her method.

•

Sperlonga—beach near Rome

•

. . .

In old age, the cereberal arteries silt up—gradual diminution
of blood supply to the brain

8/20/64

. . .

Influence of photography on painting:

1. Off-centering: main subject is in a corner
   ([*the Italian director Michelangelo*] Antonioni,
   [*the Swiss-American photographer*] Robert Frank).

2. Figures in motion: [*the nineteenth-century
    English photographer Eadweard*] Muybridge.
    Previously, all figures are either at rest (in repose)
    or at the end of a motion (e.g. farthest the limb
    can be extended)

Compare dancing figures in Breughel with Degas's *Horses at
Longchamps*

3. Understanding of focus: eye can't see focusing,
    since it does so automatically, it's a function of
    attention.

All painting prior to photography is in even focus. As the painter's
eye traveled from plane to plane, each went into focus.

•

Quality of film [stock] is important—whether grainy or not;
old stock or new ([Stanley] Kubrick used WWII unused newsreel stock for War Room sequences in *Dr. Strangelove*)

•

Mont Blanc fountain pen (Fr.)
Italic script (get book on)
Read Poe on "Magnetism," and "The Imp of the Perverse."

•

[*This is highlighted:*] Off-centering big technique in modern
fiction and poetry

•

Words have their own firmness. The word on the page may not reveal (may conceal) the flabbiness of the mind that conceived it. > All thoughts are upgrades—get more clarity, definition, authority, by being in print—that is, detached from the person who thinks them.

A potential fraud—at least potential—in all writing.

How revealing to meet [Richard] Eberhart, [Paul] Tillich, Dwight Macdonald, Mary McCarthy!

Jonathan [Miller]: "I take Trilling's ideas less seriously since I know him."

•

Sensibility is humus for the intellect.
There's no syntax for sensibility—hence, it's ignored.

•

Reading criticism clogs conduits through which one gets new ideas: cultural cholesterol.

One's ignorance is a treasure, not to be casually spent ([Paul] Valéry)

•

Body type [*SS is describing herself*]:

- Tall
- Low blood pressure
- Need lots of sleep

- Sudden craving for pure sugar (but dislike desserts—not a high enough concentration)
- Intolerance for liquor
- Heavy smoking
- Tendency to anemia
- Heavy protein craving
- Asthma
- Migraines
- Very good stomach—no heartburn, constipation, etc.
- Negligible menstrual cramps
- Easily tired by standing
- Like heights
- Enjoy seeing deformed people (voyeuristic)
- Nailbiting
- Teeth grinding
- Nearsighted, astigmatism
- Frileuse (very sensitive to cold, like hot summers)
- Not very sensitive to noise (high degree of selective auditory focus)

Pills one takes for reducing hypertension are depressants
Alcohol is a depressant

8/22/64   Paris

The incredible pain returns again and again and again.

8/23/64

Finished the story. "An American Destiny," for the moment. I see now that it's mined from the vein that produced [*SS's first novel*] *The Benefactor*—it's a sort of miniaturized Frau Anders story, more drastically comic.

[*In the margin:*] My pop art story

Gains

- Third person rather than first
- Fantasy America, rather than fantasy France (because I'm in Paris?!)
- Use of slang,—active verbs

8/24/64

Great art has a beautiful monotony—Stendhal, Bach. (But not Shakespeare.)

A sense of the inevitability of a style—the sense that the artist had no alternatives, so wholly centered is he *in* his style.

Compare [Gustave] Flaubert and [James] Joyce ("voulu," constructed, intricate) with [Choderlos de] Laclos and [Raymond] Radiguet.

The greatest art seems secreted, not constructed.

•

Camp: irony, distance; ambivalence (?)

Pop art: only possible in an affluent society, where one can be free to enjoy ironic consumption. Thus there *is* Pop art in England—but not in Spain, where consumption is still too serious. (In Spain, painting is either abstract or social protest realism.)

•

Armature—in sculpture

•

[*Josef von Sternberg's 1930 Hollywood film starring Marlene Dietrich and Gary Cooper*] *Morocco*:

Dietrich: clean, solid—movements never weak or floating or petty—sparse
Von S: profuse

[*In the margin:*] They highlight each other by their differences

•

"Fagotage" (m.)—botch; ridiculous way of dressing >
"Fagoter" (verb)—to dress (a person) ridiculously > Is this where "faggot" comes from?

•

Movies seen since Aug. 11:
The Crowd (King Vidor)—Cinemathèque
Bande à Part ([Jean-Luc] Godard)—Gaumont Rive Gauche
Une Femme est une Femme (Godard)—Cinemathèque
La Grande Muraille (Jap[anese]?)—Normandie
Maciste Contre Le Cyclope (It[alian]?)—Ciné Gobelins

•

[*The French director Georges*] Franju's first feature, *The Keep-ers* [*La Tête contre les murs*], about insane asylum—horrible, stupid, vicious director
([*parallel*] to *Les Yeux sans visage* [*Franju's next film*]

Gothic horror in films
The institution—cf. [*Robert Wiene's 1920 Weimar film* The Cabinet of Dr.] *Caligari*, etc.

8/28/64

"The Primary and most beautiful of Nature's qualities is mo-tion, which agitates her at all times, but this motion is simply the perpetual consequence of crimes, it is conserved by means of crimes alone."

—[Marquis] de Sade

Humanism = moralizing the world, thereby refusing to ac-knowledge the "crimes" of which de Sade speaks.

•

What one is *is* the idea one has of oneself. If one thinks one is loveable, one is; beautiful, talented, etc.

8/29/64

[*The American sociologist Philip Rieff, to whom SS was mar-ried between 1950 and 1959*] P. [hilip Rieff]—

Everyone else not real—very distant, small figures. I would have to swim a thousand miles to reach the margin of the relationship, on the other side of which might lie other people, and it was too far, I was too tired.

The almost infinitely extending network of that relationship; its dense weave
That's what held me—

Not (at least nowhere as strongly as I. [Irene Fornés])
The sense of P.'s uniqueness, value, preciousness—

H. [*Harriet Sohmers Zwerling, who was SS's lover when she was a student at the University of California, Berkeley, and then the lover of both Irene Fornés and SS in Paris in 1956 and 1957*]—very sloppy, loosely woven relationship—hence possibility of friendship, much later.

•

If one knew one would live 200 years, would one be as tired at 35?

Is the being tired a spontaneous complicity with death—a beginning to let go at what one judges to be about the right time, half way?
Or is it objectively so, that one would anyway be tired at 35 and spend the next 165 years "se traînant?" [*"moping around"*]

•

If one could amputate part of one's consciousness . . .

What appeared to Annette [*the American film scholar Annette Michelson, whom SS met in Paris in 1957*] as narcissism six years ago: I was still so unawakened, so out of focus. So dead, or, rather, unborn.

•

I will never just outlast this pain. (Healing passage of time, etc.) I am frozen, paralyzed, the gears are jammed. It will only recede, diminish if I can somehow transpose the emotion—as from grief to anger, from despair to assent. I must become active. As long as I continue to experience myself as done to (not doing) this unbearable pain will not desert me—

•

Persistent motive in my writing:
X speaks, asks, demands—but if doesn't answer, turns away. X tries to make the best of it.

[*A note, undated, is inserted:*] I will be alright by 7:00 am *this morning*

•

M. [Mother] didn't answer when I was a child. The worst punishment—and the ultimate frustration. She was always "off"—even when she wasn't angry. (The drinking a symptom of this.) But I kept trying.

Now, the same with I[rene]. Even more agonizing because for four years she *did* answer. So I know she can.

Those four years! That huge length of time—its weight, its almost palpable thickness—obsesses me. "How can she . . ." etc.

I'm so stuck on the "was" of people—

. . .

8/30/64

Yves—
Fragile
Hypochondriac, thin, needs 10 hours of sleep a night—lives on pills

From provinces—Nantes, Poitiers
Petit bourgeois
Father—had a small clothing factory, makes uniforms for the army
Mother—an antique dealer

Red hair, white skin, regular features

Works for army on rockets—big center in banlieue

"Je sais que je vais vieillir trop tôt et . . ." [*"I know that I will grow old too early, and . . ."*]

Paranoid—
Stole money from bank (father's friend) + from queer art gallery dealer (Annette's friend)

"Denise"—calls her Régine—she's 20, works this summer in Paris for an airline.

First time he was with Annette: "If only someone could see me now." For the last three years.—Annette: "Elle n'est pas ma reine à moi" [*"She's not my very own queen"*]

•

From parataxis (loose association of clauses) to hypotaxis (more precise indications of logical relationships + subordination)

•

. . .

Play:
Doctor
World is a body

•

Writing is a little door. Some fantasies, like big pieces of furniture, won't come through.

•

In ancient religion all significant behavior was acc[ording] to a divine prototype.

Man > arena of forces, battleground
Gods = names of important things

A) Homer on volition (cf. Snell [*the German classicist Bruno Snell, author of* The Discovery of Mind in Greek Philosophy and Literature])

B) Tragedy
A *causal* analysis
A god wills > humans act

No conception of roles

Modern idea of individuality < > role-playing (i.e. self-consciousness)

Compare *Hamlet* and *Oedipus*

9/3/64

How beautiful [*von Sternberg's 1935 film*] *The Devil Is a Woman* is! It's one of the most *extreme* films I've ever seen. Dietrich is completely object—almost lacquered, embalmed. Research into the absoluteness of décor: style obliterating personality . . . Dietrich is "mounted" inside her costumes, her huge hats—behind the confetti, the streamers, the doves, the grilles, the rain . . . Décor is "surcharge," both beautiful and parodic—

Compare with [*the Italian director Luchino*] Visconti (*Senso, The Leopard*) +, of course, *Flaming Creatures* [*made in 1963 by the American experimental filmmaker Jack Smith. SS had written an essay on the film, which would appear in her first collection of essays*, Against Interpretation *(1966).*]

•

[John] Donne's "Sermon Preached at White-Hall"—Feb. 29, 1627

•

My faults:

- To censor others for my own vices*
- To make my friendships into love affairs
- To ask that love include (and exclude) all

*but, perhaps this becomes most hectic and obvious—reaches a climax, when the thing in myself is deteriorating, giving way, collapsing—like: my indignation at Susan [Taubes's] [*SS's close friend from Cambridge, Massachusetts, days*] and Eva [Berliner Kollisch's] [*a friend of SS's and Taubes's*] physical squeamishness.

N.B. My ostentatious appetite—real need—to eat exotic and "disgusting" foods = a need to state my denial of squeamishness. A counter-statement.

. . .

9/8/64

"I got away, but I had to leave my arms and legs behind . . ."

Not to look back means cordoning off all sorts of things in the present which are too full of memories that can't be suppressed. To disinfect my life of ————, of this nearly mortal grief, I find myself refraining from this, and this, and this. The greatest loss is sex. That, and so many other things, remind me of ————.

I can't afford to allow the present any depth or ballast, because that means (for me) the past, and the past means all that was shared with ———.

I feel—when I'm not sorrowing—so dry, like powder, like a helium balloon that's been let go—
I've forbidden myself to think, to feel, because thinking and feeling—

How can I go on this way?
And how can I not?

•

"Dearest ———
"I'm sorry not to have written. Life is tough, and its hard to talk while one is gritting one's teeth . . ."

•

Color in films
[*Teinosuke Kinugasa's 1953 film*] *Gate of Hell*
Senso
[*Alain Resnais's 1963 film*] *Muriel*

Two palettes: one based on skin color, one not (city, plastic, neon)

The orgasm—repeated overexposed sequence in [*Resnais's 1961 film* Last Year at] *Marienbad*

Relation of parody + self-parody in camp

[*The twentieth-century French artist Jean-Robert*] Ipoustéguy's sculpture—the heroic figure (large head, arms outstretched, pubic hair like a badge—penis rides free), in bronze, but cracked, fissured . . .

•

"I don't want to know about your past. I have a feeling it
would weigh too much."
"But we're not on a balance."
"But we are."

•

Marxism a position vis-à-vis culture

—[Theodor] Adorno, *Philosophy of New Music*
[Arnold] Schoenberg = progress
[Igor] Stravinsky = fascism (whom A. identifies with just one
period, the neo-classical)
[*In the margin:*] NB parallels [between] Stravinsky + [Pablo]
Picasso—raiding the past [in their] different styles—no
commitment to progress

—[Georg] Lukács
[Thomas] Mann = realism = sense of history = Marxism
[Franz] Kafka = allegory = dehistoricization = fascism

—[Walter] Benjamin
Cinema = abolition of tradition = fascism

(Use this as introduction to Lukács essay)

•

Read the two novels of [*the contemporary French novelist Jean-Marie Gustave*] Le Clézio

"J'ai besoin de beaucoup de tendresse." [*"I need a great deal of tenderness."*]

"Écrire veut dire aller jusqu'au bout. J'ai renoncé à ça dans ma vie, mais dans ce que j'écris, je dois prendre un risque." [*"To write means to go all the way. I've renounced this in life, but in what I write, I must take risks."*]

"C'est trop et c'est juste assez pour moi" (Jean Cocteau) [*"It's too much and it's just enough for me"*] Motto of *Cahiers du Cinéma* American Cinema issue (Jan. 1963)

. . .

Lineage of *Le Bavard* [*by Louis-René des Forêts*]: Poe [Jorge Luis] Borges says: [G. K.] Chesterton, [Robert Louis] Stevenson, + early films of von Sternberg

9/10/64

Do essays on:

- The first person narrative, the récit
- Von Sternberg
- [Herman Melville's novel] *Pierre*[*: or, The Ambiguities*]
- Style + silence Gertrude Stein, etc.

.

All great art contains at its center contemplation, a dynamic contemplation.

Camp is one of the species of behaviorism in art—it is, so extremely, it has no norm to reflect.

•

Modern aesthetics is crippled by its dependence upon the concept of "beauty." As if art were "about" beauty—as science is "about" truth!

•

[*The contemporary American artist R. B.*] Kitaj: "found + assisted object"

•

. . .

For Sarraute piece, read early essay by [Pierre] Boulez (printed by "Domaine Musicale") "On Hedonism."

For [*SS's essay on the contemporary French anthropologist Claude*] Lévi-Strauss, read [Paul] Ricoeur essay in *Esprit*

. . .

[*The contemporary German composer Karlheinz*] Stockhausen's work abolishes the notion of *composition*—proposes

1) Any rhythmic structure may be organically adapted to any tempo; 2) unlimited cycle of permutations.

Boulez rejects (1) + (2)

. . .

9/23/64   New York

Inspiratory emphasis

Inhale > lower (flatten diaphragm) > suppress sensation—
pelvic, i.e. sexual

Therefore secret of a feeling is learning to breathe *out*

·

Spiritual chemistry . . .
Effect irradiates into other zones . . .
Cut the dialogue into panels and make a great screen of . . .

10/3/64

Flaming Creatures is sexual, sexually stimulating (not just a
spoof on sex) in the same sense that sex is also silly, grotesque,
awkward, ugly.

One man thinks before he acts. Another man thinks after he
acts. Each is of the opinion that the other thinks too much.

A murder: like a flashbulb (panoramic photo) going off in a
dark forest, lighting up all the obscure, frightened woodland
life. (Dallas—Nov. 1963)

•

Subject: the second birth of the self

Through the mad "project"

Shedding the past—exile—aborting the self

•

Principle of redundancy
(e.g. traffic lights)
red < > green
up < > down
stop < > go

Get more precise communication

English is so precise because it's so redundant . . . > cf. [*the twentieth-century English literary critic and poet William*] Empson on complex words: words have resonances, halos, vibrations. Literary work is strung on them. "E.g. "fool," "honest"

Vs. a telegram

Redundancy necessary to convey info—but what is the connection with beauty, the non-utilitarian

Mathematicians say of a certain equation "it's beautiful" because it is so simple, so *non*-redundant.

Connection between style (stylishness) and redundancy [—]
e.g. films of von Sternberg

Connection between redundancy and "the replicate."

•

Women are "politically transparent" in the 19th century.

•

We have all the elements—just have to bolt them down, then attack the warhead—then launch it.

•

Seep
Catenary curve

So much in modern life that can be enjoyed, once one gets over the nausea of the replicate.

Moralists like [*the twentieth-century American writer on urbanism Lewis*] Mumford vs. aesthetes like [*the contemporary American architect*] Philip Johnson.

Seriousness—the highest form is the same as irony.

11/1/64

I was *afraid* of my mother, physically afraid. Not afraid of her anger, afraid of her decreasing the little emotional nourishment she supplied me, but afraid of her. Afraid of Rosie [*SS's nanny, Rose McNulty*], too.

Mother slapped me across the face—for talking back, for contradicting her.

I've always made excuses for her. I've never allowed my anger, my outrage.

•

If I can't bring judgment against the world, I must bring it against myself.

I'm learning to bring judgment against the world.

•

As a writer, I tolerate error, poor performance, failure. So what if I fail some of the time, if a story or an essay is no good? Sometimes things *do* go well, the work *is* good. And that's enough.

It's just this attitude I don't have about sex. I don't tolerate error, failure—therefore I'm anxious from the start, and therefore I'm more likely to fail. Because I don't have the confidence that some of the time (without my forcing anything) it will be good.

•

If only I could feel about sex as I do about writing! That I'm the vehicle, the medium, the instrument of some force beyond myself.

I experience the writing as given to me—sometimes, almost, as dictated. I let it come, try not to interfere with it. I respect it, because it's me and yet more than me. It's personal and transpersonal, both.

I would like to feel that way about sex, too. As if "nature" or "life" used me. And I trust that, and let myself be used.

An attitude of surrender to oneself, to life. Prayer. Let it be, whatever it will be. I give myself to it.

Prayer: peace and voluptuousness.

In this, no room for shame and anxiety as to how the little old self rates in the light of some objective standard of performance.

One must be devout about sex. Then, one won't dare to be anxious. Anxiety will never be revealed for what it is— spiritual meanness, pettiness, small-mindedness.

•

Q: Do you succeed always?
A: Yes, I succeed thirty percent of the time.
Q: Then you don't succeed always.
A: Yes I do. To succeed 30% of the time is always.

•

Aristocratic	Clowning
Cynic	Cynic
(George Sanders,	(Zero Mostel, Sydney Greenstreet,
Vincent Price)	Charles Laughton)

| In style of personality breaks moral law, but observes aesthetic one | Breaks moral and aesthetic law |

| Elegant | Farts in your face, always handling you, poking in your guts |

| One fears him—fears being thought clumsy, ill-bred, low-class (that's his power) | One believes he knows the secret of fun—doesn't want to be thought a bore by him |

| Admits he's evil | Hurts you—then makes you laugh. Shameless, but denies his own evil. Acts like a naughty, adorable child. |

•

Check:

Article by Lévi-Strauss on Christmas in *The New Society* (mag[azine])

[Marcel] Proust, "About Flaubert's Style," in *Pleasures and Days*, ed[*ited by the American literary critic F. W.*] Dupee (Anchor [Books])

Hermes—new French mag[azine] on mysticism ([Mircea] Eliade, [Alan] Watts, [Henry] Corbin, etc.)

[*The contemporary French writer Michel*] Butor, *The Four Seasons*, *New World Writing* (Rothko—soft Mondrians)

[*SS marked an X in the margin:*] Any trans[lation] in English of Louis-René des Forêts ([*published by John*] Calder in London)

•

Science fiction—
Popular mythology for contemporary *negative* imagination about the impersonal

Otherworld creatures = the it, what takes over

•

Essay: style, silence, repetition.

•

Kurt Goldstein, *Language and Language Disturbances* (Grune & Stratton, 1960)—

aphasia   read

•

Noble feelings / ignoble feelings
Dignity
Respect
Loyalty to oneself

•

. . .

Comparison between [Paul] Klee + Valéry
Theory + art

•

[*The Russian-born American constructivist sculptor Naum*]
Gabo: negative space

To "construct" something is to carve the space out of it (to
disclose the space).

[Gabo:] "We deny volume as an expression of space . . . We
reject solid mass as an element of plasticity." (1920)

Gabo: Must see the sculpture from all sides—it's three dimen-
sional.

Innovations: Use of new materials—plastic, celluloid, wire; +
making sculpture move (either to see it / or because the movement *is* the subject) > e.g. *Kinetic Construction* (1920)

Bring sculpture close to architecture.

•

[Marcel] Duchamp: Readymades as not art, but a philosophical point

•

Style:

Circular style ([Gertrude] Stein) > read Donald Sutherland's book [*the American critic, playwright, and librettist, who, in 1951, wrote* Gertrude Stein: A Biography of Her Work]

Cf. [Jean-Paul] Sartre on "the white style" of [Albert] Camus's *L'Étranger* [*The Stranger*]

. . .

•

W[illiam] James acknowledged that "morbid-mindedness"—defined it, rather—as ranging over "a wider scale of experience" than healthy-mindedness

—the "value" in what is evil or lunatic

•

[Erik] Satie's "furniture music"—background, not meant to be listened to with all one['s] attention

Andy Warhol's films

•

Read [*the contemporary American literary critic J.*] Hillis Miller book

Art is a form of consciousness

•

. . .

One difference between *naming* a feeling ("I feel terrible")
and *expressing* it ("Ohh . . . .") is the response you get: "Why?"
or "What's the matter?" By naming a feeling *in order to give
vent to* it—a practice very much promoted by psychoanalysis—you make a co-reasoner out of your consoler.

•

Use of markings on a roll of film (the "leader") as part of the
content of the film: Bruce Conner's *A Movie* (like exposing
the structure of a building, or—Brecht—the mechanism of
the set)

Cross-cutting between old film quote + event in film:

Godard, *Vivre Sa Vie* [featuring] Renée Falconetti + Anna
   Karina
[*The American experimental filmmaker Kenneth*] Anger, *Scorpio
   Rising* [*where he crosscuts between material from Cecil B.*]
   DeMille's *King of Kings* + motorcyclist's orgy (sound track:
   "Going to a Party" [*actually "Party Lights"*])
[*The Spanish director Luis*] Buñuel's *L'Age d'Or* [*with its*] use
   of Christ to illustrate De Sade episode

•

Paul Ricoeur, "Structure et herméneutique," in *Esprit*, Nov.
1963

3 other essays on Lévi-Strauss in same issue, plus interview

•

. . .

18th century the great period ιof camp—distributed through whole culture

[Alexander] Pope—Spurious passage in "Epistle to Dr Arbuthnot": ". . . And he himself one vile Antithesis."

[William] Congreve—Symmetrical (like billiards): passion A, passion B

Molière?

. . .

18th century drama: no development—whole character *there*—instant feelings summed up in an epigram—love born or dies

. . .

•

Characteristics of art nouveau paintings + drawings:
Symmetrical composition, attenuated curves, spare use of color, *slender* bodies.
Le Rouget's restaurant—Art Nouveau décor near Gare Montparnasse

•

. . .

Pornography

De Sade, Andrea de Nerciat, Restif de la Bretonne >>> triumvirate of 18th-century French libertines

Earl of Rochester [John Wilmot], John Cleland >>> English (N.B. [Laurence] Sterne, John Wilkes, + Robert Burns all belonged to erotic secret societies. Wilkes the Medmenham Monks, Burns the Caledonian Muses)

18th century—no guilt; atheism; more philosophical,
    polemical
19th century—guilt, horror

Andrea de Nerciat—career officer in French army
    (father was Italian); got to be colonel:
Two great philosophical works:

[*Radiguet's novel*] *Le Diable au Corps* (3 vols.)—alternates between narrative + dialogue; starts with countess (slut) + marquise (the heroine—like [*Proust's character*] Duchesse de Guermantes—beautiful, worldly, rich; everyone curries her favor)
Affair between the two—+ contesse tells stories.
Sex never condemned, always pleasurable
A lot of social satire

[*Andrea de Nerciat's novel*] *Les Aphrodites* (3 vols.)—a secret sexual society; tells stories.

Also a novel, *Monrose*; and *Félicia* (best known book—erotic but gallant, not pornographic)

•

. . .

Death = being completely inside one's own head
Life = the world

. . .

11/4/64

Proust, in a letter:

"What's more, ever since Hervieu, Hermant, etc., snobbish
has been so frequently represented from the outside that I
wanted to try to show it inside the person, like a wonderful
kind of imagination . . ."

Like camp

•

One criticizes in others what one recognizes + despises in
oneself. For example, an artist who is revolted by another's
ambitiousness.

•

Underneath the depression, I found my anxiety.

•

History of film

This is the first generation of directors who are aware of film
history; cinema now entering era of self-consciousness

Nostalgia

[*The German film scholar and writer Siegfried*] Kracauer:
movies—anti-art; anti-auteur

•

. . .

Femininity = weakness (or being strong through weakness)

No image of strong woman who is just strong, + takes the
consequences

. . .

11/17/64

Conceiving all relationships as between a master and a
slave . . .

In each case, which was I to be? I found more gratification as
a slave; I was more nourished. But—master or slave, one is
equally unfree. One cannot step away, get out of character.

A relationship of equals is one not tied to "roles."

•

Where I detected envy, I forbore to criticize—lest my motives
be impure, and my judgment less than impartial. I was benevolent. I was malicious only about strangers, people who
were indifferent.

It seems noble.

But, thereby, I rescued my "superiors," those I admired, from my dislike, my aggression. Criticism was reserved only for those "beneath" me, whom I didn't respect . . . I used my power of criticism to confirm the status quo.

•

Wayne Andrews, [*Architecture, Ambition and Americans: A Social History of*] *American Architecture*
John Cage, *Silence*
Sir Oliver Lodge, *Raymond*
Daisy Ashford, *The Young Visitors*

11/22/64

Read Max Beerbohm, "Savonarola Brown," [*Ronald Firbank's 1926 novel*, Concerning the Eccentricities of] *Cardinal Pirelli*, Diary of Nijinsky

Soft-focus thinking (as in the 4 lectures) whose virtue is aliveness, being improvised, being contemporary to the situation in which it's uttered; ——— vs sharp-focus thinking (writing) which is more accurate, complex, unrepetitive, but has to be prepared in advance—like a Greek statue with blank eyes

•

Say I have a dreary feeling (Z) which I want to combat—a feeling which gives rise to something I repeatedly do or say that I wish I didn't.

If I merely *suppress* the behavior (if that's even possible) I recharge the feeling behind it.

Recipe for killing the feeling: *Act it out* in an exaggerated form.

The chagrin one feels then is far more memorable and therapeutic.

•

"depends where I get flung off . . ."

read [*the Austrian-British art historian Ernst*] Gombrich, *Wilhelm Meister* [*Goethe's second novel,* The Apprenticeship of Wilhelm Meister, *published in 1795*]

•

Injured, scarred *in the face*

Marked Woman [*1937 Hollywood film directed by Lloyd Bacon and Michael Curtiz and starring Bette Davis, Humphrey Bogart, and Lola Lane*]

Bette Davis—M.

- smoking at beginning (sign of independence from boss—Johnny Vanning / blows smoke in his face).

•

Nietzsche: "no facts, only interpretations."

Art is never a photograph.

•

Mimetic theory of art: art < > reality

Plato: measures art by the standard of *truth*

Aristotle: emotional effect of lying.

•

Social facts > "fact"

Psychological facts > "imagination"

Many different relations between art + fact

1) reportorial
2) ironic—pop art [—] Andy Warhol's *129 Die*;
   front page of [*Hearst-owned New York tabloid
   that folded in 1963*] *Daily Mirror*
3) Patronizing reality: *New Yorker* fiction; some
   passages in *The Group*

•

Problem as a writer:
Never think of model
Don't think of units of art as facts

"factless"

•

Erwin Straus, "The Upright Posture," *Journal of Abnormal Psychology*, 1942

•

. . .

Resurrections (in literature):

Osamu Dazai, *No Longer Human, The Setting Sun*

[Jan Potocki,] *The Saragossa Manuscript*

[Ghislain de Diesbach,] *The Toys of Princes*

[Machado de Assis,] *Epitaph of a Small Winner*

[Witold Gombrowicz,] *Ferdydurke*

[Stendhal,] *Armance*

[Knut Hamsun,] *Pan*

•

"Another merry day"

"Acting up a storm"
. . .

On [Antonin] Artaud–[Jacques] Rivière correspondance, pp. 45–52 of [Maurice] Blanchot, *Le Livre à Venir*.
. . .

Read [Thomas] Carlyle, *Sartor Resartus* on the dandy [—]
"the dandiacal body"

"J'ai le cafard" [*"I'm blue"*]

12/3/64

Interesting new sculpture rejects the pedestal ([*the American
sculptor George*] Sugarman etc.)

Refinement, finesse: Camp, based on an exaggeration of this
value, makes this central; it isn't. Vigor, vitality is at least as
important. But it is important. Cf. Jasper Johns

Essay on camp an example of the larger point—the
imp[ortance] of—the idea of—sensibility. Talking about
Camp a way of making this point.

Modern art related to 20th century revolution in the graphic
arts. We are first generation in human history to live sur-
rounded by print artifacts (comics, billboards, newspapers)—
a second nature.

[*The American art historian Meyer*] Schapiro one of the first
to be interested in [Jackson] Pollock, [Willem] de Kooning
(late 40s)

Find Schapiro essay on modern art in *The Listener*, 1956

•

Warhol ideas: single image (monotonized); the impersonal

•

"What is it?" before "Is it any good?"

•

André Breton, a connoisseur of freedom

•

DUCHAMP

•

Meyer Schapiro

"The Nature of Abstract Art," *Marxist Quarterly*, vol. 1, no. 1 (1937) reply by Delmore Schwartz, a reply to that by Schapiro, op. cit., vol. 1, no. 2 (April–June 1937)

"Style" (Kroeber vol.) [*Schapiro's essay in Alfred Louis Kroeber's* Anthropology Today]

On Modern Art, *The Listener*, 1956

"Metaphysics for the Movies," *Marxist Quarterly*, Vol. 1, No. 3 (Oct.–Dec. 1937)—attack on Mortimer Adler

- "On the Aesthetic Attitude in Romanesque Art," in [K. Bharatha Iyer,] *Art & Thought* . . .

•

. . .

Priest and Worker: The Autobiography of Henri Perrin
Translated and with an introduction by Bernard Wall

. . .

•

[*There is a box drawn around this:*] Style

Style as mode of change in art.
Consciousness of style the same as consciousness of historicity
     of the art work
Velocity of styles in contemporary painting

Contra "style," aestheticism—cf. [*a friend of SS's beginning
in the 1960s, the French critic Roland*] Barthes, "Les Maladies
du Costume de Théâtre"—*Essais Critiques*

. . .

•

Work of Art

An experiment, a research (solving a "problem") vs form
of play

. . .

•

[Michelangelo Antonioni's film] *L'Avventura*

Hard to believe [it was made] only four years ago . . .

Only learn at the end that Claudia is poor

. . .

A's scenes always have the same duration on screen as they w[oul]d in life—no manipulation of time in the cutting—

"Abandon the supernatural casuistry of positives + negatives"—A's refusal to make a villain of Sandro

Makes films about emotions, but refuses to let his actors "emote" (à la [*the Italian film director Federico*] Fellini + Visconti)—that w[oul]d be "rhetoric"

New style: "Against Rhetoric"

. . .

A's films are "literary" in that they are full of complex refer-ences

Self-conscious film-making—Fitzgerald[*'s* Tender Is the Night] in *L'A*[*vventura*]

. . .

(They have literate scripts) but not like traditional stories

> A's films: a kind of writing ("caméra-stylo" [*literally "camera-pen" of the French film critic and director Alexan-dre*] Astruc) done by the director who "uses" the actors

- Why does one "write"?
- Answer—idea of a film as *recording, incarnating*

Material must necessarily be diffuse, non-dramatic (hence, failure of [*Antonioni's 1957 film*] *Il Grido*)

•

. . .

[*The next three entries have a box drawn around them.*]

A number is the set of all sets which are equivalent to each other

A cardinal number is the class of all similar classes

To every finite set can be assigned a cardinal number

12/6/64

My friendships (Paul—[*SS's friend the American artist Paul Thek*] etc.) are weightless. Now, since ————, I experience them as maintenance problems. I'm juggling my schedule, paying dues . . .

"Every life is a defense of a particular form." [*—the Austrian composer Anton*] von Webern

(Kitaj painting)

•

Read:

Buy: OUP editions of [*the Welsh alchemist and Rosicrucian Thomas*] Vaughan, [Andrew] Marvell, + [*the metaphysical poet Richard*] Crashaw.

Vaughan sermon on dying

[*The French writer Alfred de Musset's 1834 play*) *Lorenzaccio* . . .

Walter Benjamin's book on the baroque.

Frederic Farrar, *History of Interpretation* (1886)

Poe—stories

Iris Murdoch, "How I Write a Novel," *Yale Review*, spring '64

Franz Borkenau, book on 17th century (1934)—Pascal, Racine, Descartes, Hobbes [*The Transition from the Feudal to the Bourgeois World View*]

• John Cage, *Silence*

[*The Russian filmmaker Vsevolod*] Pudovkin on film [*Film Technique and Film Acting*]

. . .

12/19/64

Novel: discovering the life of the body (posture, gesture Carolee's [*the American performance artist Carolee Schneemann*] "I had to deal with the fire," [*the Swedish sculptor*] Claes Oldenburg's "very involved these days with hallways") . . . two characters—one who makes it, one who doesn't.

1965

[Undated loose sheets:]

Language becoming a series of dead "white" tones

•

A person who (as a human being) has (?) perfect pitch

•

I don't care about someone being intelligent; any situation between people, when they are really human with each other, produces "intelligence"

•

Writers think words mean the same thing—

•

[SS's journals in the 1960s were copious but increasingly dated haphazardly or not at all. The following notes are from a note-

book marked "1965——, Novel, collated notes," but which are otherwise unspecified as to date or sequence. I have reproduced here those entries that seemed to me to tell something about SS that had a wider resonance than that usually found in book outlines.]

[Crossed out but legible:]
Note how Burroughs in *Naked Lunch* shifts from 1st to 3rd person, and back without any formal announcement.

Note, too, the use of erudition in parentheses

[Crossed out but legible:]

What sex is the "I"? Does one have to believe that God is a Woman to say "I" as a woman and be writing about the human condition.

Who has the right to say "I"? Is that a right that has to be earned?

The oneiric element.

[Crossed out but legible:]

drug ecstasy[——]cf. [Francis] Picabia's painting *Universal Prostitution* universal fornication

The rendering of the erotic fantasy: "neither beautiful nor ugly" no affective weight, nothing other than it is—just "exciting"

This as subject for novel—the fantasies being interlaced like dreams in *The Benefactor*

. . .

I'm not looking for a plot—I'm looking for a "tone," a "color,"
and the rest will follow

What if everything were the same, but no one talked.

. . .

Novel as a *game* (Burt) [*SS's friend the American novelist Burt
Blechman*]—set up "rules," which then determine character +
situation

A problem: the *thinness* of my writing. It is meager, sentence
by sentence. Too architectural, too discursive.

Jasper [Johns's] [*with whom SS had a relationship in the mid-
1960s*] formidable reticence—it's awe-inspiring—plus his
argumentativeness

"In modern America. In modern America"

Whiper Baroney Gospel Church (in So[uth] Carolina)
Blob's Park—Max E. Blob Park—near Baltimore
Tibetan Museum on Staten Island

. . .

What makes someone move?
He's being chased
He's looking for something
He's running away
He's restless

He's crazy
He's jealous

. . .

[*The twentieth-century French writer Georges*] Bataille died
of syphilis (inherited)—in early sixties—
Was a librarian—
could put such a character in a novel . . .

Bataille: connection betw[een] sex + death, pleasure + pain,
cf. *Larmes d'Éros*

[*In the margin:*] *only goal in life is ecstasy, exaltation, bliss*

. . . fantasy (erotic) is, by definition, an open form . . . fantasy
can be perpetually re-exciting by adding details—décor,
clothes, each movement and gesture
Obsessed regard of [*the contemporary French novelist Alain*]
Robbe-Grillet's novels is (suppressed) erotic consciousness
Point is—it has to be made explicit

PLOTS & SITUATIONS

Redemptive friendship (two women)
Novel in letters: the recluse-artist and his dealer and
a clairvoyant
A voyage to the underworld (Homer, Vergil [*and in
Hermann Hesse's novel*] *Steppenwolf*)
Matricide
An assassination
A collective hallucination (story)

[*Crossed out but legible:*] A dialogue between
    Orpheus and Eurydice

[*Crossed out but legible:*] The construction of a
    fantasy: accidental stimulus—gradual
    refinement + elaboration—going over + over
    it—new inventions—need a détente

A theft

A work of art which is really a *machine* for
    dominating human beings

The discovery of a lost mss.

Two incestuous sisters

A space ship has landed

An ageing movie actress

A novel about the future. Machines. Each man has
    his own machine (memory bank, codified
    decision maker, etc.) You "play" the machine.
    Instant everything

Smuggling a huge art-work (painting? Sculpture?)
    out of the country in pieces—called "The
    Invention of Liberty"

A project: sanctity (based on SW [Simone Weil]—
    with honesty of [*the poet*] Sylvia Plath—only
    way to solve sex "I" is talk about it

[*Crossed out but legible:*] Theme of the changeling—
    a child

Letters between SW (in Mississippi) and Bataille . . .

Jealousy

Regenerative experiences:

    Plunge into the sea
    The sun
    An old city

Silence
Snow-fall
Animals

Angelic apprehension of the past—neutrality—
All one's experiences are equally important, singular
(ps[choanalysis] teaches one to judge one's experiences, judge
one's past)

. . .

Each generation has to reinvent spirituality

Ardent reason

Greatest subject: self seeking to transcend itself (*Middle-march*, *War and Peace*)
Looking for self-transcendence (or metamorphosis)—the
cloud of unknowing that allows perfect expressiveness (a sec-
ular myth for this)

On the "I":
Use of WE

> The married couple
> The royal we
> News broadcast
> The nurse-patient (child) relation: "Aren't we cranky
>   today?" "Oh, we have a high temperature, don't we?"
> The parental "we": "We always want what is best
>   for you"

To found a leper colony

Sci-fi fiction the last storytelling (giving sense of otherness, "dépaysement" [*"being out of one's element"*])

. . .

The necessity of the "récit" form: because the "I" is composite

. . . The dissociated consciousness (cf. [Sartre's] *Les Mots*) that sees itself, is a spectator of itself.

acts > "acts"
agent > "agent"

"I" am playing the part of myself.

In the future, one could be re-wired or re-programmed [—] more euphoria, more repose [—] by drugs [—] destructive associations undone [/] voluntary, selective amnesias.

LSD: very wide-angle lens: flattening but a loss of depth perspective (things far away seem within reach)

. . .

A person of low vitality (20-watt personality)—cf. [*Theodore Dreiser's novel*] *American Tragedy*—deficit of energy (+ wit) coupled with extra refinement > bewilderment, blanking out, euphoria, self-flogging
A rheumatic heart in childhood—has to take care of himself

. . .

Imagination not harmonious

With the body > fantasy becoming absolute destroys the body: s-m (Sade), drugs > decay of flesh (Burroughs)

Religious vocabulary puts a boundary around total fantasy—this is gone now.
Also analogies of body + nature (perceiving person as a *body*—e.g. a tree) have been lost.

. . .

How hard it is to get people to accept "novel" as object. People who'll take Larry Poons or Frank Stella are mystified by G[ertrude] Stein saying "One + two + three + four . . ."

Most interesting poetry today is prose-poem form ([Henri] Michaux, [Francis] Ponge, [Blaise] Cendrars, [Vladimir] Mayakovsky)

. . .

What would rigorous form be in the novel?

Couldn't be mathematical, abstract (as in music + painting). There is the "material." (Same problem in films)

Could you have Infinite Variation in the novel . . .

One formal ideal: multiple sense. E.g. haiku. Take *Ulysses*, [*Robbe-Grillet's novels*] *La Jalousie + Le Voyeur*

Form has to be organic to the material. The letter-form of [Algernon Swinburne's] *Love's Cross-Currents is* the story, not just Swinburne's idea of putting the story in epistolary form. The story *is* the idea that this woman is so powerful, so forceful that, merely by letters and with little face-to-face contact, she can manipulate people's lives, prevent lovers from eloping. The story *is* Lady Midhurst's rhetoric—a rhetoric so seductive and compelling in its meanness, its intelligence, its accuracy, its suppleness, that she can manipulate at a *distance.*

Whereas to put the Thomas Faulk material [*SS's novel project at the time, ultimately abandoned*] in epistolary form would have been arbitrary. Just a way of closing off or limiting the narrative choices (as is the "récit," except when it is about a man *thinking*. It wouldn't have been organic to the story.

. . .

A work in which every part is written in a different style? But what's the relation *between* the different styles? And why *this* order? Joyce made an academic stab at it in *Ulysses*.

. . .

. . . To do in the novel what [Michel] Foucault suggests— depict the *complexity* of madness.

Imagine a man who has lost his mind. What has he lost? More like the ability to *stop* his mind.

Madness as a defense against terror.
Madness as a defense against grief.

. . .

Situation: parent writing about an extraordinary child— keeping a diary or log.

JS [John Stuart] Mill sort of child (cf. letter he wrote at six to [Jeremy] Bentham)

This w[oul]d be an organic justification for journal form

Rearing the Buddha-child

. . .

. . . Kafka the last story-teller in "serious" literature. Nobody has known where to go from there (except imitate him)

dream > science fiction

1/5/65

Think of novel in cinematic terms: close up, medium shot, long shot

Problem of lighting

Example: [William] Faulkner's "Red Leaves."

•

My self-absorption, my "turning off"—interrupting, telling an anecdote or memory of my own which ———'s story has reminded me of.

•

. . .

Mannerist painters: Jacopo Pontormo, Georges de la Tour, Monsù Desiderio, Luca Cambiaso

•

My feeling that nobody (or just a few people) has a mind = my feeling that nobody (x x) *cares*

Route 43. My mother had something beautiful (the Chinese furniture) but she didn't care enough to keep it. Eva [Berliner] didn't care enough about [*the late-eighteenth- and early-nineteenth-century German writer Heinrich von*] Kleist to buy his "Collected Works." Etc.

•

Mannerism: "The awareness of style as such."

Bousquet, p. 26 [*the French art historian Jacques Bousquet's* Mannerism *published in English translation in 1964*]

•

. . .

"Man can embody truth, but he cannot know it"
                              —[W. B.] Yeats (last letter) d. 1939

. . .

. . . been sheared off
. . . worked into the grain of
. . . pounded flat by
grudging

spurned
incredulous
spew
launch
unfits one for . . .
equivocal
evinced
pollute
reshuffled
choice insult . . .
debased
dispersed
makeshift
despondent

1/16/65   Minneapolis [*SS's thirty-second birthday*]

Becoming inhuman (committing the inhuman act) in order
to become humane . . .

Realizing that one must go against one's instincts (or training) in order to get what one wants.

An insect identifies light with air, exit—so, an insect in a tube
will fling itself to death against a glass wall on the other side
of which is a light, ignoring the exit which lies behind him in
the dark.

•

Robbe-Grillet: a biologist until age 30

Interest in relationships between persons and *things*

a) refusal to interpret (anthropomorphize) things
b) emphasis on exact account of their visual and topographic qualities (exclusion of other sense modalities *because* there is not an exact enough language to describe them—only for that reason?)

•

Cal's [*prep-school nickname of the twentieth-century American poet Robert Lowell, by which in adulthood he was known to his friends*] viciousness periodically awakened by his madness.

His malady applies a lens to certain of his qualities which are always there—

"Stereoscopy"

•

Uncork them . . .

Dickens' characters are single-motive puppets, "topped" with a humour—their character *is* their physiognomy (hence, relation to history of caricature)

•

History of notion of human as machine: mannerist drawings; caricature; [*the nineteenth-century French illustrator J. J.*] Grandville; Burroughs; [*the twentieth-century French painter Fernand*] Léger; [*Laurence Sterne's novel*] *Tristram Shandy* (?)

•

All capital cities are more like each other than like the rest of the cities in their country (people in NY more like Paris than [those] in St. Paul)

•

Cal: In madness, a machine operating at 5 times its normal rate, without its governor—sweating, farting, pouring out words, lurching back + forth.

•

Contempt

The contempt I feel for others—for myself different, less internal than *guilt.*

It's not that I think (or have ever thought) I was bad—through and through. I think I'm unattractive, unloveable, because I'm incomplete. It's not what I am that's wrong, it's that I'm not *more* (responsive, alive, generous, considerate, original, sensitive, brave etc.).

My profoundest experience is of indifference, rather than censure.

•

Style: the manner in which things appear to us as designed for *pleasure.*

•

Buy: [Ludwig] Wittgenstein's *Notebooks*

1/25/65

Carolee's [Schneemann] story about her studio burning down. "I got interested in what had happened to my work,"—how she used it—

———— [*it's unclear who this is*] is very stubborn—but it doesn't deteriorate his character

[*The American actor, playwright, and theater director, a close friend of SS's*] Joe C[haikin] holds back, thinks he has to hold back, to allow something in himself to come out

•

Not to give up on the new sensibility (Nietzsche, Wittgenstein; Cage; [Marshall] McLuhan) though the old one lies waiting, at hand, like the clothes in my closet each morning when I get up.

•

Novel:

A painter

Relation to his work

Kinds of "problems"

So-and-so wants his work to be beautiful

Impurities

The object

What people are on one's map*—

Every act is a compromise (between what one wants + what one thinks is possible)

*Inferior people lower the average

. . .

[The following entries are undated in the notebook, but are almost certainly from either late January or early February 1965.]

acronym:
e.g. laser (light amplification by stimulated emission of radiation)

St. Thomas Aquinas: "To love anyone is nothing else than to wish that person good."

John Dewey—"The ultimate function of literature is to appreciate the world, sometimes indignantly, sometimes sorrowfully, but best of all to praise when it is luckily possible."

Doué [*"gifted"*]

Basculer [*to switch*]
Couches de signification [*"layers of significance"*]

[Daniel] Defoe's characteristic form, the pseudo-memoir

2/17/65

What's good about *An American Tragedy*?

Its intelligence (about Clyde, etc.)

The patience + detail of Dreiser's imagination

Its compassion (Tolstoy)

Art is a form of nourishment (of consciousness, the spirit)

Sometimes one wants steak, sometimes oysters

Essay:

Four American books: *Pierre*
                       An American Tragedy
                       [Gertrude Stein's] *Three Lives*
                       Naked Lunch

[*This is circled:*] Style

[*This is circled:*] Medium is the message

"Styles must have location, even if they have no names . . .
There must be a home—even if it is seldom visited."
                       ([Thomas B. Hess], *Location* #2, p. 49)

"The work as object"}
"The medium as message"} in our period of liquidated political ideologies

[Robert] Rauschenberg canvas—very large—called *Axle*—
depicting [John F.] Kennedy (several times) on its cinemati-
cally organized fragmented surface—

St. Cunegund

Allowing "accidents"—work an "object"

"swish pan"

Read:

Cesar Grana, *Bohemian Versus Bourgeois: French Society + the
French Man of Letters in the 19th C.* (Basic Books)
            Ask [*the American critic*] Irving [Howe]

3/26/65

"All visible objects, man, are but as pasteboard masks."
            —*Moby Dick* (Holt, Rinehart, Winston), p. 161

"hip"—

*[The following four quotes are from John Wilcock, "The 'Hip'
Four Hundred" in* The Village Voice, *March 4, 1965:]*

"If you're hip you have an awareness of being of your own
time and the ability to communicate it." ([*the American filmmaker*] Shirley Clarke)

"[It's] someone who is aware, very much aware of what should happen + what could happen in his particular flow of experience + who's acutely sensitive to what's phony + pretentious." ([*the American journalist*] Nat Hentoff)

"—political + social consciousness . . . and someone who believes in + takes part in the sexual revolution of today." (Peter Orlovsky [*the American poet Allen Ginsberg's lover*])

•

New anti-literary establishment (painting, architecture, city planning, movies, TV, neurology, biology, electronics engineering)

Buckminster Fuller >> summer yacht seminar—"ekestics" sponsored by Greek millionaire Doxiades [*sic*]

Marshall McLuhan
Reyner Banham
Sigfried Giedion
György Kepes
[*In the margin:*] Unpolarized names!

{(But) Not: [*the American art critic*] Harold Rosenberg—too political; or [Lewis] Mumford—too political and / or too literary}

First key: [*the British neurophysiologist and histologist Sir Charles*] Sherrington—dist[inguished] between distance (haptic) + immediate senses

Eye an incarcerated organ—open to blandishments—doesn't grab, demand immediate satisfaction.

Recent painting (Pop, Op)—cool; least amount of texture possible—light colors

Need to have canvas, because you can't float colors off in space.

"Ekistic" group—
Interested in programming
A "sensory mix."
What are the sensory mixes of the future?
Completely non-political.
Total break with Matthew Arnold (exclusively literary—
    literature as criticism of culture) critics of the past

Hence, also dist[ance] between high + low culture (part of Matthew Arnold's apparatus) disappears.

Feeling (sensation) of a Jasper Johns painting or object might be like that of The Supremes.

•

Pop Art is Beatles art

•

Another key text: Ortega [José Ortega y Gasset], "The Dehumanization of Art"

Every age has its representative age group—ours is youth. Spirit of the age is being cool, dehumanized, play, sensation, apolitical.

•

Jasper Johns = Duchamp painted by [Claude] Monet

•

Op Art: "trompe l'oeil" kinetic art

Programming sensations

Could get a new art movement every month just by reading *Scientific American.*

•

"printed circuits"—what makes transistor radios possible.

•

"moiré"

•

Pour qui tu me prends? [*"Who do you take me for?"*]

•

[What follows are undated notes written on loose pages and tucked at the back of the notebook. They were almost certainly written in the summer of 1965—there is a list of movies seen in August.]

Pure narration (oral) >>>>	More + more complex forms of narration (writing!)
Chinese fairy tale	Mucking everything up!

"She wanted to be a horse. So she was a horse."

Already in Homer: concern with cauality (i.e. plausibility)

What happens is linear, cannot be other than it is.

Sprouts / shoots off from main line: something is *like* something else (similes)

Narration just traces the event, which is (was) there

•

. . .

Monet's "Waterlilies" would look pretty much the same upside down—space is verticalized.

"One note painting" (20th century) already appears in the 1880s.

. . .

[Edvard] Munch *The Kiss*—grain of wood has higher order of reality than figure represented.

4/20/65

To see more—(PROJECTS)

For instance, colors + spatial relationships, light

My vision is unrefined, insensitive; this is the trouble I'm having with painting

Another project: Webern, [*the American writer Paul*] Bowles, Stockhausen. Buy records, read, do some work. I've been very lazy.

To give no interviews until I can sound as clear + authoritative + direct as [*the American writer*] Lillian [Hellman] in the *Paris Review.*

Read (buy):   >Paris this summer
[*The French writer, composer, and musician André*] Hodeir
    book
Adorno on music
Barthes on Michelet

Annette [Michelson]:
I don't like paintings I have to "read"—hence I don't care much for Flemish painting (Bosch, Breughel)—want to be able to take in whole structure at one look

Neo-Pythagorean character of contemporary music (Boulez, etc.)

Interest in work of art with total structure (totally structured, (totalizing).

. . .

new sensibility > more encumbered *attentiveness*

uomo di cultura [*"man of culture"*] ([*the twentieth-century Italian writer Cesare*] Pavese)

A Rosenquist [the American painter James Rosenquist] *White Cigarette*, which had some of the dead nocturnal poetry of [*the 1955 Robert Aldrich film based on Mickey Spillane's crime novel*] *Kiss Me Deadly*

Biomorphism of [*the twentieth-century Catalan painter Joan*] Miró

New development: plastic-based paints

Changing the scale of the image ([Larry] Rivers, [Roy] Lichtenstein, Warhol)

[*The nineteenth-century English art critic John*] Ruskin: forms of art are moral . . .

. . .

5/20/65   Edisto Beach [*SS was visiting Jasper Johns at his house in South Carolina*]

Subject: painting + écriture

For something to be "very strong"—what?

The object is unimportant; but the painting is an object (Johns)

Already it's a great deal to see anything *clearly*, for we don't see *anything* clearly

A painting is an object, music is a performance, the book is a code. It has to be transcribed into ideas + sentiments + images (?)—

Drawing > oil painting > lithograph (3 versions of same—)

"The arrogant object" (Johns)

One doesn't learn from experience—because the substance of things is always changing

There is no neutral surface—something is only neutral with respect to something else (an interpretation? An expectation)— Robbe-Grillet

Rauschenberg's use of newsprint, tires

Johns: broom, hanger

Somebody said, "[John] Cage showed me that there are no empty objects."

The only transformation that interests me is a total transformation—however minute. I want the encounter with a person or a work of art to change *everything*.

. . .

5/20/65—South Carolina—

green—oaks, pines, palmettoes—furry grey-green Spanish moss, huge ropes [of] it, hanging from the branches of every tree—*dense*

The ocean is calm, shallow, very warm—

Reading Schoenberg's letters at midnight

Barefoot skinny Negroes walking along the road—small heads

Hollywood, So[uth] Carolina—the cabbage capital of the world

Mint juleps in frosted (iced) metal "glass"—need a napkin to hold it

A cardinal in the yard—cicadas, a crescendo, like a siren; quail ("bobwhite")

Ants, gnats, horseflies, daddy longlegs, snakes, hornets (yellow + black)

White sheets, thin white bedspreads, white walls + ceilings (wide boards)

Okra cut up, fried in deep fat, steak (well done), salad

A marmoset ("Jenny") in a large cage who sleeps in a soft wide-brimmed man's hat

Shells: conch, scallop, clam, oyster

Muddy bank—dark brown velvet mud—thousands of little holes—+, if you look closely, scurrying in + out of them, thousands of fiddler crabs

Sandspurs: "sea tail" (edible) growing at edge of beach

Basil, tea, mint growing in the yard; poison oak

Antennas on TV with small aluminum foil flags

•

JJ [Jasper Johns] allowing himself, now, de Kooning's white alongside of pink—a patch of it

Rauschenberg:

"As the paintings changed the printed material became as much of a subject as the paint (I began using newsprint in my work) causing changes of focus: A third palette. There is no poor subject (Any incentive to paint is as good as any other)."

"A canvas is never empty."

"Duplication of images" (symmetry?)

A poetry of infinite possibilities

Combine-paintings, combine-drawings

"If you do not change your mind about something when you confront a picture you have not seen before, you are either a stubborn fool or the painting is not very good."

"I am trying to check my habits of seeing, to counter them for the sake of a greater freshness. I am trying to be unfamiliar with what I'm doing."

5/22/65   Edisto Beach

Novel about thinking—

Not dreams this time (they were a metaphor for introspection, a pretext—*not* meant realistically, psychologically) [*in* The Benefactor]

An artist thinking about his work

A painter? A musician? (I'm slighty less ignorant about painting)

Not a writer—cf. [*Vladimir Nabokov's novel*] *Pale Fire*—for then I'd have to give the text of the work, as Nabokov does.

. . .

[*In the margin:*] *A spiritual project—but tied to making an object (as consciousness is harnessed to flesh)*

. . .

Dante: idea that the punishment fits the crime
Cantos 21 + 22—the "gargoyle cantos"

Idea of *distance* in art

How "far away" can you be?

One way is through abstraction—discovery of structure in nature—like X-ray (cf. [Paul] Cézanne)

New way—Rauschenberg, Johns—is through literalness—extending vision to include intense look at things we look at but never see

Johns' flag is not a flag—
Paul's [Thek] meat is not meat

Another (?): chance (transcending "intention")

In a painting, everything is present at once (*not* in music, fiction, film)

Difference between "going to be a painter" and "being a painter"

A painting is a certain kind of gesture—generous, terse, chaste, ironic, sentimental, etc.

. . .

5/24/65

. . .

Susan T. [Taubes]: rather give up sex
—otherwise can't work, doesn't want to move outside the eroticized sphere.

. . .

6/5/65   Paris

. . . Kafka's refusal of lyricism; it suffices to name the objects

Chinese porngraphic novel (1660) translated by [*the French writer and artist Pierre*] Klossowski: *La chair comme tapis de prière* [*Flesh as a Prayer Mat*]. Pauvert, 1962

Restaurant on rue Beaumarchais (#21?): L'Enclos de Ninon [*sic*]

. . .

6/8/65   7 a.m.

After 25 hours of work (dexamyl—uninterrupted except for an hour with [*the American journalist Herbert*] Lottman and, later, [*Godard's film*] *Alphaville*) I think I've sorted things out.

There are at least two projects here:

A. A *novella* about Thomas Faulk (or Darnell) whose center is the breakdown sequence I wrote yesterday afternoon.

In it—stuff about grief, trauma, domination—getting scared. It's he who has the dreary boarding house, California childhood, etc.

B. A *novel*, God willing, about a spiritual aristocrat, "R." No breakdowns for him.

He *is* a painter. He has the fire(s).
Forget about his childhood, except references "in situ." It demeans him.
He works with wax, etc. Is close to his older sister. Very laconic, gruff.

No one quite sure where he was born.
Sister claims she doesn't know.

Parents were active Nazis? Or is it his sister, whom he forgives? (He was in Sweden during the war.)

The German thing: morbidity, perversity

He takes injections for something—a hypochondriac?

Insanity = a deficit in behavior (rather than liberation)

Archbishop of Naples (1920s) said the earthquake at Amalfi was caused by the anger of God at the shortness of women's skirts

Baby Face—a film [*directed by Alfred E. Green in 1933*] with Barbara Stanwyck—she makes her way up, floor by floor, through a large corporation

. . .

7/16/65   Paris

I haven't learned to mobilize rage—(I perform militant actions, without militant feeling)

Never *anger* but either *hurt* (if I love) or aversion, *distaste* if I don't

I never telephone anyone; I would ask someone leaving my apartment to mail a letter for me, if I could possibly help it—

I don't trust anyone to do anything for me—I want to do everything myself, or if I let anyone act as my agent in any matter, then I resign myself (in advance) to its not being done right or at all

The mornings are the worst.

People are cardboard, selfish—but it doesn't matter, I can take it. "They don't mean it personally."

Am I deteriorating these last two years—drying out, becoming stern, withdrawn?

Seething with resentment. But I don't dare show it. When it mounts, I just absent myself (Annette, etc.)

No image of the future.

I wouldn't want to day-dream. What! And get my hopes up?

My career is my life as something external to myself, + so I report it to others. What is inside is my grief.

If I expect as little as possible, I won't be hurt.

. . .

7/22/65

. . . Connection between sunlight and passivity "In the day the inward eye is blind" (Clytemnestra [*in Aeschylus's* Oresteia])

8/1/65   Paris

In [*SS's projected*] Borges essay, emphasize:
debt to Robert L[ouis] Stevenson (see B's essays on)—e.g.
[Borges's story] "Pierre Menard[, Author of the *Quixote*"],
fantastic stories
Idea of flat writing—transparency of the word—"degré zéro
de l'écriture" [*the reference is to Roland Barthes's concept
of a "zero degree of writing"*]
Tradition of Kafka (in translation) vs. both Joyce + Robbe-
Grillet

Read Blanchot, *L'Attente, L'Oubli*
[Jean] Reverzy
[Bataille] *Histoire de l'Oeil*
[Pierre Louÿs] *Trois Filles de Leur Mère*

French as anti-language, hence Blanchot's novels . . .
Jansenist tradition of Robbe-Grillet . . .

Robbe-Grillet's novels are about *action*

8/19/65   Corse [Corsica]

art = making concrete abstract and abstract concrete

music has the purest historicism (it's been done—can't do it
again)—because it's the most abstract art (in this respect, like
math)

The frontality of Bastia [in Corsica]—straight streets, rect-
angles—6–8 story buildings of grey that seem a faded pas-
tel color

[Stéphane] Mallarmé had no heirs (except a woman poet, Saint-Elme)—i.e. no *obscure* French poetry, When [Gerard Manley] Hopkins is translated into French, he becomes completely clear. Very French, the notion of Descartes that a true idea may be defined (!) as one that is clear and distinct—

Is literature one of the arts?
(read the Sartre essay)

[*Eisenstein's*] *Film Form*   "the parallel"

e.g.'s > massacre of the strikers // slaughter house [Eisenstein's] (*Strike*)
        > liberation of prisoners // ice melting ([*Pudovkin's*] *Mother*)
        > eagle // Napoleon ([Abel Gance's] *Napoleon*)
        > slow train // snail ([Gance's] *La Roue, The Avenging Corsican*)

The first works—is both consubstantiation and emotional reinforcement

[The] second, third and fourth don't: are merely illustrative

Another e.g. father being blackmailed // shot of a vise (*La Roue*)

Just a technique of silent films?

•

"The ellipsis"

in time
in space   this is what cutting is

•

"The flashback"
when does this come in?

"Establishing shot"
showing spatial relations of people, things

N.B. difference when it [*entry trails off*]

8/22/65

... Noël [*Burch, the American film critic and director, who had
moved to France in 1951*]

8/24/65

Corsica—

—People speaking 2 languages all the time, switching back
from one to the other

—Cactus; eucalyptus + plane trees; thistles; palms

—Churches + other old buildings with regular pattern of square
holes left by scaffolding (manner in which they were built:
throw up wooden scaffolding the shape of the building first)

—Violent summer storms; frequent power failures

—Steady depopulation; recent repatriation of "Pieds-Noirs" [*French settlers in Algeria, who in some cases chose to leave for France and in some cases were forced to in the wake of Algerian independence in 1962*] who farm, run restaurants

—10 main names on the island (very inbred (Mattei . . .)

—The "maquis" [*"dense brush" of the Corsican interior*], the fires

—Eau d'Orezza ("pétillante" [*"sparkling"*], from natural spring in interior of the island)
Sirop d'orgea (coconut plus water, very sweet)

—Charcuterie de Corse (4 kinds of ham)

—Casino: [In Corsican] U Casone

—Pale pinkish brown color of stone houses—*faded* red-tile roofs

. . .

Bataille: connection between sex + death, pleasure + pain (Cf. *Larmes d'Éros*)

The point about a confidence-man is that he *NEVER* drops the mask. He always *SEEMS* reliable, attractive, friendly, etc. You can never square your *EXPERIENCE* of him with what you come to *KNOW* about him.

Irene: my *EXPERIENCE* of her for 4½ years was of limitless lavish love. What I might force myself (via [Diana]

Kemeny etc.) to think about her—her need to dominate, to subjugate, to undermine—my understanding, in brief, is always being short-circuited by my experience. Hence the: *HOW CAN (COULD) SHE?* Etc.

Can one overwhelm experience by understanding? Or only replace it by another experience?

Irene:

—her perfect assurance (no "I think" or "this is probably stupid, but" or "Maybe"—just constatation

[*In the margin:*] The auto-didact

—her freedom from guilt + regrets (no "I wish" or "I wish I hadn't" or "Why did I?")

[*In the margin:*] Cult of spontaneity
[Norman] Mailer ethic—Jane, Ricardo, Meg

—her consistency

—her generosity + willingness to put herself completely at another's disposal

The perfect combination: I delivered myself into her hands—

She loves me
She knows better than I (about life, sex, etc.)
She is eager to put her knowledge + herself at my disposal

Result:

When I need something, I am served (in fact, I learn needs
    I didn't know I had—through having them fulfilled
    without having to ask)

When we disagree, she is right

When I am wrong, she will teach me

When I try to help her—or take the sexual initiative—
    or correct her, I am wrong, clumsy, inapposite

When I improve, I will make her happy

So I take + take—both supremely nourished yet somehow
undermined, restless, resentful.

I frustrate her—but she is so good, a martyr to me, patient—I
feel at turns guilty and complacent + anxious.

I want to make her happy, but this has become a kind of presumption on my part. I'm not good enough—YET—to make
her happy.

Yet she loves me. Why? Because she believes my apprenticeship will work out—or just because she can't help herself?

It doesn't seem as if *I* make her happy—or make love to her.
Only that she allows it; it's all she. When she is passive sexually, it's not that I take her (or *ever* seduce her); she has con-
sented to let me play the active role + then I do it.

·

Useless to reason that this subtle, supple, ingenious form of
domination—reducing me to a panicky, hostile, dependent
child—is Irene's way of procuring for herself *love*. The only
way she knows. (First the lavish tenderness, the superabun-

dance of caresses + bathing + feeding + sex + going over one's problems > etc. etc.) And also her means of becoming powerful (through *giving*, she triumphs + emasculates!) + of over-coming her sense of her weakness.

Useless—because I *experienced* it as love.

Irene, the *first* person to act to me in a loving manner, + the *only* person from whom I gratefully accepted love.

I am left with a complete paralysis of my sexual life—she rejected me because I was no good in bed, I *am* no good in bed—and a terrible anxiety about taking from people (even cups of coffee) except when it appears to be totally impersonal.

•

Irene was jealous of David because that was the one part of my life she couldn't completely take over.

If I hadn't had David, would she have stayed as long as she did?

If I hadn't had David, would I have survived the 4½ years?

One thing I know: If I hadn't had David, I would have killed myself last year.

•

I was terrorized (but didn't know it). I am, still, terrorized. (Irene has quality; I don't. Irene doesn't love me because her standards are high. She won't settle for what I, or most people, would settle for.) And I would be in a continued state of mortal terror—of her anger; of her leaving me; of her finding me stupid, inconsiderate, selfish, sexually inadequate—if she ever came back.

Does she get a *kick* out of my groveling in the last two years? That's what Kemeny (+ Noël [Burch]) says. I can't believe it—of someone I love(d). She'd be a monster then—

I've always thought (at worst) that she felt *nothing*—that she'd had to harden + blind herself, fantastically, so as to break free—so as not to feel guilty.

But what if she actually got *pleasure* from it?

I can't make myself imagine that—which everyone finds obvious.

•

Can I say: I am *disappointed* in Irene. She is not what I thought, believed she was (is)?

No?

Why not?

Because she got there first—she is disappointed in *me*.

•

My "masochism"—caricatured in the exchange of letters with Irene this summer—reflects not the desire to suffer, but the hope of appeasing anger and making a dent in indifference through demonstrating that I suffer (and am "good," i.e. harmless).

What Kemeny means by always citing the "I'm so good that it hurts" story.

If Mommy sees she's really hurt me, she'll stop hitting me. But Irene isn't my mommy.

8/25/65

[*The twentieth-century French writer André Pieyre de*] Mandiargues says the two best erotic books ever written are: *Histoire de l'Oeil* + *Trois Filles de Leur Mère*. They are the two poles: the first, reserved—each word counts—chaste language—laconic, lean; the second, obscene—décontracté, bavardé [*"relaxed, chatty"*]—endless.

N.B. last part of the Louÿs [*Trois Filles*]—petites scènes de théâtre (like [*Jean Genet's*] *Le Balcon*)

Picaresque form of the Bataille [*Histoire de l'Oeil*] (an adventure) vs. two-room set of the Louÿs: the door, the bed, the stairway

Thomas Faulk making dummies in wax in So. Carolina, but they get blurred

Prefigures Prof. ———'s dummy of him

Why can't (don't) I say: *I'm* going to be a sexual champion? Ha!

8/27/65   Avignon

Art is the grand condition of the *past* in the present. (cf. architecture). To become "past" is to become "art"—cf. photographs, too

Works of art have a certain *pathos*

Their historicity?
Their decay?
Their veiled, mysterious, partly (+ forever) inaccessible aspect?
The fact that no one would (could) ever do *that* again?

Perhaps, then, works only *become* art—they *are* not art

+ they become art when they are a part of the past

a *contemporary* work of art is a contradiction
we assimilate present to the past? (or is it something else? a gesture, a research, a cultural souvenir?)

Wittgenstein // [Arthur] Rimbaud

Renunciation of the vocation:

W.—schoolteaching, being a hospital orderly
R.—Abyssinia

Description of their work as trifling—

School of Fontainebleau painting.

Erotic painting
"Mannerist"
(all converging on a breast, e.g.)

Avignon (Musée Calvet):

>> [Jacques-Louis] David, *Mort de Joseph Bara*
　　[Jean-Baptiste] Greuze
　　[Jean-Honoré] Fragonard
　　[Jean-Baptiste-Siméon] Chardin
　　　　(cf. in Louvre)
　　[François] Boucher
　　[Antoine] Watteau

[A. J. T.] Monticelli + [J. M. W.] Turner—precursors of impressionism

•

"0 Degree" writing: see through to the matter, which is "dépaysant" [*"disorienting"*]
e.g. sci-fi novels

"0 Degree" films
e.g. B-films—no formal elaboration; instead, the violence of
　　the subject
Medium is transparent

Novel, narrative, text (two viable traditions or possibilities *now*)

(1) 0 Degree: Kafka, Borges, Blanchot, sci-fi, [Camus's] *L'Étranger* ("récit")

2) Unfinished legacy of Joyce—novel as language, texture, materiality of discourse—[Djuna] Barnes, Beckett, early [John] Hawkes, Burroughs

Music

Get complete works of Webern

Hodeir, Adorno books

[Claude] Debussy—*Jeux, La Mer*

. . .

Two traditions

Music to be *heard* (with increasingly complex formal structures)
Conceptual music—composer not interested in how it sounds, but in the concepts or math relations it expresses
Cage, Varèse are something else again, because they are interested not in music but in sound (def[inition]: music = organized sound)

For [*the French experimental composer Jean*] Barraqué, e.g. final test is how it sounds—not for [*the Ukrainian-American mathematical biophysicist Nicolas*] Rashevsky, where intervals which dist[ribute] one sequence from the next may be 29 seconds, 30 seconds, + 31 seconds—imperceptible to the *ear*

New resources opened by electronic (taped) music

. . .

To rehear: [Henry] Purcell, [Jean-Philippe] Rameau, [Ludwig von] Beethoven's Fifth, *La Mer*, [Frédéric] Chopin, late [Franz] Liszt, [Franz] Schubert's Eighth

19th C. full of retrograde work (i.e. post-Beethoven, but which doesn't move on from late Beethoven) which nevertheless develops something—e.g. Schubert—who in his life-time practically exhausts the possibilities of *melody* (pure tonal melody). His heirs: [Johannes] Brahms, [Pyotr Ilyich] Tchaikovsky, [Gustav] Mahler, [Richard] Strauss (?) e.g. trio of *Rosenkavalier*, Act III, arias in *Ariadne* [*auf Naxos*]

Dist[inguish] *melody* from *lyricism*

The *Rosenkavalier* trio is perhaps the climax of *lyricism* in music (surpasses the "Liebestod")—But its greatness is in the play of the voices against each other—the harmonies, the orchestration—the exalted emotionalism of the melodic line: things which are much more complex (and decadent?) compared with pure melody in the Schubert sense

Philosophy is an art form—art of thought or thought as art

Comparing Plato + Aristotle is like comparing Tolstoy + Dostoyevsky [or] Rubens + Rembrandt

Not a question of right or wrong, true or false—like diff[erent] "styles"

Last good novels in English:

    [Ford Madox Ford,] *The Good Soldier*
    [F. Scott Fitzgerald,] *The Great Gatsby*, *Tender Is the Night*
    [E. M. Forster,] *Passage to India*
    [William Faulkner,] *Light in August*

Transitional "novels":

> [Virginia Woolf,] *Mrs. Dalloway*
> [Djuna Barnes,] *Nightwood*
> [Jean-Paul Sartre,] *Nausea*
> [Italo Svevo,] *Confessions of Zeno*
> [Ernest Hemingway,] *The Sun Also Rises*
> [Hermann Hesse,] *Steppenwolf*
> Nathanael West

New "novels":

> [Blanchot,] *Celui qui ne m'accompagnait pas*
> [Burroughs,] *Naked Lunch*
> [Joyce,] *Ulysses* + *F*[*innegans*] *W*[*ake*]
> Early Hawkes
> [Robbe-Grillet,] *Dans le labyrinthe*
> [Burt Blechman,] *Stations*

8/28/65   Marseilles

. . .

Two Canadian doctors report making a skin graft on a woman patient of skin donated by one of the doctors—after several sessions of hypnosis in which the woman was told the graft would definitely take.

My fascination with:
Disembowellment
Stripping down
Minimum conditions (from *Robinson Crusoe* to concentration
    camps)
Silence, muteness

My voyeuristic attraction to:

Cripples (Trip to Lourdes—they arrive from Germany in sealed trains)

Freaks

Mutants

Can use A as an idea of *form* in art, not just "subject matter"— form as a gesture of the will—: if I will it strongly enough, it will work "for" a literary text, if it's organic enough . . .

Are A and B connected? Parallel? (as I have thought, for the first time, to arrange them here)

Is B the sadistic element in my sensibility which compensates for all the blessing of people? (as Kemeny has often said).

A sadistic vision carefully detached, unhinged from any sadistic acting-out?

Compare [X] who discovered he liked to play a sadistic role in sex by noting that he liked the same things—looking in medical books, at cripples, etc.

Or is there something more? Such as:

Identifying myself with the cripple?

Testing myself to see if I flinch? (reacting against my mother's squeamishness, as with food)

A fascination with minimum conditions—obstacles, handicaps—of which the mutilated person is a *metaphor*?

A systematic research into myself:

I note, this summer, a mild claustrophobia: feeling oppressed in small rooms, needing the window open, + to sit either by window or door in restaurants

Do I show my contempt for other people's weaknesses? (Noël said I did—when he was being "sea-sick" + hypochondria-cal—but then he feels contempt for himself.)

Has my uncultivated ("California") manner outlived its use-fulness? (I lack dignity.) It has become an accomplice to my tendency to defer to authoritative self-confident people, + it perpetuates my strategy of deceiving people as to the extent of my aggressiveness, pretending that I'm not aggressive or competitive at all.

It's time I stopped reassuring people—and leading them on (this spring + summer:
George [Lichtheim, *the German refugee critic and historian of Marxism, who was in love with SS*], [*then literary editor of the British radio magazine*, The Listener, *May*] Derwent, Noël!)

8/29/65   Tangier

[SS spent the last days of August and the first half of September 1965 visiting Paul and Jane Bowles in Tangier, Morocco. By then, Alfred Chester, from whom she was already somewhat estranged, was living in the city and was involved with a young Moroccan man, Driss Ben Hussein El Kasri.]

. . .

Ravi Shankar

The reason I'm not paranoid (but counter-paranoid, even) trusting, eternally surprised at the malice (Alfred, "Edward [Field]–Nadia [Gould]") of people I haven't harmed: I was (felt) profoundly neglected, ignored, unperceived as a child— perhaps always, until or with the exception of Irene—

Even persecution, hostility, envy seem to me, "au fond" [*"at bottom"*], more *attention* than I feel myself likely to receive. I trust the good intentions of strangers, acquaintances, and friends whom I have treated courteously because I can't believe I matter that much to them—that they're paying that much attention to me—to behave "back" otherwise than courteously. To be the subject of envious fantasy . . . who am I?!

Remember—how surprised I was that Irene even mentioned my existence to "Kate" last summer; that Alfred (just now) found me "important" enough in a letter to Edward to mention that I was coming to Tangier.

Alfred's novel:
No time sequence, *yet* the narrative is sequential
No protagonist or central character, but an ensemble

. . .

Alfred:

Underneath the bully, the charmer, the wit, the sage, the betrayer—Tiresias, Oscar Wilde, Isidore—was this hysterical, ill-tempered child who cannot finish a sentence or answer a question or listen to what anyone else is saying.

Yet Alfred always was looking for an oracle (St. Stanislaus, Irene, Edward, Paul Bowles).

Now he has burnt his wig [*Chester was entirely hairless*] + talks about having a small cock + no pubic hair. He has always felt hideous, + now he talks about it, wants to talk of nothing else.

Was he ever wise? Or has he lost his wisdom? (It being a "number," like his charm.) And he looks for "meaning" ("symbols," romance) where there is none. —Pseudo-problems!

Like Susan T[*aubes, who committed suicide in 1969 by drowning herself off Long Island; SS identified the body*] not being able to concentrate on what someone is saying because she wants to understand what the connection is between that + the leaf at her feet—and she can't.

Pseudo-problems!

Nothing is mysterious, no human relation. Except love.

I couldn't fall for Alfred as I am today—even if he were still what he was (+ no longer is).
Because I respect myself now.

I always fell for the bullies—thinking, if they don't find me so hot they must be great. Their rejection of me showed their superior qualities, their good taste. (Harriet, Alfred, Irene)

I didn't respect myself. (Did I love myself?)

Now I have really known suffering. And I have survived. I am alone—unloved + w[ith]o[ut] someone to love—the thing I feared most in the world. I have touched bottom. And I survive.

Of course, I don't love myself. (If I ever did!) How can I, when the one person I ever trusted has rejected me—the person I made the arbiter, + the creator, of my loveableness. I feel profoundly alone, cut off, unattractive—as I never did before. (How cocky + superficial I was!) I feel unloveable. But I respect that unloveable soldier—struggling to survive, struggling to be honest, just, honorable. I respect myself. I'll never fall for the bullies again.

. . .

The Benefactor: "portrait of a prophet"!

Jane [Bowles] + Sherifa [Bowles's Moroccan lover]:

"She's crazy. Isn't she crazy, Paul?"
"She doesn't ever shut up!"
"She doesn't want to be treated as a servant."
"How old is she, Paul?"
"If she moves any closer to me I'll scream."
"She's a primitive, you know."
"Don't you think she's ugly?"
"She's very excited by you, by your being here. Any woman excites her."
"They're like monkeys, aren't they?" (Sherifa + Mohammed)

Paul + his "friend" (Sent him down to see if the taxi had come).
Gordon [Sager]: "Should I give him money?"
Paul: "Don't. You'll spoil him."

The Bowleses
Alfred + Driss
Ira Cohen + Rosalind

Targisti—Brion Gysin
Bob Faulkner (with Jane B. + John Latouche, one the bright
    young things of th[ei]r mid-thirties)
Gordon Sager
Alan Ansen
Alec Waugh + Earl of Jermyn, "Irving" from NY via
    Havana
Liz + Dale
Charles Wright + elderly lush

(past: Stein, Djuna Barnes, Bowles, [Allen] Ginsberg, [Gregory] Corso, Harold Norse, Irving Rosenthal)

S-M-L:
Opium—morphine—heroin
Peyote—mescaline—LSD

The world of [Evelyn Waugh's] *Decline + Fall* + [Ronald] Firbank + [James Purdy's] *Malcolm* + [Jane Bowles's] *Two Serious Ladies* is a real world! People like that exist, live those lives! *Here* (The Bowleses, Alan Ansen, Gordon Sager, Bob Faulkner, etc., etc.)! And I thought it was all a joke—that obsessiveness, that heartlessness, that cruelty. The international homosexual style—God, how mad + humanly ugly + unhappy it is.

[*The American writer*] Alan Ansen will make a pun in classical Greek on a line of Sophocles to a shoe-shine boy in Athens. 300 books, records for his summer in Tangier which must be carted back. The Athens–Tangier circuit (for "boys")

Is [*the [Anglo-American] poet W. H.*] Auden the only writer of this world who, partly, transcended it (spiritually)?

9/5/65   Tangier, Tetouan

Burning incense (holding a stick betw[een] thumb + forefinger) in the cab all the way to Tetouan. (Ira Cohen, Rosalind, me.)

Make an opera out of the story of Gilles de Rais [*medieval Breton knight infamous for the serial murder of children*]
The Arab flipper-case sitting in a tea-shop howling with laughter at a picture of the Venus de Milo someone had shown him.

Brocaded (silver + gold threads) silk "kaftans"—long (to the floor), cut wide, long full sleeves

Kif melts the brain; dexemyl sharpens the edges. (Kif makes you drift—makes you forget what someone said a minute before—hard to follow a long story or joke, makes you react *less* to other people (one isn't "considerate," i.e. you don't *anticipate* people's reactions)—

Younger Moroccans are turning away from kif ("people who smoke kif never do anything"—aren't successful, ambitious) to alcohol. (Just the reverse!)

Many jokes about Corsican laziness, which is proverbial. Man getting on another's shoulders to screw in light bulb. "Now Turn."

Burroughs also involved in erudition (as "the fantastic"), like Borges.

Insanity: proliferating + melting of thought. Like wax. (T Faulk's images)

Alfred symptoms:

Electricity image
"I'm wired wrong"
"The wiring is wrong"
"I feel I'm radioactive"
"The car is wired—everybody's listening"

Obsession with memory (anything he can't remember seems terribly important), numbers, coincidences, people having same name, etc.

Belief in magic, telepathy [e.g.] Paul Bowles wrote [Chester's] book, some connection with Truman Capote book.

Lapses of memory: forgetting what was said 5 minutes earlier

Paranoid: afraid of police car behind[;] "everyone looking at me"; "why are there so many cars?" "why is everything we say being broadcast?"

Theme of the changeling (Alfred: "I'm not human" (because of hair): "I'm a changeling.")

. . .

Kif = "grass"
High = "stoned"
Hashish = "hash"

Eating in a soup-kitchen at 7 am in the Medina. With your hands—afterwards, you wash (proprietor pours water in a small plastic container over your hands into a tin pail + then offers you the lower part of the apron he's wearing to dry them on).

1 9 6 5

Walls blackened by smoke—
One pattern of tiles on floor, another for walls (a "dream ma-
    chine") windows opening out from rooms onto central
    court—

Read *The Arabian Nights* in the Burton translation.
Purity. Leading a pure life. No mail, phone; don't ask, wait;
don't publish everything you write (Noël cited the example of
des Forêts)

Tetouan: the long narrow garden in the Spanish part of the city.
Many different kinds of trees. (Gaudí garden in Barcelona).
Esp[ecially] one kind, light grey bark, very tall—the trunk +
branches not round or tubular but indented like an arm with
two tibias or two fibulas. And the roots drip, melt over the
wall—reach across + join with the roots of the next tree.

. . .

Consciousness of other countries through radio. Can get all
the Spanish stations (Sevilla, etc.) perfectly clearly on a small
transistor in Tangier.

. . .

Scholastic definition of time as the actualization of possibilities.

There is a kif mentality which I have encountered many
times + never identified (because I hadn't experienced it myself). Joe Chaikin is one version, Ira + Rosalind two others.
Slowed down. Easy-going. All things are equally important,
nothing is very important. Trivial connections, coincidences
seem remarkable. Feeling of being protected: everything will

turn out for you. Other people come in + out of focus. Hard to stay with one subject very long talking—the mind drifts. Big oral appetite, often hungry. Powerful languor—want to sit or lie down, Very easy to change your plans, go with the moment. Cotton in your head—everything is "beautiful"—you glide toward it, away from it.

This is what the beat generation is about—from Kerouac to the Living Theatre: all the "attitudes" are easy—they're not gestures of revolt—but natural products of the drugged state-of-mind. But anyone who is with them (or reads them) who isn't stoned naturally interprets them as people with the same mind you have—only insisting on different things. You don't realize they're somewhere *else*.

I would never work—write—if I took a lot of kif. I feel a loss of energy, And I feel isolated, lonely (though not more un-happily so)—

Noël?

9/6/65   Tangier

For a year (age 13) carried the *Meditations* of Marcus Aure-lius always with me in my pocket. I was so afraid of dying—+ only that book gave me some consolation, some fortitude. I wanted to have it on me, to be able to touch it, at the moment of my death.

Tell Kemeny of my great decision—the conscious decision I took when I was 11, entering Mansfield [Junior High School in Tucson, Arizona]. Never to have another catastrophe like

Catalina [Junior High in Tucson]. ([*SS's childhood friend*] Arvell Lidikay etc.) "I will be popular." And again, more capably, at NHHS [North Hollywood High School]

I understood the difference between the outside + the inside. No point in trying to teach 6-year-olds that the collar-bone was called the clavicle, or [*SS's sister*] Judith the 48 capitals of the 48 states (me age 12, the bunk beds).

I was Gulliver in Lilliput + in Brobdingnag at the same time. They were too strong for me and I was too strong for them. I would protect them from me. I was from Krypton, but I would be meek, mild-mannered Clark Kent. I would smile, I would be "nice" . . . And politics came into it—was that a supporting cause, or a product of the unhappy consciousness? I felt guilty because I was more "fortunate" than others (Becky: the ditch digger ex–high school classmate I spotted on the canyon as I was driving to UCLA in Mother's Pontiac).

Annette decided to be illegible to the others, the little folk. (The accent, the manner, the displayed erudition). I didn't insist. I became legible.

·

Well, what's wrong with projects of self-reformation?

The four senior living writers:
Nabokov, Borges, Beckett, Genet

His mind is perforated.

"Informal painting."

Jasper [*Johns on Duchamp*]: "painting of precision + beauty of indifference"

Is photography an art? Or just a bastard, an abortion of cinema. Noël says when he looks at a beautiful photograph, he thinks: Damn you, why don't you move?

<pre>
                    Photography
        Painting ^   ^ Cinema
      (Lewis Carroll)   ([Henri] Cartier-Bresson,
                              Robert Frank)
</pre>

Maybe the only photography that is satisfying is the painterly, posed, artificial kind. (Like Lewis Carroll in the 19th C.)

Is it a defect of a film when it seems to be a series of photographs, of "belles images" ["*pretty pictures*"]? (As Harriet said of [*Sergei Eisenstein's 1927 film*] *October* in East Berlin in 1958)
Cf. Blanchot's essay on "The Athenaeum"

. . .

Novalis . . . saw that the new art was not the total *book* but the fragment. The art of the fragment—a demand for a fragmentary speech, not to hinder communication but to make it absolute. (Hence, the past, ruins become available to us.)

. . .

Alfred:

Every thing goes blank in the middle of a sentence—

"there's nothing"

"I feel the whole world is listening to everything I say"

"Susan, what's happening? There's something very strange going on."

"You're hiding something from me."

"I think I have syphilis. Or cancer."

"Susan, you look so sad. I've never seen you look so sad."

Tangier:

Rif mountain country in skirt [of] red + white striped cotton, white cotton over it on the top—a broad-brimmed straw hat with four braids coming out to brim from the top—brown leggings of skin

[You] can hear cocks crowing at dawn in Tangier—donkeys (burros) all over town, camels just outside.

The municipal hospital in the Medina—at the wall overlooking the sea. Must have been a fort: there are huge rusty cannons in the courtyard.

Beni Makada—the city mental hospital: [they] give everybody electric shock treatment.

Orson Welles of his 9-year-old daughter: she might become a professional; she's a very nice girl, she has very good manners. Professionalism is a kind of good manners . . .

. . .

[Alan Ansen said that] in *Naked Lunch*, a substructure of narrative, characterization + place description fades into "routines"—heightened fantastic projections of people, places, + actions, on the one hand, + into learned footnotes on drugs, diseases + folkways on the other.

What makes fantasy pleasurable
bearable
for most people is that, usually, one doesn't want—really—for the fantasy to come true. (Sex, dreams of glory, etc.) I find fantasies—of love, warmth, sex—unbearably painful because I'm always aware it['s] "just" a fantasy. I want—I turn up the wanting—but it isn't going to happen. I want, too much.

[Vladimir Nizhy,] *Lessons with Eisenstein* (London: George Allen & Unwin, 1962)

Tangier:

Old man in white turban with long bright orange beard (henna)

The banyan tree + the old cannons (ca. 1620s) in the garden off the Socco Grande

Water-carrier selling pure spring water which she pours in a glass—then drops a few shiny laurel leaves for taste

Hamid—Driss' brother—emaciated—sitting in striped pajamas—legs hanging over bed in hospital ward—moustache—one foot, with gangrene, in a sock—henna on all the nails of one hand—his mother + sister, Fatima, have brought him bread

Eating in common out of a huge bowl or skillet—with one's hands—each with a piece of bread to dip in

Indian movies (spectacles) dubbed in Arabic, European movies dubbed in French + Spanish (Ciné Lux, Ciné Alcázar, Ciné Rif, Ciné Vox, Ciné Goya, Ciné Mauretania, etc.)

A Municipal Casino off the Boulevard Pasteur

9/7/65   Tangier

high = "stoned," "bombed out"

Alfred: Has decided not to eat any meals outside his house (fear of being poisoned), wouldn't take coffee from Driss the other night; is going to sell his car; thinks he doesn't have a valid passport anymore (the photo); broke Driss' watch because he thought there was a microphone concealed in it—

["Shitan"] = Arab word for the devil (cf. Satan)—comes to you in dreams, prevents you from crying out

. . .

Country people on donkeys leaving Tangier late Sunday afternoon—have come in for market—down the street that leads from the Medina to the Avenida de Espana at the port

. . .

Waiter in rest[aurant] sprinkling rose water on people to whom he's just served mint tea—then in the tea

"nana" = mint
"attay" = tea
b'salemma = goodbye (shalom)

. . .

sprinkle cinammon + sugar (separate) on couscous

Alfred thinks he's a hermaphrodite.

Last year, when he had his "flip-out," he sent 50 copies of his book of stories to his family + neighbors—"so they should know me, because I'd always been hiding because I'm so ugly; I wanted to expose myself further"—incl[uding] to his father (c[are] o[f] his lawyer) who died when he was 14

"I guess I'm a failure as a writer. My books don't sell. I'm not as good a writer as I thought."

"You know, nobody writes a book alone. All books are a collaboration."

"I thought, 'I deserve to die. I've betrayed the Jews.' And then the next evening, Absalom (works at the Lion + Lizard) offered me a glass of Malaga wine."

. . .

Visitors to Tangier: Samuel Pepys, (cf. diary), Alexandre Dumas, Pierre Loti, [Nikolai] Rimsky-Korsakov, [Camille] Saint-Saëns, Eugène Delacroix, [André] Gide > Gertrude Stein, Djuna Barnes, Tennessee Williams, (Socco Chico in *Camino Real*), Paul Bowles, etc. etc.

Portuguese occupation of Tangier (1471–1662)—expelled by English fleet of the Earl of Sandwich + troops of Count Peterborough in 1662. English, after destroying most of the city, left in 1684—chased away by army of Ali ben Abdal-

lah—remained governed by his family until 1844, i.e. was
"Moroccan"

[Alan Ansen on] Burroughs—

The Soft Machine: the entire work takes place at action stations (its ideology runs past us on its way to expendability).
Briefly, original vitality is seized on by writers of life-scripts,
who impose on lively organisms deathical [*sic*] patterns
(though it is possible to downgrade a life-script, even the best
life-script is inhibiting and so inimical) for the purpose of
self-aggrandizement. The victims revolt by talking out of
turn + throwing the word + image back

Ian Sommerville's Flicker Machine
Brion Gysin's Dream Machine

Place on a turntable with a lighted electric bulb at its center a
perforated cylinder (some or all the perforations may be cov-
ered by diaphanous material of diff[erent] colors) + start the
turntable revolving. Watch the cylinder intently

The result sh[oul]d be a fragmentation of the image track
equivalent to the fragmentation of the sound-track achieved
in cut-up. (Another "control," suggestive rather than minutely
regulatory, is an early consideration of the interconnection of
sound + image tracks—Rimbaud's sonnet on the vowels.)

Moroccan whose throat was cut lying on his back at dawn in
the back of a tea-shop in the Medina: someone had put fig
leaves on his neck to cover the wound

The infinite sadness of the Villa de France dining room—
"Moroccan" décor, Hungarian 3-man combo (piano, violin,

man who doubles on bass + xylophone). "French cuisine," stiff lower-middle class English tourists plus freaks (the mad, red-faced German woman with glasses who eats alone + complains about the food; the two American men, one about 4'8" with a huge head, the other tall, crew-cut + glasses, prematurely middle-aged like an ass[istan]t prof. at some cow college)
—the whole scene like a 2nd class dining room on the *Carpathia* mid-1930's. The slim Moroccan waiters wearing fez who speak to you in bad French—

An old lady of 70: One of the Alexandria crowd who came here when Egypt went modern 10 years ago—

One of the reasons I couldn't not have a job + just write (as Alfred did in NY) is that I can't stand to ask, to become indebted to people—as one does, when one begs, borrows, + steals to live. Need to be independent, i.e. not to trust. Not just middle-class timidity—

Verbs: ducked, spreading, bolted, humored, shoved, flopping, shook, shimmied, trailed behind, shooting out, heaving, splurting, clattering, sparked off, clutching, hissed, clicked his tongue (Sp[anish]), his breast swelled, sparkle, charge, sniffed, slithered, gnawed, seeped . . .

. . .

Puvis de Chavannes painting in the Panthéon (Paris)

How much sh[oul]d artist know? (with Noël in Corsica)

Self-consciousness vs. tabula rasa—Wittgenstein, etc.

Dostoyevsky thought Eugène Sue was a great writer—can one now?

Films of George Cukor . . . [*A complete list follows.*]

Rhyming slang (Cockney): Hamsteads = Hampstead Heath = teeth, fire alarms + charms, arms, German bands + hands, loaf of bread + dead

. . .

Tangier—People looking for an experience of radical dépayse-ment [*"disorientation"*], in which context they can give full vent to forbidden addictions (boys, drugs, liquor)
If you flip, everyone is sympathetic but basically indifferent. It's your responsibility—Isn't that what you came for? Every man for himself—

I felt I had wandered into Charenton [*the insane asylum on the outskirts of Paris where de Sade was held*]. Never felt as alien, astonished, revolted, fascinated—completely "dépaysé" [*"disoriented"*]—since that first weekend with Harriet in S[an] F[rancisco] when I was 16

Communism—by definition—rules out the possibility of "dépaysement." No strangeness. (No alienation—it's explained away, something to be overcome.) All men are alike, brothers.

Never realized how much conceptualization I take for granted in ordinary conversation, until I talked to Driss. "How long has Alfred been this way?" involves "how long" and "this way"

Under majoring + pot, everything happens twice. You say something, then you hear yourself say it.

. . .

Send Noël:

[Erich Auerbach] *Mimesis*
Eliade, *Yoga*
Thomas gospel
Stations
[Wittgenstein] *Philosophical Investigations*

. . .

Novels about erotic *obsession*: Balzac, *La Fille aux Yeux d'Or*,
Louÿs, *La Femme et le Pantin*, Rachilde, *Monsieur Venus*
(Raoule the demented successor of Mathilde in [Stendhal's]
Le Rouge et le Noir)

Where to place [Théophile Gautier's] *Mlle. de Maupin*?

9/16/65   Paris

The main techniques for refuting an argument:

    Find the inconsistency
    Find the counter-example
    Find a wider context

Instance of (3):

I am against censorship. In all forms. Not just for the right of
masterpieces—high art—to be scandalous.

But what about pornography (commercial)?
Find the wider context:
notion of voluptuousness à la Bataille?

But what about children? Not even for them? Horror comics, etc.

Why forbid them comics when they can read worse things in
the newspapers any day. Napalm bombing in Vietnam, etc.

A just/discriminating censorship is impossible.

9/9/65   Tangier

*[This notebook has a photo of Virginia Woolf taped on the first
page, with Webern quoting Friedrich Hölderlin's phrase "to
live is to defend a form" on the second, and on the third a photo
of the dancer Rudolf Nureyev, with the words "lived by a
bridge, a tunnel" written under it.]*

Guaon, Jellalah, Ishiwa, Hamacha >>> Trance-groups (cults,
each with their separate santo)

Jellalah (or Djellalah): 12 in all, 9 men + 3 women

At the height of the dance (sometimes), they embrace cactus
trees, pick up (eat?) hot coals, drink blood, tear apart live
chickens + eat them, whip themselves or cut themselves with
knives

One of the women put a gag in her mouth

One retched, had spasms after, another sobbed. —In severe
cases, a massage; if that doesn't work, artificial respiration—
and a glass of water

One woman, after, saluted everyone in the room with a smile
and a kiss. (Grateful?)

The first woman to "go in" was embraced—(women take care of women, and men . . .)—then people got gradually less affectionate and solicitous with each other

Man (Negro) who shaves his head, who took off his white turban + kept wiping his head. (Sitting on the floor.)

Long grey garment on women

She undressed her from behind w[ith]o[ut] impeding her movements.

3 possibilities:

an independent story or novella—"The Dance"—about an event + someone watching it + trying to interpret it (like in [Kafka's] "The Penal Colony")*

Part II of "The Organization"—the antithesis to the Jews of Part I (i.e. a substitute for or alternative to the Org) [*SS wrote a story called "The Organization" and during the mid-1960s considered making it the foundation of a novel based in some degree at least on the Gurdjieffian circles she encountered in London through the British theater director Peter Brook and the American actress Irene Worth.*]

An interpolation—someone tells a story—in the novel about T[homas] F[aulk]

*an onlooker who wonders:

1. Is it art?
2. No, it's psychotherapy
3. No, it's sex

4. No, it's religion
5. No, it's commerce, entertainment
6. Or is it a game?

12 players
Each has his own rhythm (all the rhythms are very similar,
    have the same root——: can tease——who's It?

It's your turn. They push her forward.

Why does she go back a second time?

    not enough——needs more (like medicine)
    the group is punishing her——makes her go through
        it a second time (can't escape)
    showing-off, competition as to who's toughest
    gluttony

Can do several things with this:

Once told from the outside——another time ("The Dance")
from the inside

What hero of "Org" sees in Part II is *one* of the many interpretations raised by spectator in "The Dance"

*[Here, SS returns to the dance she saw in Tangier, though it is
not clear where the description of what she witnessed ends and
the sketch of a work of fiction begins.]*

Dancer may "turn down" one instrument (e.g. hand cymbals)
and move in close——bury her head between the flutes.

They're playing for her; they exchange knowing glances—they feel their power—they "have" her.

Sometimes they seem to take to take pity and a less violent interlude for a moment—

Her eyes are closed—her mouth hung open.

She wore no brassiere—

Under the handsome grey djellabah was a red-striped Rif wraparound. Was she ashamed?

I thought she was going to kiss her and she did—

They're pleased with themselves—

They burn incense (jawi) + hold the pot under the dancer's nostrils. Actually, there are two types of incense—one stronger, + more expensive, than the other. Does it or does it not intoxicate?

They're talking about groceries—while he "goes in"; it's not *their* rhythm. A moment ago . . .

At many points the spectator feels sexually excited.

They're praising the saint, someone tells him

9/17/65   Paris

[Bataille's] *Mme Edwarda* not just a récit [*the word "work" is crossed out in the entry*] with a preface but a two-part work: essay and récit.

Barthes, *Michelet*

Honor. Honor. Honor. To be at one's best all the time (like Léon Morin [*in Jean-Pierre Melville's 1961 film*, Léon Morin, Prêtre]).

The American bitch
The woman whose higher ethical standards the man must eventually accede to, to be "worthy" of her love. (As in Fritz Lang's *Fury*, Spencer Tracy + Sylvia Sidney)

Two types of women, uniquely American myths

9/17/65   (on plane to NY)

Ideal, for Hemingway: "grace under pressure"

Sartre: "When people's opinions are so different, how can they even go to a film together?"

[Simone de] Beauvoir: "To smile at opponents and friends alike is to abase one's commitments to the status of mere opinions, and all intellectuals, whether of the Right or Left, to their common bourgeois condition."

Compare:

Grief cannot be converted into any other currency

There is no currency with which personal grief may be converted

9/22/65   NY

How to end chapter I:

T[homas] F[aulk] has vision of sister as a mannequin or dummy

. . .

Baroque style: the conceit

[Richard] Crashaw (poetry)

[Gian Lorenzo] Bernini (sculpture)—cf. *St. Theresa*

10/4/65

Go from black + white to color (films):

[Michael Powell,] *Stairway to Heaven*

[Akira Kurosawa,] *High and Low*—yellow smoke

[Monty Berman and Robert S. Baker,] *Jack the Ripper*—blood

[Samuel Fuller,] *Shock Corridor*

[Joris] Ivens, *A Valparaiso* 2/3 [*in black and white*] > blood > 1/3 [*in color*]

[Sergei Eisenstein,] *Ivan the Terrible, Part II*

[Alain Resnais,] *Night and Fog*

[Michael Powell,] *Peeping Tom* (color film; memory [black-and-white] shots are in the past)

[The next film entry is prefaced by SS's annotation "added, June, 1966":]

[Sergei] Paradjanov, *The Horses of Fire* [*aka* Shadows of Forgotten Ancestors]

Work out principle in each case

Conversation with Paul [Thek] at Ratner's [*an all-night delicatessen in New York's East Village that was popular in the 1960s*]

T[homas] F[aulk]'s work:

The inside + the outside
—a caterpillar
—the form of a caterpillar, but the skin not organic (like a case, a box) + bright, polychrome

Metamorphosis
—faces, made of wax—
verisimilitude?
Sprouting hair, in the process of turning into the Wolf-Man
—serpent forms—huge—yet mechanized

An art which is sadistic toward the object (imprisoning it) rather than the audience

Putting the subject behind bars—connection with voyeurism, repressed sexual sadism

[Here, SS returns to the Thomas Faulk project:]

T.F. likes to look at freaks, atrocity photos, etc.

[*In passing, SS notes:*] Every art incarnates a sexual fantasy—

T.F. is not acting in the gap between art + life, but adding to "life"—taking up the possible unfulfilled options on an imaginary scale or gamut—like a man with a chromium collar + gills from his shoulders (cf. Burroughs' space men, *The Ticket That Exploded*)

"It doesn't exist, therefore I make it"

Legalism of American society:
Final appeal: "It's the law," and it works. Appeal to law substitutes for appeal to tradition, authority of a social class, etc. And in no other country do the courts—Esp[ecially] a Supreme Court—have so much power.

There is no message in this novel ["Thomas Faulk"], but rather (as Valéry said of certain of certain of Glück's operas) a perfect "mechanism to move the emotions."

Dist[inguish] sensation + emotion

[*Next to this entry, SS wrote two question marks.*] "new novels are Humean, atomistic in the wrong way"

. . .

Camus (*Notebooks*, Vol. II): "Is there a tragic dillettante-ism?"

What moves me most in art (in life): nobility. This is what I love most in [*the films of the French director Robert*] Bresson—his concern with man as noble being.

For "T.F.": The elevation + equanimity of Sartre's essay on [Paul] Nizan

I realize, rereading that essay, how important Sartre has been for me. He is the model—that abundance, that lucidity, that knowingness. And the bad taste.

. . .

10/13/65

Two arguments against discussing *formal* nature of art + against "art" concept itself (as taken for granted in my Style essay)

. . .

10/15/65

Get Poe stories!

Attrition of success: dispersion of energies

The catastrophe (for an artist) of having a retrospective; all his subsequent works become posthumous

work of art as a game
conceptual paradoxes in modern painting
Critic: using up his sensibility

The critic + the Creative Artist—two different stances. One cultivates his objectivity (knowledge), the other his subjectivity (ignorance?). The critic subjects himself, allows himself to be bombarded by contradictory stimuli. He has to remain open, yet one w-o-a [work of art] *may* cancel another out

Try to see [*1964's* Tomb of] *Ligeia* ([Roger] Corman) + [*1933's* Mystery of]*the Wax Museum* (original version + remake [*André de Toth's 1953* House of Wax] w[ith] Vincent Price):

Wax w[ith]o[ut] armature melts man w[ith] a handsome face—tries to rape a girl—she claws at his face—it peels off—underneath, a monster

10/17/65

The energy of [*the twentieth-century Italian writer Carlo Emilio*] Gadda—+ the sexuality of his response to people

Have I done all the living I'm going to do? A spectator now, calming down. Going to bed with the *New York Times*. Yet I thank God for this relative peace—resignation. Meanwhile the terror underneath grows, consolidates itself. How does anyone love?

A long convalescence. I *am* resigned to that. Under Diana [Kemeny]'s tutelage, I'll find my dignity, my self-respect.

A moment's backsliding: the news from California. Judith's reunion with Bob ("happy ending") made me dream for an hour of ———

But I must not think of the past. I must go on, destroying my memory. If only I felt some real energy in the present (something more than stoicism, good soldierliness), some hope for the future.

I'm not seeing anyone, really. Paul [Thek] growing distant, tapering off. I stayed home this evening. The phone didn't ring. That's what I wanted, didn't I? Not *these* people . . .

The detective story (Gadda, "Un Crime"). All told from his point-of-view.

[*Conversation with the American writer Stephen*] Koch [on] Borges:

Indefinite postponement of revelation (: opposite of poetry; cf. Rimbaud: poetry must be revelation or nothing)

[Borges's] *Ficciones* = illustrations of the problematical relation of (+ to) the "real" world; part of a highly reasoned dialogue with the "world"; all examples of a fundamental human act. (World is a pattern of irresolvable ambivalences, of which his aesthetic is an interpretation). Allegories of complete ambivalence. Unity only exists at the end of the labyrinth.

Hence, Borges an artist of ideas. But *resists* the conventional art-life distinction.

Career based on faith in the Word, an eternal *Logos*. (cf. studies of Carlyle, Hawthorne, Pascal). A series of metaphors, all images of infinite regression . . . God is infinite regression: He is hidden, but His endless labyrinthine depth is also his diversity.

Problem of "meaning." (Not passion)

Posits for the artist an ideal impersonality. (Hence, B[orges] often accused of coldness). B[orges] the greatest living artist of the contemplative.

Read [*the Dutch historian Johan*] Huizinga's essay, "The Task of Cultural History."

10/18/65

T. Faulk, like Hippolyte [*the protagonist of* The Benefactor], ends imprisoned in his own house. The only difference is that in the new novel the *coercion* + *pain* of that "decision" (defeat) are exposed.

But still, it's the same story. Hog-tied + flayed by the terrible parents, disguised as the ageing mistress and older friend (then) and now as older sister and older friend (now).

10/21/65

A marvelous title for T. Faulk:

The Eye and Its Eye (a book pub[lished] by Surrealist writer Georges Ribemont-Dessaignes after WWI)

buy: Georges Lemaître, *From Cubism to Surrealism in French Literature* (Harvard U.P., 1947)
Julien Levy, *Surrealism* (NY: Black Sun Press, 1936)

More stills: [*SS collected film stills.*]

Dietrich in tux
[*A shot from the Russian director Abram Room's 1927 film*]
    Bed and Sofa
[*Laurence Olivier in*] *Wuthering Heights*

Two kinds of wax:

pure beeswax: it's white, translucent; when melted down, becomes clear + transparent

Carnauba wax (more exp[ensive]): opaque—shellac, light-brown color—comes in shards—when melted down becomes translucent—melts at higher temperature

[Salvador] Dalí: "The only difference between myself and a madman is that I am not mad."

11/7/65

Picasso: "a work of art is a sum of destruction"

With D.G. [*Richard Goodwin, American writer and former speechwriter and aide to President Lyndon Johnson who later worked for Robert Kennedy, and who drafted the 1966 State of the Union; SS was briefly involved with him*] a whole new continent of neurosis sailed into view. (Atlantis) Who I am. I won't let "them" take it away from me. I won't be annihilated. (Something I didn't understand! She [*SS's mother*] only saw that I flirted a little, and exaggerated *that*.) Women accept that I am a person—most, anyway; the Jackie Kennedys don't bother me because they're so exotic—while "they" see me as woman first, person second.

Greatest influence on Barthes: reading [Gaston] Bachelard (*Psychoanalysis of Fire*—then books on earth, air, + water), second [*the French sociologist and anthropologist Marcel*] Mauss, structural ethnology, + , of course, Hegel, Husserl. The discovery of the phenomenological p-o-v [point of view]. Then you can look at *anything*, + it will yield up fresh ideas. *Anything*: a doorknob, Garbo. Imagine having such a mind as Barthes has—that always works . . . But Blanchot really started it.

Two greatest and most influential critics—Valéry; then Blanchot

11/8/65

Through 2/3 of [The] *Private Potato Patch* [of Greta Garbo *by J. Roy Sullivan at the Judson Poet's Theater*] I wanted to *be* Garbo. (I studied her; I wanted to assimilate her, learn her gestures, feel as she felt)—then, toward the end, I started to want her, to think of her sexually, to want to possess her. Longing succeeded admiration—as the end of my seeing her drew near. The sequence of my homosexuality?

[*The American actress*] Joyce Aaron: She expresses everything she feels. Instant outlet. (To be in touch with one's feelings. Not to have them always lagging behind—chronic "esprit de l'escalier.")

Make a play (with songs?) out of [*SS's short story*] "The Dummy." Transformations (Joe's [Chaikin] work).

. . .

In NY, little or no "community," but a great sense of "scene." What's started in London now—last couple of years.

My biggest pleasure the last two years has come from pop music (The Beatles, Dionne Warwick, The Supremes) + the music of Al Carmines.

I told [*the American cartoonist*] Jules Feiffer last night at the Fellini party that I was going to sue him!

In the next apt. I'll have lots of plants, massed together.

Write an essay for Don Allen's anthology, "Toward a New Poetics."

Joe [Chaikin] is not very sensuous.

D[ick] G[oodwin] says you know if you can trust someone to be discreet if he or she 1) has a strong character; 2) is a shrewd judge of people; 3) doesn't gossip himself. For example, Lillian [Hellman] doesn't pass the test because she is 1) + 3) but not 2).

11/12/65

Movies, since I've been back in NY (Sept. 17)

[At the New York Film] Festival:

Kurosawa, *Red Beard*—[Toshirō] Mifune
Visconti, *Vaghe Stelle . . .* —[Claudia] Cardinale
Franju, *Thomas L'Imposteur*

[Jerzy] Skolimowski, *Walkover*
[Marco] Bellocchio, *Pugni in Tasca*
Godard, *Le Petit Soldat* —[Anna] Karina

[*Seen elsewhere:*]

[Richard] Lester, *Help*—Beatles
[Jean] Renoir, *The Lower Depths*—[Louis] Jouvet, [Jean]
    Gabin
[Roman] Polanski, *Repulsion*—Catherine Deneuve
Visconti, *La Terra Trema*
[Arthur] Penn, *Mickey One*—Warren Beatty
[Frédéric Rossif,] *To Die in Madrid* [*produced by SS's*
    companion of the late 1960s, early 1970s, Nicole
    Stéphane]
[D. W.] Griffith, *Lady of the Pavements*—Lupe Velez
[Bert I. Gordon,] *Village of the Giants*
[Otto] Preminger, *Bunny Lake Is Missing*—Olivier, Keir
    Dullea
[Walter Grauman,] *A Rage to Live*—Suzanne Pleshette
[Jack Arnold,] *The Mouse That Roared*—Peter Sellers
[Charles Crichton,] *The Lavender Hill Mob*—[Alec] Guinness
[Clive Donner and Richard Talmadge,] *What's New,*
    Pussycat?—Peter O'Toole
Fellini, *Juliet of the Spirits*
[John Schlesinger,] *Darling*—Julie Christie, Dirk Bogarde
Sternberg, *The Last Command* (1928)—Emil Jannings
Lang, *Beyond a Reasonable Doubt* (1956)—Dana Andrews,
    Joan Fontaine
Lang, *Rancho Notorious* (1952)—Dietrich, Mel Ferrer,
    Arthur Kennedy
Sternberg, *The Docks of New York* (1928)—George
    Bancroft, Betty Compson, Baclanova

[Don Sharp,] *The Face of Fu Manchu*—Christopher Lee
[Franklin Schaffer,] *The Warlord*—Charlton Heston
[William Castle,] *I Know* [*What You Did*]
Mervyn LeRoy, *Quo Vadis*—Robert Taylor, Deborah Kerr, Peter Ustinov, Leo Genn

A problem: the *thinness* of my writing—it's meager, sentence by sentence—too architectural, discursive

Subjects:

The "ritual" murder of a helpless old tramp—ceremonial execution of a derelict performed by unknown butchers in a deserted house near The Elephant + Castle—or the murder, by a coven of louts, of a neglected baby in a pram

A father tyrannizing over a daughter

Two incestuous sisters

A space-ship has landed

An ageing movie actress

McLuhan—Art is a DEW, a Distant Early Warning system.

Paul [Thek's] problem at the moment: a square snake, metal skin, bloody flesh ends. How to make the organic ("meat") + anti-organic (the square cylinder, the metal + metal-spray paint) go together

What interests me in narrative are:

The *elements* of narration (hence, I like to break up the narrative in short sections—continuous text seems problematic to me, perhaps even fraudulent)
The inessential detail—what fractures reality (rather than versimilitude)

. . .

11/13/65

Jasper Johns [*on Duchamp*]: "painting of precision and beauty of indifference"

The Zero zone: the zone of our boundless expectations

A prologue à la [Laura] Riding story:
In the beginning was the Org—the strong people + the weak people—

11/14/65

The book is getting clearer in my mind, and I want to do it fast, in first draft, by January. If I do five pages a day, in sixty days I'll have 300 pages.

. . .

11/16/65

. . .

Laura Riding: sign above her bed: GOD IS A WOMAN

. . .

LSD: everything decomposes (blood, cells, wire)—no struc-ture, no *situations*, no involvement. Everything is *physics*.

. . .

11/20/65

Keep an *image-log*. One a day.
Today: five brides motionless (in tableau) on a bare white
    stage, one Negro—high cheek-bones
Light from above is kind, light from below is cruel. Of one
    woman, when the light shone from below, you could see
    what she would look like age 60.

Tape—with echo chamber "I-I-I-I"
                    "That's not you" (boy's voice)
                    "It's me"

. . .

for "The Bird" :

Look at English novel in 18th C. form, before it hardened.
Defoe, [Samuel] Richardson, [Henry] Fielding, Sterne: You
could have mixed "media" there too—

Essay passages (erudition, etc.), poetry, etc. as well as story.

One future of the novel is in the mixed media form.
Examples:
Ulysses
Naked Lunch (film scenario, "erudition," etc.)
Pale Fire (poem, notes, etc.)
[Burt Blechman's] *The Octopus Papers*

What about "The Organization" as a mixed-media form >

. . .

Function of boredom. Good + bad

[Arthur] Schopenhauer the first imp[ortant] writer to talk about boredom (in his *Essays*)—ranks it with "pain" as one of the twin evils of life (pain for have-nots, boredom for haves—it's a question of affluence).

People say "it's boring"—as if that were a final standard of appeal, and no work of art had the right to bore us.

But most of the interesting art of our time *is* boring. Jasper Johns is boring. Beckett is boring, Robbe-Grillet is boring. Etc. Etc.

Maybe art *has* to be boring, now. (Which obviously doesn't mean that boring art is necessarily good—obviously.)

We should not expect art to entertain or divert any more. At least, not high art.

Boredom is a function of attention. We are learning new modes of attention—say, favoring the ear more than the eye—but so long as we work within the old attention-frame we find X boring . . . e.g. listening for sense rather than sound (being too message-oriented). Possibly after repetition of the same single phrase or level of language or image for a long while—in a given written text or piece of music or film, if we become bored, we should ask if we are operating in the right frame of attention. Or—maybe we are operating in *one* right frame, where we should be operating in two simultaneously, thus halving the load on each (as sense *and* sound).

Mailer says he wants his writings to change the consciousness of his time. So did DH L[awrence], obviously.

I don't want mine to—at least not in terms of any particular point of view or vision or message which I'm trying to put across.

I'm not.

The texts are objects. I want them to affect readers—but in any number of possible ways. There is no one right way to experience what I've written.

I'm not "saying something." I'm allowing "something" to have a voice, an independent existence (an existence independent of me).

I think, truly think, in only two situations:

> at the typewriter or when writing in these notebooks
> (monologue)
> talking to someone else (dialogue)

I don't really think—just have sensations, or broken fragments of ideas, when I am alone without a means to write, or
not writing—or not talking.

I write—and talk—in order to find out what I think.

But that doesn't mean "I" "really" "think" that. It only means
that is my-thought-when-writing (or when-talking). If I'd
written another day, or in another conversation, "I" might
have "thought" differently.

This is the most useful extrapolation / interpretation one can
give to what Socrates said about "dialogues" vs "treatises" in
the Seventh Epistle.

This is what I meant when I said Thursday evening to that
offensive twerp who came up after that panel at MOMA [*the
Museum of Modern Art*] to complain about my attack on [*the
American playwright Edward*] Albee: "I don't claim my opinions are right," or "just because I have opinions doesn't
mean I'm right."

. . .

11/21/65

Gustav *Klimt*—painter (contemporary of [Gustave] Moreau)
    —erotic
Show last year at Guggenheim—get catalogue
Most of his works are in Brussels + Vienna

Hardly any point in short fiction ("story")—practically anything good must be 100 pp. long

Carlos [*the Cuban-American film critic and friend of SS's Carlos Clarens*] (*Dorian Gray*)—all the years I've known him, he doesn't get any older-looking; what's even more amazing, he doesn't get any smarter either

. . .

Movies to see:

The Bride + the Beast (1948?)—bride was really a gorilla in former incarnation "Lulu" (Asta Nielsen) [*in Leopold Jessner's 1923* Erdgeist]

Read Sheridan Le Fanu, *Carmilla* (> [*the French filmmaker Roger*] Vadim, *Et Mourir de Plaisir*)

. . .

11/24/65

Lillian [Hellman] identified with Becky Sharp [*in William Makepeace Thackeray's* Vanity Fair]—always wanted to be a bitch, to bait people.

I never got past admiring and envying her for being able to throw the dictionary back at the drippy schoolmistress. All that manipulative stuff with men was beyond me.

Analysis: two or three cataracts have fallen from my eyes. A hundred more to go?

I come each night around 2.00 or 3.00. *The NY Times* is my lover.

. . .

Trick: Ask what would this mean if *I* were doing it. (In other words: would *I* have to, most likely, have a mean or hostile feeling toward someone to do or say that?)

I take words literally—as if they were written. Not as if they were being said by someone with a motive or a feeling about *me* behind them. I feel that would be presumptuous—hence my chronic "esprit de l'escalier"

Cause

> fear of acknowledging the wrongness of Mother's demands + behavior (then I would have to be hostile, reject her, + where would I be?)
>
> reinforced by my discovery of books— impersonal communication, words *not* addressed to *me*
>
> cultivation of objectivity > critical bias: text is independent of the author

. . .

Duchamp: "Install air meters. If anyone refuses to pay, turn the air off."

Jasper: "What if the street sign said RUN, or RUN FOR YOUR LIFE." (A woman walking across the street when the sign flashes WALK.)

. . .

11/25/65

My "ability" to absorb information; my need to orient myself in terms of facts

Where am I? I'm in Tangier, a city of 300,000 in Morocco (King Hassan II) that used to be part of Spanish Morocco + was then a free city until 1956, etc., etc.

False appeasement of anxiety—

Where am I?

Great unmade works of art: Eisenstein's *An American Tragedy*

Movies I saw as a child, when they came out:

NY

20,000 Years in Sing Sing
Penny Serenade
Blossoms in the Dust
The White Cliffs of Dover
Fantasia (1940)
Here Comes Mr. Jordan
A Woman's Face
Strawberry Blonde
[Education] for Death
For Whom the Bell Tolls
The Corsican Brothers
Snow White + the 7 Dwarfs
Yankee Doodle Dandy
Rebecca

The Wizard of Oz
Watch on the Rhine
In This Our Life (1942) sisters —[Bette] Davis
Shadow of a Doubt
Sahara
Citizen Kane (1941)
The Great Dictator
My Friend Flicka (1943)
The Thief of Bagdad
Pride of the Yankees
That Hamilton Woman
North Star
Mrs. Miniver
Young Tom Edison (1940)
*The Atchison, Topeka, + Santa Fe [SS is referring to the title of
     a song from* The Harvey Girls *(1946)]*

1943–46   (Tucson + summer of '45 in LA)

Devotion Ida Lupino
Wuthering Heights
Mildred Pierce
A Stolen Life [—Bette] Davis
Spellbound
The Best Years of Our Lives
Duel in the Sun
Brief Encounter
Notorious
The Rising Sun [*aka* Sunrise] —Sylvia Sidney
Wilson
To Each His Own
A Song to Remember —Cornel Wilde, Merle Oberon (George
     Sand played by Merle Oberon)

The Song of Bernadette
Jane Eyre
The Maltese Falcon
Jamaica Inn —Charles Laughton, Maureen O'Hara
Gaslight
Reap the Wild Wind
Casablanca
30 Seconds Over Tokyo

11/26/65

The Benefactor as a meditation on Descartes. I'd forgotten that! Until Bert Dreyfus [*a friend of SS's*] mentioned it to-day—because I've spent the last 7 years of my life with illiterates, and gotten so used to never even *mentioning* anything that depends on book knowledge.

I find [psycho]analysis humiliating (among other things); I'm embarrassed by my own banality. I feel reduced. That's one reason I'm preoccupied with its being a "professional" rather than a "personal" relationship.

Knowing has to do with an *embodied* consciousness (not just a consciousness)—this is the great neglected issue in phenomenology from Descartes + Kant through Husserl + Heidegger—Sartre + [*the twentieth-century French philosopher Maurice*] Merleau-Ponty have begun to take it up.

What is a body (human?)—it has a front + a back, an up + a down, a right + a left—is functionally asymmetrical in that it moves *forward* in space.

Relationship of the body to buildings. (What satisfies body consciousness—e.g. no obstruction, debris that impedes forward movement). Cf. last chapter of Geoffrey Scott's *Architecture of Humanism.*

11/29/65

Weekend with Jasper [*with whom SS had become involved earlier that year*]

Nothing that's *said* is true (though one can *be* the truth).

Long silences. Words weigh more, become palpable. I feel my physical presence in a given space when I talk less.

Of everything that's said, one can ask: *why*? (including: why sh[oul]d I say that?)

Everything becomes mysterious with Jasper. I think—I don't just either opine or give (or solicit) information.

Intelligence is not necessarily a good thing, something to value or cultivate. It's more like a fifth wheel—necessary or desirable when things break down. When things go well, it's better to be stupid . . . Stupidity is as much a value as intelligence.

Don't generalize. Not: I always or usually do this or that, but: I did then. Also: don't predict your future behavior. You don't know what you're going to do or feel in that situation (or: what that situation will be like). And don't, don't invite other people to generalize about themselves.

Good question: what is that man doing? (now) Do you (now) want it? etc.

The unpleasantness of the feedback—other people's reactions to my work, admiring *or* adverse. I don't want to react to that. I'm critical enough (+ I know better what's wrong).

The good thing about saying "it's beautiful" of a work of art is that when you say that you aren't saying anything.

I like to feel dumb. That's how I know there's more in the world than me.

What does it mean to say: Please go over there. Where?

Because you stink
Because I want to take your picture
Because I want to play ball with you
Because I want that beam to fall on your head

Jasper doesn't like things to be decided. ([*The American critic Max*] Kozloff's article: Duchamp is this, he's that; Duchamp is this, he's that). It closes things off.

If you decide they're not closed, they're not.

From G[ertrude] Stein—

It is the destiny of a work of art to become a classic. The principal characteristic of a classic is that it's beautiful.

But it's also the destiny of a work of art to become dead.

"Art" (+ "work of art") are categories as arbitrary + artificial as "nature"—a painting + a novel have little in common— no more than a mountain + a running brook.

Bionics (new science that attempts to equate animal behavior + senses w[ith] instrumental or technological counterparts)

Bioluminescence (in plants + animals)

12/3/65

Movies in the last week:

Von Sternberg's, *Thunderbolt*[—]George Bancroft
**** [Jacques] Demy, *The Umbrellas of Cherbourg*
[Gregory Ratoff,] *Oscar Wilde*
[Kenneth G. Crane,] *Monster from Green Hell*
[Kenneth G. Crane and Ishirô Honda,] *Half Human* [*The Story of the Abominable Snowman*]—Toho [*Japanese production company*]
[Carl] Dreyer, *Ordet*
Bresson, *Procès de Jeanne D'Arc*
Riccardo Freda, *Theodora, Empress of Slaves* (1954)
    (— [aka Robert] Hampton)

Pre-Raphaelite sets and costumes

[Herschel Gordon Lewis,] *Blood Feast*
*********David Lean, *Great Expectations*
********* John Ford, *The Informer*

Places to see:

Winchester Mystery House (San Jose, Calif[ornia])
Lola Montez' grave in Brooklyn
Klimt paintings in public buildings + houses in Vienna
Florida Everglades + Sanibel Island
Salt mine near Cracow, Poland [*the Wieliczka salt mine near Kraków*]—runs 80 miles underground, been in existence 1000 years
New Amsterdam Theatre—42nd Street—Art Nouveau frescoes + relief (1906)
Police Academy—NY—tour every Wed[nesday] aft[ernoon]
Rainbow Room—top of RCA Bldg—30s ocean liner
Tiffany Tennis Court—NYC Art Nouveau
Musée Grevin (Paris)—esp[ecially] Théâtre des Miracles
Watts Tower—LA—house near cathedral in Chartres like Watts Tower [*La Maison Picassiette*]

. . .

Art is a "situation"

Art is the biggest antique business going. Art as cultural souvenirs.

. . .

Is beauty important? Maybe, sometimes, it's boring. Maybe what's more important is "the interesting"—+ everything that's interesting eventually seems beautiful.

Cf. John Cage (Zen) text on the boring: If it's boring once, do it twice; if it's still boring, do it four times; if . . .

Read Melville's *Typee*—theory of language + communication

Device of multiple narrators (cf. movies)

Difference in art between:

> Representation, presentation
> Behavior

One of the elements that makes the difference is *duration* ("durée").

Thus, Andy Warhol's *Kiss* (or *Eat*)—but not *Empire State Building*. It's "real" time or duration. But only certain materials, like the erotic, are open to this treatment or transformation; not a building

Every aesthetic position now is a kind of radicalism. My question is: What is *my* radicalism, the one given by my temperament?

The Benefactor is the least radical book I shall ever write.

Cage, happenings, etc.

Synaesthesis: many kinds of behavior going on at the same time (sound, dance, film, words, etc. etc.) creating a vast behavioral magma—

I like the Cageian aesthetic because it's not mine. He marks a boundary or horizon that I don't want to approach but find valuable to be able to have continuously in sight. He occupies a certain position to which I, in another position, relate myself.

The only good things on theory of film: Eisenstein—esp[ecially the] essay on Dickens, Balzac, [*the German art historian Erwin*] Panofsky

If I ever write any more essays, I want to do one apiece on Breton + Cage

Meaning of "drag"—French "travestie" (disguise—+, secondarily transvestite disguise) > in art cf. [*Gautier's novel*] *Mlle. de Maupin*

Function of masks, masquerade (cf. Halloween—children disguise themselves in order to be destructive)

Story about [*the sculptor Constantin*] Brancusi told to me by Annette: B. lived next door to friends who were giving a July 14th party
    —[he had] helped [with the] preparations. The hour of the party arrives [and an] American girl with a Negro escort comes. Brancusi says, "Did you invite him? I can't possibly go." Hostess horrified; "I'm sorry, cher maître." Hour later Brancusi calls. "I have the solution. I'll come 'en travestie.'" Came—in sheets—had a great time. (He "sent himself" to the party!)

Other sexual motifs in art:
Voyeurism
s-m

12/5/65   [*SS's friend the film critic*] Elliott [Stein's] birthday

Many 19th C. arts are leading towards cinema:

> The family photo album
> The wax museum (Musée Grevin, etc.)
> The camera obscura
> The novel (?)

. . .

Elliott says voyeurs are usually stupid, + often almost impotent.

Peeping Tom isn't about a voyeur—he's a sadist.

"The morbid." T. Faulk is fascinated with that.

. . .

12/12/65

Dressing > good (means *leisure* vs work)
bad (means for *others* vs for oneself)

For me, to dress is to "dress up," play the grown-ups' game. When I'm myself, I'm sloppy.

The Jesuit device (one of many) for promoting concentration in prayer + meditation: "composition of place." You think closely about where an edifying event (say, the Crucifixion) took place—weather, flora + fauna, colors, etc.—+ thus understand its deeper meaning more easily.

"I don't like remembering things."—Ezra Pound

12/15/65

Evil cannot coexist with evil; it feeds on itself, if it cannot feed on the good. (meaning of Laclos [*Les Liaisons Dangereuses*])

The difference between the Laclos novel + the new Mailer [*An American Dream*] is not that one is moral (because evil is punished) + the other not, but that one tells the *truth* about life + the other doesn't.

The SW [Simone Weil] side of my temperament.

> The attraction of absolute selflessness
> The gaucheness in personal relations that leads
> to solitariness
> The obsession with cruelty

On 3): look at the plot of the new novel!

I am haunted. All my dreams are nightmares.

Work: trudging across endless sand-flats

. . .

12/17/65

[Each of the following three entries has two large question marks in the margin.]

Genet is "sub-moral"? Moral problem arises at the point when one acknowledges (+ prefers) adult consciousness as opposed to the childlike consciousness.

For children, the *feelings* of others aren't real. (Hence, the pleasure in fantasies of destruction.) It is the child in us that can go do this—as when we enjoy destruction in sci-fi films.

It's childlike of Genet to subordinate a cruel act to the concept of what gives him sexual pleasure.

. . .

[*The twentieth-century American composer*] Morton Feldman: music just over the threshold of audibility

Does p[sychoanalysis] damage writing?
No—it helps build a sane room (in which to live) next to
    the mad room (in which one writes)—
No need to have a house with only one room.

. . .

12/19/65

. . .

Jasper: I shun *statement*—want the experience of the spectator to be as individual as possible.

12/21/65

. . .

Relation between Breton's *Le cadavre exquis* + Burroughs'–Gysin's cut-up method: No transitions (cf. Firbank)

Read [*the Armenian-born teacher and mystic George*] Gurdjieff + [*the Indian philosopher Jiddu*] Krishnamurti

. . .

12/22/65

[Fritz] Lang, *Kriemhild's Revenge* (1924)—Klimt, [Aubrey] Beardsley, Eisenstein

Exorcizing the ghost. What was, no longer is. Being in touch with my own feelings.

I made a rule when I was thirteen: no daydreaming.

The ultimate fantasy: the recovery of the irrecoverable past. But if I could daydream about an invented happy future . . .

12/25/65

Jasper someone who finds everything "curious" or "difficult." "I have difficulty dealing with that situation." Favorite words: "situation," "information," "fantastic," "activity," "interesting," "lively"

. . .

Jap [*Jasper Johns's nickname*]: "I'm all for the future."

. . .

Machines (computers) at Univ[ersities] of Illinois + Toronto

Morton Feldman: "I'm 39—the rest of my life is redundant."

Duchamp: "I don't care what my paintings (etc.) *look* like—I care about the idea that is expressed."

Christian Wolff—teaches Greek at Harvard, now about 30—son of Kurt Wolff, the publisher—is Cage's only "student"

12/28/65

Gance's *Napoleon* the Mt. Everest of films. Full of "devices": symbolism, triple-screen, superimposition, color *and* black-and-white, different rhythms, different textures of film stock.

The direction of innovation in film has been fairly linear—the problem of "cutting"—i.e. of ellipsis. Development of greater + more sophisticated ellipses.

The other possibilities have been mostly ignored. E.g. why use same type of film stock throughout a given film (because a film is "one thing"?)

Exceptions: first scene in [Ingmar Bergman's] *Naked Night*;
Dr. Strangelove

Problem of point of view in film—

One film that has film-making as its subject: *Peeping Tom*

The one "modern" architect: Buckminster Fuller

Is there such a unitary thing as "modernist" painting? So that
one could say of someone (as [*the art critic and historian Michael*] Fried says of Duchamp): he is "a failed modernist."

Jasper says no—

Cage & [Gertrude] Stein

Annette: "modern" music, three elements, a progression:

Destiny ("musical destiny"—forms)—Beethoven to Wagner
Will—Schoenberg, Webern, Boulez
Chance—Cage

. . .

George [Lichtheim]: *German* romanticism is the only full-
blown romanticism. [It] was anti-liberal, anti-modern, anti-
urban, anti-democratic (anti-individualist, anti-Jewish)

[It] gave rise to the best in German + Central European
culture—that is to say, modern culture at its most advanced,
experimental, + theoretical.

To Germany philosophy, German music, sociology, philosophy of culture, Marx, Freud, Schoenberg, Kafka, [Max]
Weber, [Wilhelm] Dilthey, Hegel, Wagner, Nietzsche, etc.

+ also—mediated by Nietzsche + [Oswald] Spengler—when
it took a political turn, the worst: Nazism

Compare German romanticism (Hölderlin, Novalis, [Frie-
drich Wilhelm Joseph] Schelling) with Keats, Coleridge,
Wordsworth, Chateaubriand!

. . .

1966

Three stages in making a w-o-a [work of art] or a written argument:

Conceiving it
Doing it
        2a) Understanding it
Defending it

People take all three for granted—but I don't see the point of this third, posthumous, stage.

Should be: getting rid of it
One is always somewhere *else* when one has finished—than where one was when one started.

Why sh[oul]d one remain locked?—which one w[oul]d have to be in order to be in a position to defend (justify, explicate w[ith] conviction) what one has done—

This stage is stupid—

. . .

My intellectual formation:

Knopf + Modern Library
PR [*Partisan Review*] ([Lionel] Trilling, [Philip] Rahv,
    [Leslie] Fiedler, [Richard] Chase)
University of Chicago [——] P&A via [Joseph] Schwab–
    [Richard] McKeon, [Kenneth] Burke
Central European "sociology"—the German Jewish
    refugee intellectuals ([Leo] Strauss, [Hannah]
    Arendt, [Gershom] Scholem, [Herbert] Marcuse,
    [Aron] Gurwitsch, [Jacob] Taubes, etc. . . .)
Harvard—Wittgenstein
The French—Artaud, Barthes, [*the twentieth-century
    Romanian aphorist and philosopher E. M.*] Cioran,
    Sartre
More history of religion
Mailer—anti-intellectualism
Art, art-history—Jasper, Cage, Burroughs

End result: Franco-Jewish-Cageian?

. . .

The sweetness of David's cheek

I couldn't *react* to Joe [Chaikin's] news today—that he would
shortly have a very dangerous heart operation followed by
six-months' convalescence. I couldn't feel, I couldn't concentrate—even while he was talking. I mustered solicitude me-
chanically, but it was hard (harder than it used to be? Has this
always been happening?). My mind kept drifting to trivial
observations + reportage about today.

I was dead—the sound of his voice kept fading—I told my-self to be concerned—but I kept forgetting what he had just told me, it kept slipping out of my head

I started to feel anxious, depressed, restless. But not about him. About me: Where was I? Why couldn't I lay hands on my feelings?

1/4/66

The situation in painting is tight: like science. Everyone con-scious of "problems," what needs to be worked on. Each artist by his recent work issuing "white papers," on this or that problem, + the critics judging whether their chosen problems are interesting or trivial. (The [*American art critic*] Barbara Rose approach.) Thus, [*the American art critic*] Rosalind Krauss judges Jasper's flashlight, ale cans, to be the exploration / solution to a peripheral (trivial) problem of sculpture now: what to do with the pedestal (vs the object), Jasper's solution being to make it sculptural—etc. While Frank Stella's work is thought to be very interesting because it is a solution to central problems. W[ith]-o[ut] a knowledge of recent art history + its "problems" who w[oul]d be interested in Frank Stella?

Artists working hip to hip—very tight—everything chang-ing each six months, as more "work" from the diff[erent] academies comes in. One *has* to keep up, have a very keen ra-dar. (To be relevant, to be interesting.)

While in literature everything is so loose textured. One could make a parachute jump blindfolded—anywhere you land, if you push it hard enough, you're bound to find interesting unexplored *valuable* terrain. All the options are lying about, barely used, hardly thought about or discussed by writers or critics.

Think of the legacy of Joyce—[it has] hardly begun to be used, apart from Beckett + Burroughs. Or the possible conscious use of *cinematic* narrative devices in literary narrative. Apart from some Faulkner, and, again, Burroughs.
A dozen other problems.

Only in France has there been any systematic exploration of one particular problem (in the "nouveau roman" of Robbe-Grillet, Sarraute, etc.), only one, in the manner in which painters + sculptors *all* work today.

Jasper is good for me. (But only for a while.) He makes it feel natural + good + right to be crazy. And mute. To question everything. Because he *is* crazy.

Cage's writings are impossible w[ith]o[ut] Stein. In fact, he's the only American successor to Stein. But more eclectic, less rigorous. (All that [D. T.] Suzuki + [Alan] Watts—a "soft" influence.) A much less rigorous + independent mind. Essentially an impressionistic synthesis.

Wisdom. A great writer has wisdom. Where does his authority come from? Because he lives what he extols? It's not *that* simple. Why has no one bothered to learn that DH L[awrence] was a scrawny man with a squeaky voice who had a hard time getting it up + reviled + tormented Frieda for what he considered her blatant sexuality, and not bothered to find [*the American radical social theorist*] Norman Brown a thin-mouthed college professor? One gives Brown the benefit of the doubt: he is Moses, who doesn't enter the promised land. Lawrence is faking. Because there's something suspect in

Lawrence's writings to begin with—forced, sentimental, strident, inconsistent.

I'm attracted to demons, to the demonic in people. Only that? Ultimately, yes. Madness, but high-temperature anti-mainstream madness: People with their own generators. Philip [*SS's ex-husband*] was mad, and Irene and Jasper—and that girl from the Living Theatre, Diane Gregory, at Joe [Chaikin's] workshop last night. Her big hot black eyes + parted mouth, + floor-length quilted dress. Sallie's [*the American literary critic Sallie Sears, a friend of SS's*] madness was repellent—because her sensibility is so limiting + tame, + because it took the form of dependence.

Mad people = people who stand alone + burn. I'm attracted to them because they give me permission to do the same.

David isn't as precocious or creative as I was as a child, + this bothers him. He compares me at age nine with him at nine; me age thirteen with him now. I tell him he doesn't have to be as bright. He has other satisfactions.

I'm not ambitious because I'm complacent. At five, I announced to Mabel (?) [*the housekeeper when SS was a small child in New York and New Jersey; she did not accompany the family when they moved to Arizona*] I was going to win the Nobel Prize. I *knew* I w[oul]d be recognized. Life was an escalator, not a ladder. And I also knew—as the years went on—that I wasn't smart enough to be Schopenhauer or Nietzsche or Wittgenstein or Sartre or Simone Weil. I aimed to be in their company, as a disciple; to work on their level. I had, I knew—I have—a good mind, even a powerful one. I'm good at *understanding* things—+ ordering them—+ *using* them. (My cartographic mind.) But I'm not a genius. I've always known that.

My mind isn't good enough, isn't *really* first rate. And my character, my sensibility is ultimately too conventional. (I was too much infected by the Rosie-Mother-Judith-Nat [*SS's stepfather*] drivel; just to *hear* all that for fifteen years ruined me). I'm not mad enough, not obsessed enough.

Do I resent not being a genius? Am I sad about it? Would I be willing to pay the price for that? I think the price is solitude, inhuman life such as I now lead, hoping it to be temporary. Even now—I know my mind has gone a step forward by virtue of being alone the last 2½ years w[ith]o[ut] I[rene], don't have to package + dilute my responses because I share them with another person. (Inevitably, with Philip + with I[rene], they were reduced to the common denominator, the consensus.) The impact Jasper has made on me—the new intellectual thing in my life this past year—w[oul]d not have been possible if I were still with I[rene].

But why do I want—+ what good is it—to go on pushing my sensibility further + further, honing my mind. Becoming more unique, eccentric.

Spiritual ambition? Vanity? Because I've given up on human satisfactions (except for David)?

I've got this thing—my mind. It gets bigger, its appetite is insatiable.

. . .

1 9 6 6

1/8/66

. . .

We need a new idea. It will probably be a primitive one (will we be able to recognize it?). All useful ideas, for some time, have been very sophisticated.

. . .

[On the first page of a notebook dated simply "1966–67," SS lists her travels over those two years. It was something she was in the habit of doing in the 1960s and 1970s. Reproduced here is the part of the list covering the summer of 1966 as a representative sample.]

1966

June 3 left NY (Air France), arrived in London
June 3–15: London. Imperial Hotel. June 15: flew to Paris
June 15–July 8: Paris
July 8: flew to Prague, then Karlovy-Vary [Czechoslovakia]
July 8–19: Karlovy-Vary ("Hotel Otava")
July 19: drove (with Elliott [Stein], [Jiří] Mucha [*son of the Czech Art Nouveau painter Alphonse Mucha*], Marti [?] to Prague
July 19–25: Prague ("Hotel Ambassador")
July 25–26: train journey from Prague to Paris
July 26–Aug. 1: Paris
Aug. 1: flew to London
Aug. 1–6: London (18 Earls Terrace, S.W. 7)
Aug. 6: train to Folkestone, train back to London
Aug—London (153 Gloucester Rd., S.W. 7)
Aug. 11—flew to Paris

Aug. 29—train ("Le Mistral") to Antibes
Sept. 4—train to Venice
Sept. 5—arrived in Venice—first night "Gritti Palace [Hotel]," next three nights at the "Hotel Luna"
Sept. 10—train (1:35 am) to Antibes; arrived 4.00 pm
Sept. 11—Antibes
Sept. 12: train ("Le Mistral") to Paris
Sept. 12–21: Paris
Sept. 21: flew (Air France) to NY

6/26/66   Paris

Morbidity: The aestheticizing of death. Cf. the ossuary of the catacombs of Paris (which David + I visited this morning). Death is "arranged" for the spectator. Mottoes, reflections, admonitions, stone plaques on the walls between the huge packages of stacked bones. No single interpretation of death or message to the spectator—but an anthology of contradictory sentiments. (Vergil, Genesis, [Alphonse de] Lamartine, Rousseau, NT [New Testament], Horace, Racine, Marcus Aurelius.)

The pleasant white-haired old lady who was the guide said, as the tour crossed from the long tunnel into the actual "empire de la mort,"—"Think. There must be several geniuses here, among the seven or eight million people interred here."

On the origins of aesthetic feeling: What Elliott said when (the other night) he saw me playing with the "piranha" or "crocodile" clip he had on a continuity script he was carrying. "They're good for attaching to the nipple. Or the loose skin of the balls." I tested it by clamping it on the joint of my left index finger—the clip is very taut + even there began to be very uncomfortable in a few seconds. "But it must be agony on the nipples or the balls," I said.

"But someone looks so beautiful," he said, "naked, with a lot of those stuck on different parts of his body."

Horror films—compare their themes with those inventoried in [Mario] Praz's *Romantic Agony*.

•

The doubling of the self in dreams.
The doubling of the self in art.

The nightmare is that there are *two* worlds
The nightmare is that there is only *one* world, this one

•

Foucault [*from* Madness and Civilization, *translated by Rich-ard Howard*]: "Madness is no longer the space of indecision through which it was possible to glimpse the original truth of the work of art, but the decision beyond which this truth ceases irrevocably . . . Madness is the absolute break with the work of art; it forms the constitutive moment of abolition, which dissolves in time the truth of the work of art; it draws the exterior edge, the line of dissolution, the contour against the void."

•

Novels with cinematic structure:

Hemingway, *In Our Time*
Faulkner,

[Horace] McCoy, *They Shoot Horses, Don't They?*

Robbe-Grillet, *Les Gommes* [*The Erasers*]

    his first novel, + the most cinematic—a decoupage

[Georges] Bernanos, *M. Ouine*

I[vy] Compton-Burnett,

V Woolf, *Between the Acts*

Philip Toynbee, *Tea with Mrs. Goodman*

des Forêts, *Les Mendiants*

    his first novel—multiple pov [points of view]

[Barnes,] *Nightwood*

Reverzy, *Le Passage*

Burroughs,

[John] Dos Passos,

Firbank, *Caprice*; *Vainglory*; and [*Inclinations*] (trilogy)

Jap[anese] writer [Yasunari Kawabata] (N.B. visual sense, suppleness of changing scenes)—*Snow Country*, etc.

Dickens (cf. Eisenstein)—

There are people who thought with camera eye (a unified p-o-v that displaces itself) before the camera

N[athanael] West,

Blechman

"new novelists": Claude Simon, *Le Palace*

                Claude Ollier, *La Mise-en-Scène*

(all based on organization of a décor (No[rth] Africa)

read Claude-Edmonde Magny's book on Am[erican] lit[erature] [*L'Age du Roman Américain* (1948)]

Dreams > science fiction

Name: Walter Patriarca

"The double" means the self-as-an-object.

The inhuman presence of objects.

Obsession:

> To possess
> Jealousy

Haunted city—
Vast squares—stone perspectives—park
Imported classicism—river, the bridges—
Students rioting outside the cathedral—
Dazzling bed linen; the cafes + confectioners'
Shops with their chocolate + almond cakes—
High-bosomed beauties at the opera—marble—
Steel skates

The essence of things

Good signs are *arbitrary* > Barthes in *Mythologies*
Bad as "natural"

The willingness to be, to open . . .

I will tell you in whatever voice is left to me of the voices
now inhabiting. They cry. Each sentence, each breath, is a
sundering.

This fabric, this bolt of language belongs to whom?

Speech < > a person speaking

Always?

Story of Queen Christina . . .
Story of a collective hallucination . . .

Dialogue between Orpheus + Eurydice . . .

Entire novel is a voice of narrator questioning

> who he is
> where he is
> where he is
> who he is talking to
> what is going to happen next

Explores in 3) problem of science fiction
    In 5) theme of apocalypse

W[ittgenstein]:

"The limits of my language are the limits of my world"

"To imagine a language means to imagine a way of life."

[*The twentieth-century Austrian writer Hermann Broch's* The D]*eath of Virgil*: the nocturnal anguish that impels a creator, on his deathbed, to destroy his work

Person who has an extraordinary, incommunicable experience
Cf. William Gerhardi, *Resurrection* (1935)—novelist, Gerhardi, is writing a book called *Resurrection*—talks with his friend, Bonzo

Sylvia Plath:

Poet—
Husband, father
Two children—
Suicide—

1 9 6 6

July

Movies seen (July) + = Cinémathèque
(In Paris)
+ Julien Duvivier, *Poil-de-Carotte* (1932)—Harry Baur
+ Yasujiro Ozu, *Histoire d'un Acteur Ambulant* [*A Story of Floating Weeds*] (1934—silent!)
+ Mikhail Romm, *Le Fascisme Tel Qu'il Est* (1965–66)
Victor Fleming, *Dr. Jekyll & Mr. Hyde* (1941)—[Spencer] Tracy and [Ingrid] Bergman
+ Tony Richardson, *Mademoiselle* (1966)

Karlovy-Vary
(*Czech film)

Hermína Týrlová, *The Snowman* (short)
Jan Schmidt + Pavel Juráček, *Joseph Kilian* (short)
Ivan Passer, *Intimní Osvětlení* (*Éclairage Intime*) (1965)
Iulian Mihu, *Prosecul Alb* (*White Trial*) (1965)—Roumanian feature
[Rubén] Gámez, *The Secret Formula* (moyen)—Mexican (1965)
Zbynek Brynych, *The Fifth Horseman Is Fear* (1965)
Miloš Forman, *Peter and Pavla* (*Černý Petr* [literally] *Black Peter*)
Godard, *Masculin, Feminin* (1966)
Evald Schorm, *Everyday Courage*
[Jacques Godbout,] *Yul 871*
Jerzy Kawalerowicz, *Faraon* (1966)
Karel Kachyňa, *Wagon to Vienna*,
[Werner Herzog,] *Fata Morgana*
Jean-Paul Rappeneau, *La Vie de Château*
[Jaromil Jireš,] *The First Cry*
[Jean-Gabriel Albicocco,] *The Wanderer*

Věra Chytilová, *O Něčem Jiněm* (*Another Way of Life*)
Karel Kachyňa, (*Long Live the Republic*)
[Václav Vorlícek,] (*Who Wants to Kill Jessie?*)
Alain Resnais, *La Guerre est Finie*

7/5/66

Materials:

> Organization
> early draft
> Laura Riding myth
> Sci-fi ideas cf. telepathy in [*the novels of the British
> writer William Olaf*] Stapledon
> Conspiracy
> A collective hallucination

> artist—madness—breakdown exp[erience]

> T[homas] Faulk
> "Sylvia Plath"
> Foucault ideas about incommunicability
> Wax figures; skin grafts
> The inhuman presence of objects

> erotic obsession
> dialogue between Orpheus + Eurydice
> pornograph
> a "fantasy"

> ecstatic experience
> Tangier

a woman narrator
Art Nouveau—flowing hair, serpentine body

[Guillaume] Apollinaire deleted all punctuation from his first collection of poetry.

Dziga Vertov (c[irc]a 1922) called his films "Cinéma-Vérité"—then, "Cinéma-Oeil" (Antedates newsreels?)

The landscape of words (Joyce, Stein) obliterates elements of the "story"—traditional distinctions, which are non-linguistic, of character, act, attitude.

Relation between ideas of Valéry (a work of art must be necessary, or it's nothing) and of Duchamp. *Large Glass* is "the most complex art-work, technically + intellectually, of our time . . . [its] baffling intricacy of reference + implication . . . its compendious ramifications into mathematics, literature, + the laws of chance . . . Duchamp set about elevating intellectual awareness into a creative principle in itself."

*A way of continuing with "The Organization"—

There is a question as to how the members communicate with each other. By letters? (an underground postal system?) By telepathy?

Learns that chief of organization is receiving messages from the Future.

Chief relates myth of the founding of the Organization.

A scapegoat is awaited (part of myth).
Turns out to be the narrator.

7/6/66

A novel in the form of:

> letters; a letter
> a diary
> a poem plus commentary
> an encyclopedia
> a confession
> a list
> a manual
> a collection of "documents"

"Organization" is a novel or a novella?
N.B. Nothing about making a work-of-art in this. Save all that
material . . .

An ordeal, a martyrdom

A strange and sovereign language.

What is "we"? The different kinds of "we"—

Characters in "The Organization":

> narrator
> the chief
> friend, Walter
> Keeper of Archives
> A talking computer
> Narrator's mother
> A singer, Lolly Po

Throughout book, there is a war going on. Reading in newspapers of bombings—dull ache . . .

"There is another world, but it is in this one." ([*Yeats*] motto to Patrick White book, *Solid Mandala*)

In the end, narrator is assassinated. But then, who is telling the story?

Gangs of surfers; roving highway motorcyclists

The physical-ness of people, taken for granted as flesh (that smells, that itches) in Ozu's movies. Japanese culture as a whole? People continually scratching themselves, even in moments of remorse, grief, love in *Histoire d'un Acteur Ambulant* (1934).

The long love-scene between Paul and "the lady" (Balkan Queen) which is most of Elinor Glyn's *Three Weeks* is art nouveau—N.B. erotic use of long hair, flowers, woman's body curling like a serpent; eroticism as languidness, swooning, losing consciousness.

I bought the English Duden today. A treasure! Instant Raymond Roussel (lists . . .) Instant world— . . . All there is, the *whole* world, an inventory.

7/8/66   Karlovy Vary

The canal with its rushing water—the huge ochre hotels—the bust of Karl Marx in the little plaza near the spring—the tacky clothes—the absence of cars (the streets are virtually

malls; no one notices the sidewalks)—the politeness + friend-
liness of people—the inefficiency—the smell of urine + hot
asphalt. It's just funny old Europe again—

Czech movies:

> *Intimate Lighting* (Ivan Passer)
> *Long Live the Republic* (Karel Kachyňa)
> *Pearls from the Bottom* (Schorm, Chytilová)
> *Everyday Courage* (Evald Schorm)
> *Appassionata* (Jiří Weiss)
> *A Blonde in Love* (Miloš Forman)
> *The Accused* ([Ján] Kadár & [Elmar] Klos)
> *The Fifth Horseman Is Fear*
> *The Ceiling* (Chytilová)
> *Joseph Kilian* (short)
> *The Hand* (short) (Jiří Trnka)
> *Peter and Pavla* (Miloš Forman)

The new generation of [Czech] directors: Passer, Forman,
Chytilová, Schorm

[The] older generation: Jiří Weiss, Karel Zeman, Kadár & Klos

7/17/66

Methods of narration:

Intercut two independent stories—Chytilová, *Something Else*
Move "out" of

7/23/66   Prague

To become famous in order to have access to people, not be alone.

I am too "close" to David in the sense that I identify with him. When I spend a great deal of time with him, I lose the sense of *my* age; I accept the limits of his world (no sexuality, shyness, etc.).

I smile too much. How many years have I been saying that? Fifteen at least. It's the Mother-and-Judith in me—

I must learn to be alone—and what I've discovered is that being with David isn't being alone (despite my acute loneliness). It's a whole universe of its own, to which I adjust. With David, I become a different person than I am alone.

What I liked about being with [*SS's friend*] Barbara [Lawrence] is that I felt more adult with her than with most people. (The company of Elliott, of Paul [Thek], for instance, makes me childish.)

When I'm alone—after a while—I do begin to look at people. I don't, with David (he inhibits me? I'm distracted by him?); I don't with Elliott (his interests, their specificity, confuse + distract me).

These minutes, writing this in the lobby of the Ambassador [Hotel]—at a table spread with a white cloth, by the open doors on a fine Saturday morning, having just finished a big breakfast (two boiled eggs, Prague ham, roll with honey, coffee) and *alone, alone* (David upstairs, still sleeping)— watching the other people in the lobby, on the terrace, passing on the street—have been the first moments since the begin-ning of the summer in which I've had some sense of well-being.

I am alone—I ache—the novel is bogged down—and so on. Yet for the first time, despite all the anguish + the "reality problems," I'm *here*. I feel tranquil, whole, ADULT.

7/28/66   Paris

America founded on genocide
(> the uniqueness of Am[erican] slavery, the only slavery w[ith]o[ut] limits) > the genocide in Vietnam

Merely an application to the "world" of the American idea of nation-building, clearing the wilderness of natives, dark people.

The "authority" of a documentary movie is its connection with fact, an image of reality. Theatre is actors, a representa-tion rather than a presentation. What can the theatre offer that is analogous to the authenticity of the photograph? The genuine, unfeigned travail of the actor. Enactment, rather than acting. A theatre based on the martyrdom of the actor ([The Living Theatre's] *The Brig*, [Jerzy] Grotowski, etc.)

[*In the margin:*] It is this that *The Brig* and [*Peter Brook's pro-duction of*] *Marat/Sade* have in common

Vietnam is the first television war. A continuous happening. You are there. Americans can't say, as the Germans could—but we didn't know. It's as if CBS [had been] at Dachau. With panel debates in 1943 Germany, one out of four saying Dachau is wrong.

Theatre of Cruelty, happenings, Artaud, etc. based on the idea that shock, violence (in theatre, art) is efficacious. It alters one's sensibility, rouses one from torpor.

Vietnam war—a huge closed-circuit TV production—seems to prove the opposite. As the images multiply, the capacity to respond diminishes.

TV the most brutalizing single factor in modern sensibility. (TV changes the whole rhythm of life, personal relations, social fabric, ethics—all this only just beginning to be apparent. Forces one to think: *WHAT IS* AN IMAGE?)

The *punitive* labyrinth—Kafka; [Hugo von Hofmannsthal,] *Lord Chandos*; Joyce

The *initiatory* labyrinth—Borges; Robbe-Grillet; Hoffmannsthal, ——— [*name illegible*]

The *architecture* labyrinth—Roussel

The clarity + exactness Beckett

Comédie

Two women and a man (who has the hiccups)

Discoveries about myself this summer (small beer!)

>I wear pants *mainly* to hide my fat legs—other reasons are secondary
>I believe *I'm* real, valid, sympathetic; my activities are fraudulent. (Joe [Chaikin] says it's the opposite with him.)

An obsession with a person so great that it can give rise to the disbelief I felt two years ago here in Paris, seeing the young man laughing at *La Grande Muraille.*

Acting (theatre) vs being a star (movies). Movies have special-ized (though not exclusively) in actors whose appeal lies in the *continuity* of character, manner, appearance from one role to another. Garbo, [Douglas] Fairbanks, Bogart. Fritz Rasp [*the German film star who played in Fritz Lang's* Metropolis]. Garbo is Garbo, only secondarily acts a character. Characters, roles are pretexts which both obscure and reveal the star. Theatre has gloried in the absence of the actor. Someone like Olivier or Guinness, or Irene Worth, or Robert Stephens—almost totally changed, unrecognizable from one role to the next. Acting as impersonation, the actor as chameleon.

[In the upper right-hand corner of the page, above this entry, are the French words souches *("tree stumps, [vine] stock, or-gins") and* envoûtement *("bewitchment").]*

Joe, David, [*the American scriptwriter*] Marilyn [Goldin] all agree passionately that I'm more critical of people—have higher standards—than anyone they know. Joe says I look to be offended—

————'s response to [*the costume designer*] Willa Kim's "They're improving themselves." Note!

[*The German expressionist director Paul*] Leni's *The Man Who Laughs* (1928) [*the silent film that adapted a Victor Hugo novel of the same name*]
Conrad Veidt [as] "Gwynplaine"
Mary Philbin [as] "Dea"

Why are you laughing? I'm not. I can't help it. My face is always like this.

Nabokov talks of minor readers. "There must be minor readers because there are minor writers."

Buy a dictionary the size of an elephant—

Journey, to a writer, may "mean" nothing. It is a form of narration. Choice of journey in *Dans le Labyrinthe* is of this sort, says R-G; not like Kafka! "The form has made it possible for me to free myself from the philosophical justifications which served as guiding threads through my previous novels."

{40 years ago Ortega y Gasset wrote essay on the death of the novel

{plus T. S. Eliot (1923) [*Eliot's essay " 'Ulysses,' Order, and Myth," appeared in* The Dial *magazine in the fall of that year*]

The organization, the league:

   To protest the war
   To seek virtue, wisdom

A man seeking to resign—

In fact, carrying a message (secret postal system)

Only when Joe came yesterday did I realize the extent of my despair of the last two months. My heart began to pound— just sitting opposite him at the [Paris café] Deux Magots having coffee. I was talking hysterically about nothing! (Theatre,

Peter Brook, NY). And for the first time I thought: But I *could* go back to NY—give up the charter. Why has that not even occurred to me until this moment? I've been paralyzed—

Film magnate lusting hopelessly for lush blonde

Peter Brook describes film made of training at Green Beret camp in Louisiana—a "happening" they stage there: soldiers are divided into two groups, one American prisoners + the other Viet Cong captors. Viet Cong beat up Americans (. . . waiting with a bottle of ketchup).

8/4/66   London

[SS was in London largely to sit in on a workshop collaboration between Peter Brook and some of his actors—including Glenda Jackson—from the Royal Shakespeare Company, and the Polish experimental theater director Jerzy Grotowski and some of the actors from his Laboratory Theatre.]

"Come at half noon," "half three," etc.

The metopes of the Parthenon discover the *flexible* body so distinct from the *ceremonial* body. The natural (real) body as distinct from the social body—

On Egyptian statues, you can even write on the body (more accurately, on the stiff costume) giving rank of person or a prayer. Unthinkable on Greek statues.

In Parthenon metopes, the bodies of men and animals (horses) are the same—muscle, bone, veins, flesh. Same texture, same degree of articulateness, same sensual authority.

8/5/66   London

My habit of trading "information" for human warmth. Like putting a shilling in a meter; lasts for five minutes, then have to put another shilling in.

Hence, my ancient wish to be mute—because I know what most of my speech is *for*, and I'm humiliated by that.

I suffer from a chronic nausea—*after* I'm with people. The awareness (after-awareness) of how programmed I am, how insincere, how frightened.

Joe says I look at people to find their limits. As if what a house was was a roof only. Always too small. Only with one person (———) did I acknowledge limits without minding them; did I see that although the roof was small, the house was spacious—

What's wrong with my obsession, among other things, is that it prevents me from seeing what's good in other people. Their possibilities.

G[rotowski]'s work suggests that everyone has his vicious animal imago and his regressive, good, infantile one. For some people, both imagos are *grotesques*, caricatures, self-parodies, eruptions of lunacy. For others—one imagines [Ryszard] Cieslak [*Grotowski's principal actor*]—both are beautiful: purifications, improvements on the "human style"

G: Whatever is easy (possible) is not *necessary*.

Two beginning Buddhist meditations: (1) on breathing; (2) on compassion, kindness.

#2 is a sequence.

> I think of myself. I wish that I be whole, harmonious,
>   mature, happy, at peace . . .
> I think of a friend, someone I love. I wish that he or
>   she be . . .
> I think of someone to whom I am neutral, I wish . . .
> I think of an enemy . . .
> I think of my family . . .
> . . . my community etc.
> . . . all sentient beings.

[Agehananda] Bharati, "Tantric Buddhism"

8/6/66   London

Grotowski has made a practice as well as a theory of self-transcendence (spiritual, corporal) using many of the ideas I projected in *The Benefactor*. But while I distanced them, through irony—unable to resolve the contradiction between my belief that these ideas were mad + my belief that they were true—G. is dead serious. He *means* what I said.

Because he doesn't feel this contradiction? Because, for him, they're not just ideas—
He's put them into practice—

Peter Brook:

Very intense, high-pitched, pale blue eyes—balding—wears black turtle neck sweaters—warm sensuous handshake—fleshy, meaty face

Studied with Jane Heap (famous *Little Review* lady from the 20s) living at end of her life in Hampstead); a pupil of Gurdjieff; her Sunday afternoons

Brain-picker
Of Jeremy Brooke, "Oh. Do you think so. I thought he was an interesting failure."

His wife, Natasha. Married 13 years. She had TB for a while, so they've only just begun to have children. Have one daughter, age three (?). Wife about to have another child in 7 weeks.

Both parents were doctors—came to England, had to study again (humiliation, etc.) + take exams. Came from Russia.

Went to Cambridge—directed while there

Mother discovered laxative formula: Brook's ExLax

Directed Dalí *Salome* (opera), *Irma La Douce*, *King Lear*, *The Screens*, *The Deputy* (in Paris), *The Physicists* (in London + Paris), the Lunt-Fontanne *The Visit*, *Marat/Sade*

His way of gesturing, low seductive voice

[*The British playwright*] P[eter] Schaffer says [Brook] "orchestrates" people.

Can sit *very* quietly

In a group: he turns the spotlight; you're on—people are eager to perform for him.

Grotowski:

Around thirty-five

Like Caligari or magician in [Thomas Mann's] *Mario + The Magician*

No one knows anything about his sex-life

Was never a critic

Has studied Yoga in India for a time

In his company, no one brings him his or her personal problems

Obsessed with religion (hatred of R[oman] C[atholic] church); his great theme: sex + religion

Recurrent motifs: crucifixion + flagellation (somewhat Tennessee Williams, says Brook)

[Pedro] Calderón play [*The Constant Prince*]:

Cieslak as the Prince almost naked on a platform, the rest of the actors in primitive medieval costumes, moving around him

Fantastic energy flowing through company w[ith]o[ut] breaks

They whip Cieslak hard with towels—

G. says they discussed + read through play for months using a
bird for each part

To become silent, to *be* one's body

Then: Writing would be something secret, the vice of words
become residual +:
All the more intense

Cf. Stapledon—words an art form only

Grotowski + actor (Cieslak: "the instructor")

(G.) Mr. Mind:

> fat (plump?)
> black suit, white shirt, black narrow tie
> young (34?)
> dark glasses
> cutting gestures
> unlined, slightly reddish face
> dark brown hair, cowlick
> smokes

(C.) Mr. Body:

> black trunks
> maroon sweatshirt
> lean
> panting
> high cheekbones
> thin legs
> slippers
> smile, sweetness

29 years old
face heavily lined
light brown hair
wipes his chest, brow, arm pits, w[ith] white
    handkerchief
head down into chest as he walks
claps hands to get attention
speaks halting English

What if the instructor were Grotowski—+ brought along the fat man w[ith] the dark glasses to pretend to be Grotowski?

Remember [*William Castle's 1959 film*] *The Tingler*! (Grotowski!)

N.B. The dramatic effect that everything G. says has to be repeated by Brook. (For me, [it's] like watching an American movie w[ith] French subtitles. I'm equally + simultaneously interested in both.) So that the actors learn of G.'s method with Brook's voice, intonations, + gestures. The authority of Brook remains unchallenged.

8/7/66   London

Ronald Bryden in essay in *The Observer* today: "The technique of the commercial . . . is the jump-cut from wish to fulfillment. It has become the technique of the new international pop-cinema . . . And with the speeding up, automatically, goes comedy. Anything accelerated to a faster pace, as Chaplin liked to demonstrate, somehow becomes absurd. The trade mark of the new comic-strip cinema is instant, absurd satisfaction . . ."

Buddhist monk the other night ("Virya") =

    Dignity
    A rule
    The body straightens
    Speech becomes what is necessary

8/8/66   London

Puny exploits—penury

Beckett (from 3 dialogues with Georges Duthuit):

"Total object, complete with missing parts, instead of partial object. Question of degree."

[*Highlighted:*] "In search of the difficulty, rather than in its clutch. The disquiet of him who lacks an adversary."

"To be an artist is to fail, as no other dare fail . . . failure is his world/\ . . ."

Holland in the Hunger Winter of 1944–45—

The chief has a vast collection of pre-electric records

Some secret disgrace in his early life

Lolly Pop (music arranged by Big Beat Mephisto)

Title: The prisoner

Eating ideas

Novalis, *Thoughts*:

[*Highlighted:*] "There are moments when even alphabets and books of reference may appear poetical."

"A character is a completely fashioned will."

. . .

[*Highlighted:*] "Philosophy is properly home-sickness; the wish to be everywhere at home."

"To become properly acquainted with a truth, we must first have disbelieved it, + disputed against it."

"The power by which one throws oneself entirely into an extraneous individuality—not merely imitating it—is still quite unknown; it arises from keen perception + intellectual mimicry. The true artist can make himself anything that he likes."

In America, religion equals *behavior*. One stops going to church or synagogue because [of] prohibitions or excessive burden of ritual, not (as in Europe) because of a crisis of *faith* or *belief*. Hence, Midwesterner who gave up going to church when he came to NYC as young man, may very well send his kids to Sunday School when he marries + moves to Long Island. All he has to discover is that Prot[estant] church in L.I. doesn't ask him not to smoke + drink as the one back in Iowa did . . .

[After half a dozen pages of transcription of passages from Samuel Beckett's Proust *and* Three Dialogues with Georges Duthuit, *SS writes the following:]*

I would be more myself

1 If I would *understand* less of what others mean
2 If I would *consume* less of what others produce
3 I would smile less; eliminate the superlatives, the unnecessary adverbs + adjectives from my speech

Because of 2 I am not fully present in many experiences: — more armored, I can absorb more. More open, I would be filled by one or two things—I would confront them more deeply.

With 1 I'm continually darting out of myself—I am not loyal to my own plane of perception.

I vulgarize my feeling by speaking of them too readily to others. As of Grotowski to Joe [Chaikin] + to Peter Brook + to [*SS's friend, the widow of George Orwell*] Sonia [Orwell]. With each I saw how he or she w[oul]d react to Grotowski, + accommodated to that!

The English monk's name now is Virya, which means energy. Summonera Virya.

HOW TO MOBILIZE ENERGY.

G. almost always inert—doesn't waste his energy?

Or is it bad that he's like this—two switches, on + off. Is it that that makes him, when expressive, demonic?
(Dr. Jekyll + Mr. Hyde)

Theatre jargon:
"You play off yourself" or "you play off other people"

Opposite of hide *oneself* is not show *oneself* (which is the same thing, inverted) but something beyond showing or hiding (shamelessness or shame).

Hiding and showing are both primarily *self*-regarding attitudes.

Imagine an attitude in which one's total attention is fixed on an other (not just to see one's own image reflected in the eyes of the other), an attitude in which *consciousness* of self (though hardly self) is obliterated.

Is this the aim—to abolish *consciousness* of self.

Cf. Sartre, who precisely denies that this is possible.

Harvard [*Throughout the 1960s, SS, who had left Harvard having completed her coursework and exams for a PhD but without writing her thesis, toyed with the idea of doing one.*]

Thinking about self-transcendence in modern French philosophy (Blanchot, Bataille, Sartre)

More precise thesis topic:

Self-Consciousness, Consciousness of Self, and Self-Transcendence in Contemporary French philosophy
[Henri] Bergson, Sartre, Bataille, Blanchot, Bachelard

role of self-manipulation
role of language and silence
role of art, images (sight)
role of religion

role of concrete erotic relations
role of objectivity, impartiality

G. always dressed the same:
Black shoes highly polished; black socks
Always wears dark glasses indoors

C[ieslak:] several different sweaters—one baby blue, one maroon, one navy blue; several pairs of slacks; brown casual shoes

P. Brook: long skull, high forehead

There we sat, in a stupor of self-forgetfulness.

A Frenchman who had retired from the consular service + lived there quietly with his books

8/10/66   London

Elements of "Org"

It's a study of

 friendship
 paranoia

Man who is most paranoid (Aaron) is the betrayer. His remorse.

Do I have to decide if the Org is good or bad?

Leave it mixed. Like the Jews—

Emphasize that the Org has given many men of genius to the world, though often these were people who denied their Org membership—

Chauvinism of Org people—

Popular prejudice that Org people are cleverer than others—

Nowadays, tend to find them in big cities; not so in the past—

From Paul Goodman's "Down in the Mouth," notebook of 1955

"To know an 'objective truth'—this is fairly idle and for the most part a phenomenon of withdrawal from contact . . .

". . . I am not worth the truth because I have not succeeded with 'my' truth . . ."

The future of work, if I dare think of it. (To think of what's beyond makes submersion in Org less painful):

A book made up of two novellas, each about 100 pages. Each centered on a kind of "theatrical" event.

Maren in T.
The Martyrdom of Virtue (or: The Rehearsal)
(G., C., etc.)

Title: "Two Stages"

So: *The Benefactor* (novel)
    "In League" (novel)
    "Two Stages" (novellas) > "Witness," "The Rehearsal"
    "The Ordeal of Thomas Faulk" (novel)

8/23/66

I've read this summer: [Arnold Bennett,] *The Old Wives' Tale*; [Thomas Hardy,] *The Mayor of Casterbridge*; Gerhardi, *Resurrection*; Blaise Cendrars, *Moravagine*; Sheridan le Fanu, *Carmilla*; [Guy] de Maupassant, *The Horla*; [Jane Austen,] *Pride and Prejudice*; H.-H. Ewers, *L'apprenti Sorcier*; Olaf Stapledon, *Last and First Men*; Gérard Genette, *Figures*; [Giorgio] de Chirico, *Hebdomeros*; [Diderot,] *Rameau*[*'s Nephew*], *La Religieuse*

Today, watching Godard making *Deux ou Trois Choses que Je Sais d'Elle* at the HLM [*French acronym for a public housing project*]

[Herbert] Lottman, the hack + vampire, asks: "What's this movie about?" [Godard's] A[nswer]: "I don't know." Q: "Is it about anything?" A: "No." Q: "What is the general theme of your films?" A: "That's for you to say."

8/26/66

Walked around the 16ème [*arrondissement in Paris*] with David, Elliott [Stein], [and] Louis looking at buildings by [Hector] Guimard, [Jules] Lavirotte, + [Charles] Klein.

. . . Also Balzac's house, apt. building by Mallet-Stevens, etc.

. . .

Novel: about paranoia + process of *demystification*: the scared, the social, the group, what binds

. . .

9/2/66

Antibes > Monaco > Roquebrune-Cap-Martin (10th c. château / fort) > La Turbie (The Trophy of the Alps) > Antibes

. . .

9/10/66   Venice

The Italian "gentilezza," "civiltà". . .
The Ghetto: The tallest buildings in Venice (6, 7, 8 stories)—five synagogues—the plaque, its noble inscription to the victims of the Nazis on the wall of the main synagogue

The two great living writers, Borges and Beckett

Valéry: In the state of ineffability, "words fail." Literature tries by "words" to create "the state of the failure of words." (*Instants*, p. 162)

La Bussière, "le mangeur de dossiers" [*literally, "the eater of dossiers"*]—clerk who saved Joséphine de Beauharnais, among others from the guillotine. (Shown in Gance's *Napoleon*)

[Undated, 1966]
8000
6085
———
1915

6085 copies of *Against Interpretation* have been sold
1915 copies of the first printing are left

•

1967

[In a number of SS's journals, there are entries written on loose sheets of paper tucked into the notebooks. SS herself was often unclear as to the correct date of these sheets. The following entry is marked in SS's hand "old note—1967?" On that basis I have reproduced it here.]

Art is the general condition of the *past* in the present. (Cf. architecture.) To become "past" is to become "art." (Cf. photographs too.)

Works of art have a certain *pathos*—poignancy.

> Their historicity?
> Their decay?
> Their veiled, mysterious, partly (and forever) inaccessible aspect?
> The fact that no one would (could?) ever do *that* again?

Perhaps, then, works only *become* art. They *are* not art.

And they become art when they are part of the past.

(creating the past)

Therefore, a *contemporary* work of art is a contradiction.

We assimilate the present to the past. (Or is it something else? A gesture, a research, a cultural souvenir?)

The poignancy of creating the past

So much in life that can be enjoyed, once one gets over the nausea of the replicate.

Duchamp: Readymades not as art but as a philosophical point about allowing "accidents," about a work as "object."

4/11/67

. . . Cocteau says: Primitives make beautiful things because they've never seen any others. Analogous to what I did as a child. I started thinking using my mind, because I'd never seen anyone do it. I didn't think anyone had a mind except in the Pantheon (mostly dead, foreign)—Mme. Curie, Shakespeare, Mann, etc. Everyone else was like my mother, Rosie, Judith. If I'd known about the middle ground—all the intelligent, thoughtful, sensitive people, who knows? I might never have gone on + on + on with my mind. For partly I did that because I thought no one was taking care of that at all. The mind needed my help to survive.

4/18/67

Rosie: Like having an elephant in your living room. From the time I was born until the age of fourteen. And to think, at nineteen, I did that to David! (Just like Susan T[aubes]: what's good for me is good enough for my children. Really: Should my children have it any better than I did?

Rosie talking: like an endless stream of lava, like fallout. Imprinted on my head—the defilement of language, spoken and written.
"nother," etc.
That's what upset me about Irene's not being able to spell.

8/3/67　Fort de France [Martinique]

Body images.

A defended body, full of violence.

A body defined by its constant struggle to cope with the pull of gravity. Struggling against the desire to sink down, lie down, fold up. Having to "will" being erect. (Spine, neck, etc.)

Treating the "back" (of you) as if it's not part of you: Sallie [Sears]. Like the back (rear wall) of a bookcase.

8/6/67　Fort de France

Future of fiction (prose narrative) to more + more say *everything* (suppressing the anecdotal, the particular?)

Emphasizing art as an instrument of *analysis* (rather than of expression, statement, etc.)

8/9/67

... It's all this that I've always been bent on—an accomplice in lies about myself, assenting to convenient self-reductions (to guard my secret of secrets). And scavenging—being cannibalistic in all my relations. Think of it! I'll get this from [*childhood friend*] Merrill, this from Philip, this from Harriet, this from Irene, this from Annette, this from Joe, this from Barbara, etc. Gathering my treasure, I learn what they know, or I develop something through my connection with them (some talent in myself that they inspire)—then I take off. I know I haven't taken anything *from* them (they have as much of it after I'm gone), but still I was feeding. I knew I knew more—was fitting it into a larger system to which they had no access.

[*In the margin:*] *as in* [*Henry James's*] The Sacred Fount

Would I have wanted a companion? Yes. I did try with each in good faith, but then when I gave up I didn't tell what I was doing.

I tried hardest with Irene. But I found out it was hopeless: what I thought of (code) as her incapacity for "nobility." Then the relationship became a lie. I had to reduce myself to just the psychological (the case-history) me to get what she had to give. The case-history me was absolutely authentic—what a relief, a blessing it was to express it—I had kept up so many lies on that front for so long. But it wasn't all of me. I knew all the time there was a transcendental ego that had survived alongside the damaged ego of my childhood that became enslaved to Irene's ministrations—and that ego Irene couldn't understand, or join, or love.

I had to become dumb (with Irene) to become smart. I wanted her wisdom—to ingest it, to make it mine—as part of a larger sum. But I knew I had access to it only as an idiot, a client, a suppliant, a dependent. All of which I knew I was anyway—so what was the harm or the lie? But there was harm, of course. And a lie too. For I wasn't strong enough for my own game, almost did collapse when she withdrew her tyrannical support. I was always acting in bad faith. (But could I have done otherwise? Ah, I don't think so.)

Case-history stuff:

For Eva [*Berliner*], the world is *over-populated* things + people plus their hallucinatory doubles (the object is both a tie *and* a garden hose). Things and people (especially parts of the body) always fraught with the possibility of metamorphosis into demonic creatures.

Some results:

The tilted, wary walk—as if she's always looking behind her—and / or can't put her weight fully on the ground

The tilt of the head—looking at you sideways ("What am I going to see?")

Perpetual blanking-out—not seeing a lot that passes before her field of vision. Being "unobservant" (as Gert [*Berliner, Eva's former husband; a painter and photographer*] apparently used to call it) or only intermittently or unsystematically observant.

Reading-block—fear of reading as stimulus to fantasy, fear of making a "mistake" about what she's read.

Hence, too, slowness in reading—having to vocalize internally as she takes in words with her eyes, *double* checking that it is what it is.

[*In the margin:*] Resistance to absorbing information, knowledge—because this is felt to be to "general"—knowing = knowing something particular, a part (?)

Trouble sometimes in following movies—because she looks away or blanks out fairly often (when images threaten to metamorphose)

Complex systems of mistrust of people: never confident that their essence is stable, even perceptually. (What she thought was Uri [*her son*] coming in the door might be a dragon; [*her friend*] Joan's face might turn into a disembodied, obscene mouth)

Physical clumsiness. Because of not feeling at home with "things," being able to take them for granted + therefore handle them casually, probingly, authoritatively. (Again, because of their subliminal hallucinatory aura.) Inevitably sexual clumsiness, too.

Her gifts for observing + sensing of other people's feelings compromised by 1) anxiety about their reality (solipsistic universe—they're all actors in a play I wrote) and 2) anxiety about reliability of her own perceptual apparatus (requiring a supplementary move: If I were she, what I would be feeling is . . .)

Feeling of discontinuity as a person. My various selves—
woman, mother, teacher, lover, etc.—how do they all come
together? And anxiety at moments of transition from one
"role" to another. Will I make it fifteen minutes from now?
Be able to step into, inhabit that person I'm supposed to be?
This is felt as an infinitely hazardous leap, no matter how
often it's successfully executed.

More general form of this: mistrust (partly "well-founded")
of her ability to make a "commitment" to another person

From all this (there's much more) one can infer:

Brutal assault on her ego, her self-esteem, as a young child. Her
mother's insecurity, competitiveness with a bright daughter—

The "contract" Eva made with her mother—she was the
earthy, sensitive, creative one; while Eva had more brains,
cleverness. But then her father cut her down there. She wanted
to be good in school—to please her mother by fulfilling that
role set out for her—but also not to do well—because she
rightly hated her mother for this limiting definition of her,
wanted to frustrate her mother.

If a child feels the parent wants to do him in, he gets news of
a hostile persecuting universe from which he must *defend*
himself—also must placate the parent—also must deal with
his own rage and sense of impotence. Ultimately the child
has no ego but what is confirmed by the parents; if they don't
love you it must be because they think you're bad, you must
be—they can't be wrong. So you think you're bad but you
hate them anyway for not loving you—which produces guilt,
because they're good. So you start to punish yourself, which
reduces the feeling of hate (some of it is now turned against

yourself, siding with them) + makes it possible to love them more—personal love.

In Eva's case, the hallucinatory "other world" always breaking in on this one (in fantasies, flash hallucinations) is:

A symbolic statement, an iconography, of her hostile
    judgments of people around her (originally the
    parents)
A form of self-punishment—she "haunts" herself
    or has herself haunted—for these bad feelings
A symbolic imagining of the retaliation of the
    others, if they knew her true feelings

The hallucinatory images must have originated from an experience of her parents as persecutory, demonic—she "caricatures" them; these images are a form of wit—but then was extended or generalized to the whole world, so that a tree or a shadow or a chair can become a monster. But one couldn't have a *primary* experience of the whole world (the perceptual field) as demonic. First persons. Indeed, first of a part of a person—the mother's breast.

(The perception of the world *begins* synecdochally—seeing parts for wholes. The structure of true learning would be finding truer + truer wholes, w[ith]o[ut] losing the concrete perception of parts.)

Seeing parts of a body (a form of flash-hallucination, the Brobdingnagian vision) is a form of aggression, as Vera [*Eva's psychotherapist*] said to her. She caricatures the person by dismembering him, reducing him, putting him in his place; also scaring herself, giving herself license for anxiety, self-contempt, withdrawal. Simultaneously she disarms the person and makes him more threatening than before. A microcosm of the vision she must have turned on her parents—

The generalization of hallucinations about persons to the whole world of things also serves a double purpose:

It dilutes the accusation against her parents—it's not
just them, it's the whole world
It steps up the self-punishment, the cost to her in
sense of wholeness.

Thereby, reducing guilt. She is less guilty because she doesn't accuse them *that* much, or single them out. (She does it other people, to things, etc.) And because she suffers more.

But the generalized need to suffer remains. The price of that original hatred of them never seems to be paid off. Hence, masochistic fantasies—which also fit into a more specifically sexual pattern whereby one needs to feel forced—to feel one has no *choice*—in order to allow sexual sensation.

Earlier, she told me, the principal weapon of self defense was mockery. Could never say anything "straight." Fear of rejection, "betrayal." If I show you my true feelings, you won't love me [*there's a question mark in the margin*]—you'll mock me—reject my gift. So I'll beat you to it. I'll mock you.

A kind of braininess—but at the same time, one that she would mistrust. Experiencing her mind mainly as a means of aggression, as a weapon turned against other people, she w[oul]d want to get rid of her mind. Becoming mindless becomes equated with the ability (the freedom) to love. Hence, Gert. (Becoming a "real woman," etc.)

Joan gave Eva enough love to permit her to dare to speak "straight"—w[ith]o[ut] mockery.

Hence, Joan told Eva she'd make a human being out of her. And Eva acknowledged that to be true. And still somewhere fears to break with Joan, as if the license to be human might be revoked then. (Magical thinking which plays only a *part* in her tie to Joan, but shouldn't be discounted.)

(Some analogues to this in my tie to Irene.)

. . .

To transcend the "bad" seeing that I've always been aware of, that's always made me feel guilty.

I've always been "hiding behind my eyes." (Lillian Kesler saw this last year at Richard + Sandy's. [*SS's friends, the poet and translator Richard Howard, to whom she remained close throughout her life, and his then partner, the novelist Sanford Friedman.*]) Because I wanted to see but for it not to be known how much I see—the others will hold it against me—and not to tell what I see, at least only part of it.

But why will they hold it against me? Because they'd know I'm seeing past them—at my most benevolent, still locating them in a scheme I believe I can (or do) transcend; and, often, seeing their failures, their weaknesses. Shriveling them up—to a dried out piece of bacon (my dream about my mother) or a tiny well-done meatball.

But this isn't all—or I do myself (the self I've been up to now) an injustice. I also see, I have an awful gift for seeing people's unhappiness. A talent I developed as a child with my mother. She invited it, of course. It was a way of getting my love, which probably wasn't, in the circumstances, readily forthcoming. She showed me her misery + weakness. I pitied her—and it gave me a reason to love her (a means, the imperative I sought) to transcend and suppress my hatred of and resentment toward her. But it also made me—underneath—despise her, and despise myself. It created an unbridgeable distance between us. I would adore her and pity her and exercise my empathic powers upon her and forbear to burden such a weak vessel with *my* needs and *my* anger. I would be kind, I would be generous. But I also became her superior. I was the stronger. I had needs, but was strong enough not to ask or expect her (or anyone else) to satisfy them. And, with my own needs unsatisfied, except by myself, I could even try to satisfy hers. So I also was patronizing her—much as I feared her anger (living in constant terror that she would withdraw suddenly + arbitrarily from this bargain, calling in even the shoddy semblance of reliable affection for me it guaranteed). I also scorned her. And so, in a perverse way, I was the willing accomplice in a relation with her in which she was satisfying a subsequent need of mine. What became a very powerful need—to become strong; to feel, to know myself (whatever the outward appearance, the cringing, the thralldoms) stronger than "the others."

So I grew up trying both to see + not to see. Trying to use up as much of my intellectual energy, my energy for seeing, on things "outside." Ideas, art, politics, science, culture. And for the rest, seeing people, trying to mediate between those two problematic (but still seductive) ways of seeing.

Seeing people's pain > which leads to pity
(compulsive desire to become someone's
caretaker, guardian, benefactor) which leads

to, eventually, a sense of oppression, being
trapped, desire for flight from the relationship.
Seeing people's (ethical) inadequacies, lack of
nobility, + petty self-love + lack of ambition for
themselves which leads to reducing them.

Irene's advent into my life was the great turning point. She
introduced me to an idea deeply foreign to me—how incredible
it seems now!—that of seeing *myself.* I thought my mind
was only to see outside myself! Because I didn't exist in the
sense that others + everything else did. Everything else was
an "object," but how could I be an object to myself? Etc. etc.

I then wanted to learn that new kind of seeing from Irene. At
Irene's hands—with a terrible, appropriative lust.

Could I never have thought I was seen by anyone else before
in my whole life? No, I didn't. But how could I have been so
resigned? When did I give up hoping anyone would see me? It
must have been terribly early. (All those radical disruptions:
Mrs. Enright leaving after 6 mo[nth]s, then Rosie, my parents
coming + going, Rosie leaving when I was 4 or 5, then my
father's death, summer camp, my mother's absences, being
sent to Verona [*SS's maternal grandfather's house in Verona,
New Jersey*].)

[*In the margin:*] Check this

And shortly after I must have started hiding, making sure
they *couldn't* see me. (The nailbiting started at camp, the
asthma the next winter.) Always (?) this feeling of being "too
much" for them—a creature from another planet—so I would
try to scale myself down to size, so that I could be apprehend-

able by (lovable by) them. With the unwavering resolution to sacrifice nothing I "really" was in the process. That scaling down, that mashing, was just a question of my being clever and "perceptive" enough. To see what they wanted. To see what they could bear. Trying not to give them less than I might (without bad results) nor more (and overload their capacities, frighten them, make them feel stupid, alienate them, make them hate me for making them feel stupid).

But how could I have known or decided that I was "more" than they—all centered on my fabulous, cosmic voyaging mind? Even if it were true that potentially I had such a mind (but how *could* I have?) how would I have known? And how did I dare stake out such a claim for myself? With no support or stimulation or help from anyone? It seems like madness—that claim, and the steps I took to be worthy of it. (The Nobel Prize fantasy, the search for the appropriate vessel for my ambition.) And all the while searching for reconciliation with the others—to be loved, to be taken care of. But certainly I was acting in bad faith. (Wisely, I suppose.) If they didn't come across, I always had my ambition, my mind, my secret being, my knowledge of my destiny to sustain me. So I was hedging my bets. If they came across, well + good. (But I certainly wasn't going to give up the most important thing, my mind, to get their love.) And if they didn't come across, "tant pis" [*"too bad"*]. I'd survive.

I mustn't underestimate, though, what I did give up—while faithfully guarding my "real" self as I understood it. I gave up, first of all, my sexuality. I gave up my ability to understand myself as an "ordinary" person; I gave up most of the ordinary range of access to myself, to my feelings. I gave up my self-confidence, my self-esteem in personal relations—particularly with men.* I gave up being at home in my body.

Only a few kinds of relations were left—ones I specialized in particularly. Desexualized pedagogic friendship.

I renounced trying to be attractive. I renounced the right to be "bad" or frail as everyone is "bad" or "frail" from time to time. Not that I wasn't, just like everyone else! But I hated myself for it much more than [most] people do—castigated myself, dropped my self-esteem an inch lower. Wasn't I supposed to be "better" than other people? That being so, then what was good enough for them could hardly be a proper standard for me. At the same time that I also thought I didn't, in some respects, yet come *up* to their standard.

Hence, many things. My pattern of violent thirsty impulsive intimacy with people—followed by phasing out. All that unsatisfied need for contact which builds up + builds—+ then bursts out upon a new person who comes into my life and seems to "see" me at all in a new or generous way. I seduce myself with my hope, my farseeing of what's rich in that person—+ gloss over the limits that are equally discernible. And then, quickly, I can see only limits. And then comes [*sic*] the evasions, + the guilt, + the struggle to roll back the frontiers of the relation—to withdraw some of the promise of intimacy—without breaking off entirely. (When, often, rightly or wrongly, that's what I really want to do.)

This is hardly true any more. I set it down to make the record complete. But it was periodically true until very recently. My relations with Barbara and [*SS's friend the film scholar*] Don [Eric Levine], though ("toutes proportions gardées" [*"all other things being equal"*]) fraught with hazards of this kind, were both conducted in a much more perceptive, more mature way—against tremendous odds.

My universe, then, in radical contrast with Eva's, is under-populated. I don't experience the world as invading me, men-acing me, assaulting me. The primal anxiety is absence, indifference, "the lunar landscape."

From which I can infer a lot about my first five years. Obvi-ously neither my mother nor Rosie were out to get me, to break my spirit, to give me a bad opinion of myself. Nobody made fun of me or made me feel stupid or ugly or clumsy. They made me feel that the world was mechanical, usually polite (though sometimes incomprehensibly irascible), and incredibly obtuse and *stupid* people who, I must have thought, couldn't be that stupid if they wouldn't be so lazy or distracted or undermotivated. They could be intelligent, they could see, if they tried. But nobody wanted to try. They seemed so slug-gish, so inert—and so predictable in most of their responses. Their touch was bony + insensuous + badly-timed (like my mother) or oppressive + too heavy + suffocating (like Rosie). So the lesson was: stay away from bodies. Maybe find someone to talk to. Thus, my early hallucination about the family of little people in the sewer pipe who were my friends.

My early anxious attempts to make Judith a companion by stuffing some "facts" in her head . . . But it didn't work. For how long did I think it would? So instead, I had the company of the immortal dead—the "great people" (the Nobel prize winners) of whom I would some day be one. My ambition: not to be the best among them, but only to be one of them, to be in the company of peers and comrades.

Even today, so much of this remains. The ancient compulsion to populate the world with "culture" and information—to give the world density, gravity—to fill myself up. I always feel like I'm eating when I'm reading. And the need to read (etc. etc.) is like an awful raging hunger. So that I often try to read two or three books at a time.

Diana [Kemeny] said a long time ago that "facts" had been "toxic" for me. What did she mean?

And those hundreds of movie stills on my walls. That's populating the empty universe, too. They're my "friends," I say to myself. But all I mean by that is that I love *them* (Garbo, Dietrich, Bogart, Kafka, Věra Chytilová): I admire them; they make me happy because when I think of them I know that there aren't just ugly leaden people in the world but beautiful people; they're a playful version of that sublime company to which I aspire. I never "fantasize" in Eva's sense. She told me how she couldn't bear to have all those images around her— looking at her. They would always be coming alive. They would be an "invasion." For me, they're reinforcements! They're on my team; or rather, I am (hope to be) on theirs. They're my models. They guard me from despair, from feeling there's nothing better in the world than what I see, nothing better than me! They don't come alive, they don't talk to each other or look at me: they aren't, can't in any way be aware of me, much less judge me, conspire against me, etc. They're just pictures of people far away I don't know. They're just what they are. Photographs in frames on the wall of my living room which I chose, I framed, I mounted.

So the problem isn't how to keep things from coming alive that should be neutral, lifeless, unconcerned with my existence. My old solutions: "culture," my mind, my passions for thought, for art, for spiritual + ethical distinction.

I *perceive* value, I *confer* value, I *create* value, I even create—
or guarantee—*existence*. Hence, my compulsion to make
"lists." The things (Beethoven's music, movies, business firms)
won't exist unless I signify my interest in them by at least noting down their names.

Nothing exists unless I maintain it (by my interest, or my *potential* interest). This is an ultimate, mostly subliminal anxiety.
Hence, I must remain always, both in principle + actively, interested in *everything*. Taking all of knowledge as my province.

8/10/67

Mother:—

My acute anxiety + dread of her growing old, *looking* old—at
one time, I even wished to die first because I wouldn't be able
to bear *seeing* that—It would be something like "obscene."

Why was that so terrible? For one thing, because her beauty
was her one quality I genuinely admired. When I told her
how beautiful she was, I really meant it. And I was so glad, so
grateful to be able for once to say something to her I really,
wholeheartedly, meant.

And also, because I felt obscurely that I would be guilty. My
existence had always been somewhat painful to her on that
score—if I was, say, ten years old + her daughter, that set
some limit on the Dorian Gray act. (How she—and I, in
part—loved it when we were, as we often were, taken for sisters.) And if she could be made that unhappy about something, then it must be my fault. She had made me—and I had

accepted the designation of—author of her happiness. (Letting me know she didn't love Judith, making me feel she hadn't loved Daddy. There was only *her* mother, at every mention of whom she wept—and me.)

My mother came back from China when I was almost or just six this tragic woman, a Niobe, a casualty of life. And I was elected to prop her up, to give her transfusions, to keep her alive for the duration of my childhood.

How would I do this? By *befriending* her. (Sacrificing my own childhood, my needs to learn, to be dependent; by growing up right away.) By flattering her.

I was my mother's iron lung. I was my mother's *mother*. And delegated by my mother to be Judith's mother, too. I felt flattered by my mother to have been entrusted with such a grown-up task, joyful + triumphant at having beaten out my sister so thoroughly in the competition for my mother's love, and guilty over the extent of my triumph (as if *I* had made my mother not love my sister—as if I'd seduced her away from Judith—by being smarter, more interesting; by knowing how to flatter my mother) and sorry for Judith and, somewhere, deeply critical of my mother for her insensitivity + injustice to Judith. So I tried to approach Judith + make friends with her. But that didn't work.

My mother always "compelling" me to exonerate her for being a neglectful or ungenerous mother by being "miserable." Tired all the time. Was she drinking + taking pills then?

The shadow of her mother. As if, by still weeping over her death after all those years, M. was telling me—I'm a child, I'm fourteen years old (though I may look older). I'm not a woman, I'm not mother. And I was my mother's mother's successor. (I'm even named after her.) I take up exactly at the point where she left off when she died. My mother is still a young unhappy girl. I have to bring her up. (Employing great manipulative skills—to save her from the humiliation of *knowing* that's what I'm doing, that's what she wants me to do—and to save some of myself for myself, uncontaminated by frustrated attempts at "sharing," by lies, by adulteration.)

I'm afraid of my mother—afraid of her harshness, her coldness (cold anger—the rattling coffee cup); ultimately, of course, afraid that she'll just collapse, fade out on me, never get out of that bed. Any parent, any affection (though I've assented to a fraudulent contract to get it) is better than none.

My ultimate project: to keep her afloat, alive. My means: flattery, unlimited statements of how much I admire and adore her, and repeated rituals of denigration of my own worth. (I confess, to her reproaches, that I am cold + heartless + selfish. We weep together over how bad I am, then she smiles + hugs + kisses me + I go to bed. I've gotten what I wanted. I also feel unclean, unsatisfied, debauched.)

To keep her alive I also have to amuse her, to distract her from a full knowledge of her misery. (Like a parent dangling a bauble before a child about to start bawling.) Observing her narcissism, which also repels me, I encourage it, I feed it with flattery. All the while looking at her anxiously to see if my words are having the desired effect, if I'm succeeding in cheering her up.

But, of course, at the same time, I also hate her narcissism. It means involvement with herself not with me—therefore rejection of me. I feel contempt for her for being so *weak* that she cares how she is for "others"—so much that she gives so much time to washing, making up, dressing, etc. I feel *superior* to her because I'm entirely indifferent to these things—and vow I always will be when I'm grown up. I'm going to be an entirely different kind of woman. I despise her for the pleasure she takes in my admiration. She doesn't see me. Doesn't she see I *want* something from her? (even though I also do mean what I say)

And later on—in my teens—I come to feel more divided about my mother still being beautiful, still looking so much younger than her chronological age. I'm still proud of her, boast about it to friends; but secretly, it's becoming something "creepy" for me. One more instance of fraud / lie. The master-lie about who + what she is. I long for her to age + lose her looks just like everyone else. To stop being exceptional, so I can stop judging her by the special (lenient) rules.

But if I'm afraid of my mother, she is also afraid of me. On a more specific level, afraid of my judgment. Afraid I will find her stupid, uncultivated (hiding *Redbook* under the bedcovers when I came in to kiss her goodnight), glamorous, morally deficient.

And I, obligingly, do my best not to look, not to record in consciousness or ever consciously use against her what I see, or (at least) not to let her become [aware of] that + when I see.

But there's something more. Hard to describe. Like magical *powers* which my mother ascribed to me—with the understanding that if I withdrew them, she'd die. I must hang on, feeding her, pumping her up.

My own aging: the fact that I look much younger than I am seems

> Like an imitation of my mother—part of the slavish thralldom to her. She sets the standards.
>
> Like still keeping up the secret promise to protect her—that I would lie about her age, help her to look young (what better way to establish that she's younger than that I'm younger than I am?)
>
> Like my mother's curse (I hate anything in me— especially physical things—especially physical things—that's like her). I felt my tumor + the possibility of a hysterectomy as her bequest, her legacy, her curse—part of the reason I was so depressed about that.
>
> Like betraying my mother—for I look younger when it doesn't do her any good. Now she is getting old + looks it; but I'm not, I stay young—I increase the difference of age between us.
>
> Like a trap she's laid for me—so now people think David + I are sister + brother, + that pleases me immensely, turns me on. And I remember her— + I boast of my age dragging the number into conversation when it's not really necessary, adding a year on to David's age when I speak of him—and then enjoying the surprise (flattering?) on people's faces. So I can feel I'm not like her—not weak, not narcissistic—but also fear that I really am.

My task: to prevent my mother from truly seeing herself. Estimating it was a knowledge she couldn't bear. Therefore, encouraging her stupidity—once I had diagnosed it. All the while, then, knowing myself—by what I knew—to be much stronger than she. (The stronger one is he who knows more, can see more.)

[*In the margin:*] one definition

But, at the same time, being so weak. Doubly weak because 1) I was a child and 2) I had forfeited the defenses natural to a child—the unselfconsciousness, expressions of aggression + frustration, tantrums, etc. I had disarmed myself by my own seeing. (I had seen too much—her weakness, her lack of self-esteem, the weakness of her ego.) It would be too cruel to take advantage of her on the basis of what I had seen. Besides, I was trying to be her protector. Wasn't that the pledge I'd made to myself for far from selfless motives? It seemed my best chance of getting any love + attention at all.

So, destroying her—cutting her down—would defeat my purpose, which was to build her up.

And hadn't I pledged to be a grown-up—she said she didn't like children—which meant that I forfeited the right to express "childish" needs or reproach her for "letting me down" in the mother-role.

I feared her—I patronized her—she was afraid of me—I cringed to become "smaller," to hide more of myself so I wouldn't appear threatening to her—doing that, I despised her and I despised myself (for my cowardice, my neediness, my lies)—she came closer to me—then I backed away, into my private pleasures (the mind, my fantasies, books, my projects)—then she reproached me for being old + hard-

hearted + selfish—then I was overcome with guilt + remorse
for having forgotten myself (!), for having let her down—then
an orgy of fearful criticism of me + my vows to improve—she
forgives me, I'm happy, I feel good, I start my program of "being good" (being more attentive to her, producing a me she
can like)—but the rewards for this aren't as great as I'd hoped,
or I get tired of them—my attention wanes or I get distracted
or I become cocky and get "fresh"—then she gets fiercely angry, slaps me, shuts the door against me, won't talk to me for
days—I'm in agony, usually not understanding exactly what it
is I've done, i.e. what she's mad about, but she often makes me
wait in torment + suspense for hours or days—then, often
quite arbitrarily, it seems to be over—I never felt I could
change my mother's mind when she was angry, when she truly
set her mind to being angry nothing could move her (which is
why I gave up tantrums at such an early age—they got me nowhere). Only she could call her anger off, when she mysteriously pleased. So anger was the one emotion I could affect by
my ruses and manipulations of myself + her. Anger had a life
of its own. Therefore, her anger was at all times to be headed
off. (*My* anger I knew in advance to be totally lacking in efficacity!) Anything but anger—any substitute, any dishonesty.
But still, I remained terribly afraid of her—of those mostly
unaccountable rages. (I knew I must have provoked them, but
I never meant to—I felt I'd been careless, inattentive, stupid
for a moment, I slipped, it was like a mistake; I would be more
careful next time.)

Also, I despised myself for my fear of my mother's anger. For
my uncontrollable cringing + crying when she raised her
hand to strike me. (My fantasies during the war of being cap-
tured by the Nazis or Japs and remaining steadfast + stoical
under torture. The stoicism I cultivated for the weekly injec-

tions + when I was in bed with the asthma—balm to my crippled self-esteem. I *was* brave, I *could* take it.)

I didn't feel, deep down, my mother ever *liked* me. How could she? She didn't "see" me. She believed what I showed her of myself (that carefully doctored version). I felt she *needed* me, that's all. Faced with her repeated absences and trips, I encouraged that; I strove to make a "me" for her she could need, someone she could rely on more and more. Some of the time, that is. Other times, she didn't seem to need me at all + I was cast down with shame, with a sense of humiliation at my own presumption. And other times, when she needed me without my having tried to elicit anything from her, I felt oppressed; tried to edge away, pretending I didn't notice her appeal.

One of the things I felt pleased my mother was an erotic admiration. She played at flirting with me, turning me on; I played at being turned on (+ *was* turned on by her, too). Thereby, I pleased her—and I somehow triumphed over the boyfriends in the background who claimed her time, if not her deep feeling (as she repeatedly told me). She was "feminine" with me; I played the shy adoring boy with her. I was delicate; the boyfriends were gross. I also played at being in love with her (as when I copied things from *Little Lord Fauntleroy*, which I read when I was 8 or 9, like calling her "Darling.")

Since, in some sense, I was also my mother's mother (and my sister) I had from an early age—10 or so—a strong compensatory fantasy; my own future motherhood

[*In the margin:*] Wasn't it later?

I would have a boy-child—David. I would be a *real* mother. And no more female children. This was a fantasy about get-

ting out of childhood, attaining a real adulthood; freedom,
Also a fantasy about giving birth to myself—I was both myself as the mother (a *good* mother) and the beautiful gratified
child.

The old puzzle: I "see" someone. But then how can that person "see" me?

If I see someone, I'm stronger (wiser) than he? Seeing him, I
must be "more" than he is. Then how can he, at the same
time, being weaker (dumber) ever see me? He might think he
can, but he's wrong. He sees only a part of me.

This was the problem with Irene, + with Diana. Since I
thought they could see me, I'd ruled out the possibility of my
seeing (dissecting, appraising, interpreting, figuring out, judging) them.

Is my "look" always aggressive, act of hostility against the
other? No. But it is never "less" than an act of self-affirmation,
an active experience of my own strength.

But I've experienced my *strength* (my mind, my eyes, my intellectual passions) as condemning me to perpetual isolation,
separation from others. I must become "weak" to get close to
them (so they'll let me get close to them). Or I must pump
them up, fill them with substance, make them "stronger."

[*In the margin:*] Either way, closing the gap. My long series of
pedagogic relationships—not to perpetuate the master–pupil
relationship but to create a company of peers for myself.

Always the frustrating sense of the disparity between my
energies, my ambitions, and those of other people. The others

setting such low goals for themselves, so easily tired, so lacking in vitality.

In my primal landscape, there are other people besides myself. I'm not a solipsist, like Eva; I've never been tempted by the fantasy that the world is something I make up in my head, that other people aren't really real as I am, that they're all reading from a script that I wrote. No, the people *are* there—and real. But that's all. They're all minimal people, almost inert, barely alive or feeling or thinking. I have to teach them how to think + how to live so I'll have someone to talk to, someone to like, someone to admire. I have to pump them up—like blowing air into balloons. No, not really. The substance, to be convincing, must be dense, heavy, tightly packed. They're too lazy to do it for themselves. I'm sure they could if they would, if they really tried. But they don't seem impelled by the kind of vision + energy that impels me.

8/12/67

My fascination (almost obsession) with the theme of psychological vampirism. Exchanges of energy. Good + bad vibrations and emanations.

Eva's proposal for a telegram to be sent to Irene. *Guilt production called off. Last delivery made yesterday. Factory bought out by munitions cartel.*

My feeling of being "seconds." That was too radical a conversion of my being; I violated myself; it wasn't organic, it was too much an act of will (me leaping ahead, hoping the rest of me with all the baggage would in good time follow after, catch up). It still feels "inauthentic" somewhere to me. It wasn't *my* destiny, my native language. I expatriated myself. My choice, of course; but somewhere I know I'm speaking a foreign language.

Irene the author, sponsor, + therefore guarantor of my new being. My panic when she withdrew her sponsorship. My deep conviction that she must continue to sponsor me, to certify me.

But I must grasp that she didn't invent the system, though she's a very able exponent of it.

And the mystery of her giving most of it up in the last four years. Calling the system into question? But how can one (she) give it up? She's fishing; she's doing that to punish me, to make me feel guilty—an act of revenge. So I feel I've vampirized her. The gift is poisoned. I become immobilized. I start manufacturing + delivering my buckets of guilt—as penance, as restitution, as a way of placating her. But she won't be appeased. (For a while, the lure that she might come back to me if I was guilty "enough," proving that I took *all* the responsibility on myself, that I had gained "nothing" by our exchange in the way of self-confidence, self-affirmation.)

[*In the margin:*] until 2 summers ago

I had been my mother's iron lung. I wanted someone to be an iron lung to me. (Therefore, the project of building Irene up—her ego, her mind—so she could assume this role.) An end to the covert feeling from other people's energies + gifts, all that while making sure I "gave" more than I "took." Instead, an open + avowed apprenticeship in which I was not entitled to a "just" return, to anything reciprocal; because the terms of the situation were that my gifts were useless, stupid. My gifts were all potential; my return was all in the future.

What I have to see is not just Irene's natural gifts (her being a native-born citizen in the country to whose citizenship I aspired) but the fact that those gifts had become *corrupted*— and that this must have happened long before Irene + I met. From the time she got involved with the *Village Voice* ([Ed] Fancher, Dan Wolf [*co-founders of the paper with Norman Mailer*] then Mailer, Alfred [Chester], [*the American artist*] Barbara Bank, Harriet [Sohmers], etc. Being the Cuban sex-pot to the neurotic desexualized Jewish intellectuals. Mrs D. H. Lawrence bringing the enlightenment of carnality + true feeling to the urban casualties. Irene learned she could *exploit* her gifts, that they were a property, that they had a "value," a high value, in the human marketplace.

Irene falling down from our fine flights of intellectual fantasy with a paranoid thud whenever a hint of ethical demand entered (as it naturally did for me).

The project of demythologizing Irene. *Alongside* the project of resolving her hold on me in the mythic terms in which it's also, truly, posed.

Irene demanding to be described as "innocent"—refusing to be described as "good" (my offer). She wanted to be absolved of any ultimate responsibility for her acts. In a way, she insults herself . . . At that time, of course, I didn't understand any of that, any of what was at stake. I only knew (felt), dimly, dumbly, that it was so much better (bigger) to be thought "good" than "innocent." Good means you have knowledge, and yet "still" are good. I couldn't understand why she was refusing to be praised more than she wished to be praised, why she was refusing my greater tribute, what she wanted from me when she insisted that I find her innocent instead. (For me, "good" had everything good in being innocent and *more*.)

[*In the margin:*] in a taxi coming home from a 10 am Saturday screening at MoMA

When Irene + I came together, I promised always to find her "marvelous." That was one of the terms of our contract, and any violation of that was a betrayal, an assault, a rejection. But think what one would have to be (what condition of one's ego, etc.) to make that a *condition* of a relation. Limiting the free exercise of the other person's mind.

And how it fitted into my neurotic set. How I'd always wanted, longed to find someone marvelous! All my life. And no one had ever helped me enough (*made* me) do it. No one had ever explicitly denied me the right to "see" them, to stand at a distance from them, to understand them, to find fault with them. Everyone (I knew) always wanted, somewhere to be seen, to be understood. (Even my mother, even Philip.) Now, I longed for that interdiction! (Don't see me. I'll see you.) For someone with the arrogance, the certitude, the *talent* to enforce it.

All dreams are model *self-analyses*. Poor dreams are the simple-minded statements or analyses of one's "problem." The good dream is the more complex, the least reductive statement or dramatization. (Versus the common idea that a good dream is one in which you triumph, behave well, wake up . . . feeling happy etc.) The important part of the dream is the analytic statement, not the narrative resolution.

My two model landscapes: the desert (dry, harsh, empty, hot) and the tropics (wet, full, even over-full, hot). A polarity but with one thing in common—a uniform year-round single hot climate. My "surprise" at the round of seasons (feeling it's something contingent, almost a "mistake" each time winter comes round in New York). My fear of (refusal of) the *cold* being more profound, more absolute than my anxiety over the empty, "le vide."

This is a major ingredient in my swimming phobia. Fear of immersion in the ocean as something *cold*. My mother's model interior landscape—hardly anything at all of nature, except that it should be warm (to be in a light dress, or get in a bathing suit). It's a Grand Hotel. Bedroom, large bathroom, bar with dance floor, restaurant, terrace, swimming pool, maybe a golf course. Going back + forth between these places, which are close together. The continual guaranteed presence of "service," the situation of being *served*. Absolving her of the pressure of the demand to be more energetic, autonomous; to do for herself—+ others (like me). What is laziness or indolence at home doesn't count as that in a resort hotel. Also, the bland neutralized genteel kinds of contacts you have in a hotel. The system of decorum which is "given"; she doesn't have to ask for it, to create it, to be continually anxious about its being violated. She knows how to behave; presumably the others know how to behave, too, or they wouldn't (wouldn't dare) be here; they've signed a contract to behave, as it were, before they checked in. A process of self-selection; elimination of riffraff.

As Eva pointed out, if I hadn't made the grand switch from "Kant" to "Mrs. D. H. Lawrence," I would never have been able to write fiction.

The first, and absolutely essential step was—of course—to end my marriage. My life with Philip was chosen + designed to be the context in which I would go further + further along the "Kant" road. The right kind of gratifications + the right kind of deprivations. It was really, in its own terms, an immense success + showed great judgment on my part.

The trial run for the "new being" was Harriet. To get through some of the "objective" blocks (my social inhibitions + snobberies, my worldy ignorance + lack of sophistication).

Then came the true initiation—by Irene. The transformation of my subjectivity.

If the outside corresponded to the inner life in people, we couldn't have "bodies" as we do. The inner life is too complex, too various, too fluid. Our bodies incarnate only a fraction of our inner lives. (The legitimate basis for the paranoid endless anxiety about what's "behind" the appearances.) Given that they would still *have* inner lives of the energy + complexity that they have now, the bodies of people would have to be more like gas—something gaseous yet tangible-looking like clouds. Then our bodies could metamorphose rapidly, expand, contract—a part could break off, we could fragment, fuse, collide, accumulate, vanish, rematerialize, swell up, thin out, thicken, etc. etc. As it is, we're stuck with a soft but still largely determinate (especially determinate with regard to size + dimension + shape) material presence in the world—almost wholly inadequate to these processes which then become "inner" processes. (i.e., far from wholly manifested, needing to be discovered, inferred; capable of being hidden, etc.) Our bodies become vessels, then— and masks. Since we can't expand + contract (our bodies), we stiffen them a lot—inscribe tension on them. Which becomes a

habit—becomes installed, to then re-influence the "inner life."
The phenomenon of character armor that [*the Austrian psychologist Wilhelm*] Reich focused on.

An imperfect design! An imperfect being!

Of course, maybe we wouldn't have so much subjectivity if the
"outer" were better designed to register the interior life. Maybe
subjectivity as we experience it (all the pressure, the force, the
energy, the passion of it) is precisely the result of this "confinement" inside our being. (Like the pressure build up when a gas
is heated up inside a sealed metal container.)

(Is this the purpose of the disparity—the good of it? But that's
too Panglossian a thought.)

Of course, it is. That's what all the sages have known— +
when the demand of a reconciliation of "inner" and "outer,"
they always posit a subjectivity which seems (compared with
what we have at its best) radically depleted, bland, monotonous, empty. Plato, the Gnostic vision, Hesse's bead game
community, etc.

That's why the angels have no bodies (or they have "angelic"
bodies)—not, mainly out of (Christian-)neurotic aversion to
the flesh.

The source (on my side) of the guilt I feel in relation to Irene:
that I acted, from the beginning, in *bad faith*—I never "really"
gave up everything, never really abased myself, never really
thought I was stupid (as she demanded).

Over-arching the whole question of the "first self" versus the
"second self" (my new being, into which Irene initiated me)

was the larger framework: the visionary *self* was *never* ques-
tioned. The issue on which I involved myself with Irene was
"only" that of what concrete style of consciousness. Somewhere,
partly knowing it and partly not, I was cheating. I was going
to, I intended to "use" her knowledge as she could never use it
(absence of "nobility," etc.) as she could *never* put it to use. I had
a (larger —) framework in which to situate her wisdom. So I
apprenticed myself to her—wholeheartedly, true. Even when
I came to realize it meant humiliating myself, rendering up my
mind, pronouncing it incompetent + shallow + death-ridden +
no instrument for proper life—I did all that, not without
struggle but in the end, I did it. Yet all the while I knew there
was "more." More to "me." More would come after—when
I had her wisdom, when I had ingested it + made it mine.

And now I feel profoundly guilty. As, in some way, I always
have. I feel I'm a vampire, a cannibal. I feed on people's wisdom,
erudition, talents, graces. I have a genius for spotting them +
for apprenticing myself to them + for making them mine.

Does that make me a thief? Not exactly. I don't feel—ever—
that I'm taking them away from these people. I don't leave
them any poorer after I'm gone. How could I? These aren't
things you can take away. They still have them, but now I
have them, too. (These things can only be given up—Irene? . . .
by their possessors, never stolen.)

Then what's the matter? Who am I harming? Answer: them.
And me. For, even if there is no possible question of theft or
depletion or diminution of the Other, I am operating under
false pretenses. They don't know what I want from them? At
least, they don't know—can't know—how lustfully, how
single-mindedly I want it from them. And I can't tell them.
For if they did know, they wouldn't give it to me.

Don't I give in return? Sure. Lots. Maybe, in some cases, more than I get in exchange. It's a compulsive giving (benefaction, generosity) to ward off my own oppressive sense of guilt (over feeling like a predator).

And—this is the key point—I always leave them when I've "learned" all I can, when I've had my fill. I "use them up" for *myself* and then want to pass on to new sources.

I rush about the world raiding other people's wells (?) to bring back my buckets + pour all these contributions into my super-well. No one is to see the full extent, all the riches stored there. My deepest secret! They are to see only my skills and products—piecemeal—which are made possible by this laboriously accumulated resource.

9/18/67   New York

Aesthetic book: *The Benefactor*
Ethical book: *Death Kit*

And now? The third stage?

S[øren] K[ierkegaard] was right. Aesthetic isn't enough. Neither is the ethical.

New "form" out of speaking the truth (truth in existential sense, not as "correctness").

I have difficulty with describing physical movement of people—detail (?)

. . .

Less consistency or unity of tone in *Death Kit* than *Bene-factor?*

Benefactor is a reductio ad absurdum of aesthetic approach to life—i.e. solipsistic consciousness (one that doesn't *fundamentally* acknowledge the existence of what's outside the self). I was thinking of the description of the dandy in [Baudelaire's] *Mon coeur mis à nu.*)

[Undated, October]

[Gertrude] Stein—exploring what happens when you drop the idea that one thing follows another (that "this" follows from "that")

Cage + Thoreau on silence and reduction—

. . .

Questioning the idea of the "logical development" of something, something having an "internal logic." I've always taken this for granted.

11/17/67

My neurotic problem isn't primarily with myself (as with Sandy [Friedman]) but with other people. Therefore, writing always works for me, even lifts me out of depressions. Because it's in writing that I (most) experience my autonomy, my strength, my not needing other people. (Sandy has, in writing, the keenest experience of his weakness.)

Au fond, I *do* like myself. I always have. (My strongest purchase on health?) It's just that I don't think other people will like me. And I "understand" their point of view. But—if I were other people—I'd like me a lot.

Fear of contact. I "see" other people. But not in relation to me. That's opaque, a mystery—or simply flat (he "likes" me, he doesn't like me). I'm embarrassed to speak of it. It seems presumptuous.

I, in my corner, with my monstrous needs. And all of them over there! I vow not to make a fool of myself.

. . .

Constructivism [—Kazimir] Malevich, [Vladimir] Tatlin (cf. tower) [—] feeble imitation in Bauhaus, [Walter] Gropius a dope, didn't understand Russians—just wanted to make beautiful things—quickly crushed

Greatest period of modern art in Russia in early 20s, but they were too advanced + too isolated

> theatre on streets—thousands in the Storming of
> the Winter Palace [*SS is referring to the later
> re-creation of the event in Eisenstein's* October]
> Mayakovsky paper atelier (Rosta [*Russian State
> Telegraph Authority for whom Mayakovsky
> worked*])—turned out new ones every day

1968

[In the spring of 1968, SS went to North Vietnam for two weeks (May 3–17) at the invitation of the North Vietnamese government as part of a delegation of American antiwar activists—a trip that excited a great deal of controversy and also provided the basis for her book Trip to Hanoi, *published that same year. For the most part, her notes are either transcriptions of what her hosts were telling her (I have found no notations, affirming or questioning, of what SS was hearing; these notebooks are more like a reporter's than a critic's), schedules and, as she almost always did, SS made factual and historical notations about the places she was seeing and lists of Vietnamese words and their English meanings. As a result, I have chosen to reproduce only a few representative samples of such entries, while quoting in its entirety the one more introspective, skeptical, and analytical entry that I have been able to find. Indeed, it is self-conscious in a way that neither the other notes nor, in my view at least,* Trip to Hanoi *succeed in being.]*

[Undated, May, but most likely May 5 or 6 in Hanoi.]

The cultural difference is the hardest thing to understand, to overcome. A difference of "moeurs" [*"mores"*], style. (And how much of that is Asian, how much specifically Vietnamese I certainly can't find out on my first trip to Asia.) Different way of treating the guest, the stranger, the foreigner, the enemy. Different relation to language—compounded, of course, by the fact that my words, already slowed down and simplified, are mediated by a translator or if I'm speaking English to them we're talking baby-talk.

Added to that the difficulty of being reduced to the status of children: scheduled, led about, explained to, fussed over, pampered, kept under surveillance. We are children individually—even more exasperating, a *group* of children. They are our nurses, our teachers. I try to discover the differences between each of them (Oanh, Hien, Pham, Toan) and I worry that they don't see what's different or special about me. I feel myself continually trying to please them, to make a good impression—to get the best mark of the class. I present myself as an intelligent, well-mannered, cooperative, legible person.

The first impression is that everyone talks in the same style, and has the same things to say. And this is reinforced by the exact repetition of the ritual of hospitality. A bare room, a low table, chairs. We all shake hands, then sit down. On the table: two plates of half-rotten green bananas, cigarettes, soggy cookies, a dish of paper-wrapped candies from China, tea-cups. We are introduced. The leader of their group looks at us. "Cac ban [Chào đón] . . ." [*"Welcome" in Vietnamese*] Someone comes through a curtain and begins serving tea.

The first few days it seemed quite hopeless. There was a barrier that seemed impossible to cross. The sense of how exotic they were—impossible for us to relate to them, ~~understand them~~, clearly impossible for them to understand us. An undeniable feeling of superiority to them; I could understand them (if not relate to them, except on their terms). I felt my consciousness included theirs, or could—but theirs could never include mine. And I thought with despair that I was lost to what I most admired. My consciousness is too complex, it has known too great a variety of pleasures. I thought of the motto of [*the 1964 Bernardo*] Bertolucci film [*Before the Revolution*]—"He who has not lived before the revolution has never tasted the sweetness of life"—and mentioned it to Andy [*the American writer and activist Andrew Kopkind*]. He agreed.

More than hopeless. An ordeal. Of course, I was not sorry I had come. It was a duty—a political act, a piece of political theatre. They were playing their role. We (I) must play ours (mine). The heaviness of it all was due to the fact that the script was entirely written by them; and they were directing the play, too. There was no question in my mind that this was as it should be. But my acts appeared as nothing other than dutiful. And inwardly I was very sad. Because this meant I could learn nothing from them—that an American revolutionary could learn nothing from the Vietnamese revolution, as I think one can learn (for instance) from the Cuban revolution, because—from this perspective, at least—the Cubans are pretty much like us.

We had a role: we were American friends of the Vietnamese struggle. A corporate identity. The trip to Hanoi was a kind of reward, a form of patronage. We were being given a treat—being thanked for our efforts—and then we were to be sent home again, with reinforced loyalty, to continue our separate endeavors as we saw fit.

There is of course an exquisite politeness in this corporate identity. We are not asked—separately or collectively—to justify why we merit this trip. Our being invited and our willingness to come seems to put all our efforts on the same level. We each do what we can—that's what appears to be assumed. Nobody asks questions about what we specifically or concretely do for the struggle. Nobody asks us to explain, much less to justify, the level and quality and tactics of our efforts. We are "cac ban" all.

Everyone says, "We know the American people are our friends. Only the American government is our enemy." And from the beginning I want to yell with exasperation. I honor the nobility of their attitude, but I pity their naïveté. Do they really believe what they are saying? Don't they understand anything about America? Part of me is always thinking of them as children—beautiful, naïve, stubborn children. And I know that I'm not a child—though this theatre requires that I play the role of one.

I long for the three-dimensional textured adult world in which I live—even as I go about my (their) business in this two-dimensional world of the ethical fairy-tale to which I am paying a visit.

It's monochromatic here. Everything is on the same level. All the words belong to the same vocabulary: struggle, bombing, friend, aggressor, imperialist, victory, comrade, the French colonialists, the puppet troops. I resist the flattening of our language, but soon I realize that I must use it (with moderation) if I'm to say anything that's useful to them. That even includes the more loaded local phrases like "the puppet troops" (instead of the ARVN [*Army of the Republic of Vietnam, the South Vietnamese army*] and the movement—they mean *us!*—and "the socialist camp" (when I'm aching to say "communist"). Some I'm already comfortable with: like "The Front" instead of "Viet Cong" and "imperialism" and "black people" and "the liberated zones." (I notice that when I say "Marxism" it's usually translated as "Marxism-Leninism.")

It's the world of *psychology* that I miss.

Each account of something has as its pivot a date: usually either Aug[ust] 1945 (date of the Vietnamese revolution, the founding of the state) or 1954 (expulsion of the French colonialists). Before and after . . . Their concept is a chronological one. Mine is both chronological and geographical. I am continually making cross-cultural comparisons—at least trying to. This is the context of most of my questions. And they seem mildly puzzled by many of my questions, because we don't share a common context.

The first few days I am constantly comparing the Vietnamese with the Cuban revolution. (Both my experience of it in 1960 and my sense of how it has developed that I get from other people's accounts.) And almost all my comparisons are favorable to the Cubans, unfavorable to the Vietnamese—by the standard of what is useful, instructive, imitable, relevant to America radicalism. I want to stop doing this, but it's hard.

I long for someone to be indiscreet here. To talk about his "personal" or "private" feelings. To be carried away by feeling.

I remember the Cubans as sloppy, impulsive, manic (marathon) talkers. Everything here seems terribly formal, measured, controlled, planned, and hierarchical. Everyone is exquisitely polite, yet (somehow) bland.

The strongly hierarchical features of this society strike me immediately, and displease. No one is in the least servile, but many people know their place. I evoke the populist manners of the Cuban revolution. The deference I see given to some people by others is always gracious and graceful. But there is clearly the feeling that some people are more important (valuable) than others, and deserve a bigger share of the few comforts available. Like the store for foreigners (diplomatic personnel, guests) and important government people to which we were taken the third day to buy pants and tire sandals. Our guides told us this was a special store quite proudly, without shame. I thought they should see that the existence of such facilities was uncommunist.

It exasperates me that we are taken quite short distances by car—two cars, in fact—big, ugly, black Volgas that are waiting with their drivers in front of the hotel whenever we are supposed to go somewhere. Why don't they let us—ask us— to walk? Better yet, they should insist that we walk. Is it because of politeness? (Only the best for the guests.) But *that* kind of politeness, it seems to me, could well be abolished in a communist society. Or because they think we're weak, effete foreigners? (Westerners? Americans?) It horrifies me to think they might regard our walking as beneath our dignity (as important people, official guests, celebrities, or whatever). There's no budging them on this. We roll through the bicycle-crammed streets in our big black cars—the chauffeur blasting away on his horn to make people on foot and on bicycles watch out, often give way.

What would be best, of course, is if they would give us bicycles. But it's clear they can't possibly take that request seriously. Are they at least amused? Do they think we're being silly or impolite or dumb or what when we broach it?

Wherever we go in Hanoi people stare, often gape. I find that very pleasant, I don't know exactly why. It's not a particularly friendly stare, but I feel they are "enjoying" us, that it's a pleasant experience for them to see us. I asked Oanh if he thought many people would see that we are Americans. He said this wouldn't occur to many people. Then who do they think we are, I asked. Probably Russians, he said. And indeed, a couple of times people said "tovarich" and some other Russian words at us . . . Mostly, though, people don't say anything to us at all. They stare calmly, they point, they discuss us with their neighbors. Hien says the thing about us that is most frequently said is how tall we are. With good-natured amazement.

The monochromatic version of Vietnamese history that is recited to us again and again. Three thousand years of repelling foreign aggressors. The present extended backward in time. The Americans = the French colonialists = the Japanese (briefly) = millennia of "Northern feudalists"—read "Chinese." There was even a Tet offensive in the [*thirteenth century*]. The great sea battle on the Bach Dang river in 1288 is related as another version of the victory over the French at Dien Bien Phu.

Speaking all the time in simple declarative sentences. All discourse either expository or interrogative.

Whatever we do, we are locked within ourselves. And yet the doing of anything marks the extent to which we make contact with what is not ourselves.

It is a very complex self that an American brings to Hanoi.

Vietnam seemed most real when I saw it at [one] remove, in a film, Joris Ivens's *17th Parallel.*

When Viet[namese] children play "capture the pilot," the tallest must be the American.

The first North Vietnamese feature film was made in 1959. There are now four film studios in the country.

I was lucky to have started the trip in Phnom Penh [in Cambodia]—where I spent four days waiting for the ICC [International Control Commission] plane—and even luckier (though Bob [*Robert Greenblatt, a mathematician from Cornell working full-time for the antiwar movement*], Andy, + I cursed our bad luck) to have been stranded in Vientiane [in Laos] for four more days. That at least has given me some perspective.

. . .

Hanoi approximately 1 million people before the bombing, now (1968) about 200,000 . . .

Pham Van Dong [*then prime minister of North Vietnam*]: speech of 2–3 years ago against the "disease of rhetoric" among cadres—generalities—advises political cadres to pay more attention to literature—wants to improve Vietnamese language . . .

Revolution betrayed by its language

. . .

Sentimentality

Austerity: Vietnamese ingenuity—a society . . . [in which] everything [is] for use

Chastity: nurse slept in room w[ith] the guides, drivers
Fidelity
No shorts or bare chests as in Cambodia

AK [Andrew Kopkind] wonders: where is Ego set among Viets?

[In Hanoi:]

No bonzes

The poverty of [the city]—same colors (no green, red, yellow)—dark blue, beige, khaki

Organization of DRV [Democratic Republic of Vietnam] life—discipline—elitist?

Militia unit training in garden square

Sirens on opera house use

*Contrast: independence of DRV + independence of East European satellites

Loudspeaker goes on at 10:30—announces alerts + music—song by printing workers

Adults shooing away kids who follow us

5/7/68

Evening: 8–11pm

Visit to exhibit of US weapons used in North Vietnam.

Regular bombs (explosive)—100 to 3000 lbs.

Anti-personnel weapons—a) dum-dum bullets,
b) fragmentation bombs—CBU, i) cylinder,
ii) round—shrike, butterfly bombs—c) incendiary
weapons, i) white phosphorous, ii) napalm—
Napalm A, Napalm B, iii) thermite, iv) magnesium

CBW—chemical-biological warfare—defoliants,
toxic chemicals, poison gas

Photos of victims, skulls, cross section of brain, napalmed rice

5/10/68

Mr. Trung, editor of *Nhan Dan* [*the official newspaper of the
Communist Party of Vietnam*]:
Love for US
Very soft-spoken
Effect of US movement—LBJ wrong in evaluating our strug-
gle and sentiment of US people. Those in US for aggression a
minority

To make war you must have finance, troops, weapons, support
of large masses of people—people's war—started w[ith]o[ut]
weapons.

Likes teach-in—draft resistance—"tradition of freedom in
the US"—likes signatures + ads in paper—different forms +

tendencies in the movement, but richness in character—500,000 April 15 or storming of Pentagon—must have strong organizational character—able to call the movement Communist—

["]We know our Communist friends in the US are not in great number["]—

Movement to safeguard the freedom + prestige of the US—"the other America"—not just US troops

["]Movement helped send Mr. Averell Harriman to Paris["]

5/12/68

from Writers' Union evening:

Morrison [*Norman Morrison, the Baltimore Quaker who immolated himself on November 2, 1965, below Secretary of Defense Robert McNamara's Pentagon office in protest against America's involvement in Vietnam; he was a hero in North Vietnam during the war*] is patriot + benefactor for DRV.

Ho [*North Vietnam's leader, Ho Chi Minh*] in 1945: "People are good, only governments are bad."

. . .

Morrison is a great man because he solved the problem outside of himself—he is not Viet, he is not a Communist—he did not (have to act) in that way.

. . .

[The following notes were made by Andrew Kopkind and recopied into the notebook in SS's hand. I have included only a few excerpts, among them some references to SS's activities in North Vietnam as recorded by Kopkind.]

5/13/68   Morning

Coffee—Discuss with Oanh about Russians. Oanh says "we know" that there are divisions in Russian embassy. Some Russians "depraved"—[Tom] Hayden says they're like "Americans in Saigon"—Oanh says Viets were surprised to find out about Russia—"product of bad education" in USSR—Oanh also has news of 2nd Paris [peace talks] meeting; agreement on question that only N. Viets + US citizens [*sic*] be allowed. Also news of general strike in France in support of students.

An alert—all clear in a few minutes—no time for shelter (or interest)

Raining lightly—drove few blocks to ministry of education ... old French villa or bureau—Ushered in to meet smiling director and six young teachers—khaki, green and blue shirts—around long table—tea, cookies, candies, cigs—bare electrical connections on wall—teachers in various disciplines.

Prof. Ta Quang Buu—signed Geneva agreement
Professor: Before 1956, no higher education—go back to 17th C. + before—then higher education w[ith] national characteristics—French made effort to wipe out trad[ition] (Prof. corrects Oanh's translation)—I have been formed un-

der French domination—know French + English. Students educated since '54 . . . know Russian

. . .

Despite atrocities of war, profs and students have not been mobilized [*this sentence is highlighted*]—6000 teachers in colleges—5000 teachers in [secondary] voc[ational] schools— c. 200,000 students in all (voc. [schools] + college[s]) *not* drafted. Gov[ernmen]t + party pay special attention to formation of technical + eco[nomic] planning cadres, + improvement in quality—

[Professor:] Most important difficulty is intellectual isolation—but we have been developing in both theoretical + applied science—

. . .

SS gives outline of US edu[cation]—educ[ation] for first 12 years but not serious—needs rev[olution] to change society + polit[ical] conditions that produce it

. . .

Meeting hall in hotel—near shelter—long table—c. 30 people, mostly men, few women—v. light room, fans spinning, Hien translates—man w[ith] wires out of ears alongside (deaf?)

. . .

(interruption by long—10 mins.—alert. No one goes to shelter, but conversations stop)

Q[uestion]: Poor people's march [*This is referring to the mass protest in the United States in the spring of 1968 organized by Reverend Ralph Abernathy, who became the leader of the Southern Christian Leadership Conference after Martin Luther King's assassination.*]

Psychology of the US (long SS answer).

[Q:] What do common people think of war, effects of Tet double standards for US people + Viet? Does SS expect US people not to believe propaganda?—Vast majority of Viets don't question propaganda either.

. . .

Dinner + then to small theatre . . . R[obert] G[reenblatt] + I left at half time . . . SS stayed—came back + talked w[ith] Swedes + students. [*The American journalist*] Mark Sommer v[ery] naïve—at dinner we had talked again about his patronizing attitude—he had complimented the Viets on their humanity (their not being dehumanized by the war, the cruelty of the Americans)—like praising Negroes for their sense of rhythm—Viets' humanity is not at issue; ours is. Long discussion of *our* complicity in US society—SS attacked Mark—he really is rather callow + mindless— After SS returned, we talked again about the "barrier" here—but the barrier is itself an expression—surface reflection—of the Viet reality. There is also something else beneath, but we cannot discount what is on the surface—

. . .

SS goes to see [U.S.] prisoners—2 of them, 1 in for 3 years, 1 for 1 year— No place given or no indication of where they were being kept—both bow—one (3-year) very low, the other per-functorily—both in "pyjamas" but different—striped + solid

3-year was more "obsequious," other curt. Oanh + three others in room, at small military post, about 10 men from hotel . . .

Both [POWs] said they got mail from the US at regular inter-vals—pictures of family

High rank Lt. Col. and Maj[or], both w[ith] long Air Force service—Korean War + older—in WWII. Older said he knew nothing of Geneva Accords. They get information— They know about Poor March, Abernathy, RFK, etc.

SS told them about US political changes—

SS saw them separately . . .

One understood a little Vietnamese—responded when officer said in Viet that he could take fruit + candy

[The POWs] were given material to read about [the] war— Felix Greene book [*Greene, a cousin of Graham Greene's, was a reporter for the* San Francisco Chronicle *in the early 1960s, an opponent of U.S. involvement in Vietnam, and a North Viet-namese sympathizer*], *Vietnamese Courier.*

[The POWs] bow as they leave.

. . .

[From here, the entries are SS's.]

Love of "revolution" for Westerners: final romance of primi-
tivism, simple life [/] people

decentralized, honest society w[ith] love

. . .

[Undated, June]

Diana [Kemeny]—no neg[ative] transference; doesn't permit
anger, tears; my accomplice; tell me something in detail

One of my strategies:
Disarm people: people are dangerous, must be placated

. . .

[Undated, other than "July 1968 Paris"]

"Minimal" cinema
(Warhol's aleatory cat in *Harlot*)

Bertolucci: Make each shot autonomous; thereby reduce
montage

Make film about language—each person speaking his own
language.

. . .

Keats: "Though a quarrel in the streets is a thing to be hated,
the energies displayed in it are fine."

Buy Barbara Miller Lane, *Architecture + Politics in Germany 1918–1945*

. . .

8/7/68   Stockholm

I see now that my pattern of association with male homosexuals has one more, very important meaning than those I've already understood (de-sexualizing myself; having male company—which I long for—that's still safe, not threatening, etc.). It also means the roundabout recovery or preservation of my femininity! Everything "feminine" is "en principe" [*"in principle"*] poisoned for me by my mother. If she even *would* . . . do it, I don't want to do it. If she liked it, I can't like it. That includes everything from men to perfume, attractive furniture, stylish clothes, make-up, fancy or ornate things, soft lines, curves, flowers, colors, going to the beauty parlor, and having vacations in the sun!

[*In the margin:*] Not to mention alcohol, card games, + TV. Thank God my mother didn't like children, food, movies, books, and learning!

Poor me. But I've rather cleverly found a back door to some of those things by becoming close to a series of men who admire and imitate "feminine" things. I accept that in them. (They—not women, not my mother—validate it.) Therefore, I can accept it in myself. And so in the last decade I have gradually been adding more "feminine" things, tastes, + activities in my life. I can love "art nouveau" (all curves, opalescent glass, insane flowers). I can enjoy flowers. I love to dance. I love beautiful clothes. I want to (well, in my head I do, though in fact I don't!) go to and give parties. I want a beautiful apartment with stunning furniture. I [enjoy] wearing bright colors.

How different I was until eleven years ago (through the end of my marriage): no flowers, no colors (my clothes were just black, grey, + brown material to hide in—to cover up as much of myself as I could), no lightness of any kind. The only good was work, study, my intellectual + moral ambitions, becoming "strong" (because my mother is "weak").

So, as I suddenly saw this morning—it was just waking up in the hotel here, picking up an already read issue of *La Quinzaine Littéraire*, glancing at a review of the new [Carlos] Fuentes novel, reading a description of a woman character who collects "art nouveau"—my involvement with the male homosexual world in the last eleven years isn't just something bad for me, a neurotic symptom, a retreat, a defense against the emergence of my own sexuality + full maturity. It's also been—given my initial problems—something very positive. I've been helped by it—though I think I've gotten all I can from that unconscious strategy by now, and it's of no *further* use to me. Because I can be more genuinely a woman (but still strong, still autonomous, still an adult) more genuinely than any man can!

How odd to have thought of all this—instantaneously, though it's taking me a half hour to write it down—just on seeing three sentences about "art nouveau." (When I think of the many whole books I've read, + own, on "art nouveau"— the conversations with Elliott [Stein], etc.)

I've had such enormous difficulties thinking about myself, being connected with myself this last year. Only the same old

stale reflections. No new ideas or insights since the big package a year ago in Martinique . . .

It's mostly to do with Diana's absence from my life, I suppose.
Never have I written so little in my journal—so that I've had
the *same* notebook—this one—for over a year, + still am not
close to filling it up.

Another mini-thought. When I had this idea (me with a new
idea!) this morning in bed, I was so delighted at having a new
thought—it's been so damned long! I've been sure this year
that my mind was shot to hell, + I was becoming just as stupid as everybody else—I wanted to do something to express
my pleasure. So I spoke out loud, rather self-consciously:
"Well, what do you know. An idea!" Or something like that.
And the sound of my voice in this room with nobody but me
here profoundly depressed me.

I never talk out loud to myself—I never even try—and now I
see why I don't. I find it very painful. Then I *really* know I'm
alone.

Maybe that's why I write—in a journal. That feels "right." I
know I'm alone, that I'm the only reader of what I write
here—but the knowledge isn't painful, on the contrary I feel
stronger for it, stronger each time I write something down.
(Hence, my worry this past year—I felt myself terribly *weakened* by the fact that I couldn't write in the journal, didn't
want to, was blocked, or whatever.) I can't talk to myself, but
I can write to myself.

(But is that because I *do* think it possible that someday someone I love who loves me will read my journals—+ feel even
closer to me?)

"I want to be good."

"Why?"

"I want to be what I admire."

"Why don't you want to be what you are?"

9/19/68   Stockholm

Italian Trotskyist magazine, *La Sinistra* (ed. Savelli)

Read in the last month: eleven stories of Chekhov; Melville, *The Confidence Man*; [Maxim] Gorky, *Mother*; [Evgeny] Zamyatin, *We*; Tolstoy, *The Kreutzer Sonata*; Nabokov's *The Waltz Invention*; Conrad's *Nostromo*; three Agatha Christie's

Get Schoenberg, *Style and Idea*

Essays still to write: Artaud, Adorno, Psychotechnics (Spiritual Liberties + Psychological Disciplines), Notes Towards a Def[inition] of C[ultural] R[evolution]

. . .

1969

[Undated, June. The journal in which these entries appear is marked "Politics" on the front cover.]

"Without revolutionary theory there can be no revolutionary movement." Lenin (1902)

Was Rosa Luxemburg "a spiritual ally of the Mensheviks" (Lichtheim) or a good communist ([*the American antiwar activist*] Staughton Lynd)? How to decide this.

The double experience of 1968—The French May, the Czechoslovak August.

"The solution lies in the effective insurrection of minds." Saint-Just. Read Saint-Just's *Esprit de la Révolution*, etc.

("Insurrection . . . must be the permanent state of the republic." Sade)

"1848 was amusing only because people make utopias like castles in Spain." — Baudelaire

Ivan Illich [*the Austrian Catholic social critic, whom SS met in the late 1960s*] mentioned what a radical transformation would be wrought in a society if one passed one simple law: that nothing within the borders of the country could move faster than 30 m.p.h. Think what a change that would make in the priorities + quality of goods produced. Such a country would produce cars that would last for 50 years.

"One becomes stupid as soon as one stops being passionate." ([Claude Adrien] Helvétius)

Whatever doesn't land you in jail gets co-opted.

Read on:

> The Chaco war (1935)
> The slaughter in Madagascar in 1947
> The massacre of 45,000 Algerians at Setif in 1944
> The North Italian factory occupations in 1919–20
> The Bosnian student movement before WWI

. . .

1970

2/4/70   Paris

The thought is never (?) "heavy"—it's the anxiety along-side it.

The longing to touch / be touched. I feel gratitude when I touch someone—as well as affection, etc. The person has allowed me proof that I have a body—and that there are bodies in the world.

Being a big eater = desire to affirm that I have a body. Identifying refusal of food with refusal of the body. Irritation with people who don't eat—even anxiety (as initially with [*SS's lover during this period*] C[arlotta del Pezzo]) and revulsion (as with Susan [Taubes]). Lesson of last 5 months: I don't have to eat a lot.

2/10/70   New York

Long conversation with Stephen [Koch] this afternoon—immensely helpful.

I haven't so many alternatives as I thought—in fact, only two: uproot the feeling, tell her [Carlotta] to go to hell—or jouer le jeu [*"play the game"*].

Of course, it will be the second. The age of innocence is over.

This is not the end of the story—only the beginning of Phase Three.

Phase One was July–August: passion, hope, longing. Phase Two dates from my return to New York on Sept. 2 until this last week in Paris: intensified longing, obsession, suffering, paralysis in work, magical chastity, innocence (still), joy at the feeling of being loved, being patient waiting for our life together to begin.

Now Phase Three. The time of playing the game. Carlotta cannot be the center of my life, only (possibly) part of a plural center that will include work, friends, other affairs. I must allow her her liberty to be with me when she wants to and then go away again. I must learn to use, and genuinely enjoy, the liberty that such a situation allows me.

I must appear to be strong—which means that I really must be strong. I must not offer her my suffering, my longing for her, as a proof of my love. I must not even tell her so often that I love her. I must not try to persuade her, with words, that it will be good for her to be with me. (This awakens her fear of dependence.) I must not ask her to reassure me, to tell me she loves me. I must not ask her when she is coming to New York, only [say] that I hope she will come.

Above all, I must not act as if what has happened this week is decisive (to ask her to reassure me that it is decisive). Nothing is decisive for her. But if I ask her to tell me that it isn't, she will feel cornered—as if she is being asked for a commitment.

I must show that I am interested in (get pleasure from) my work, David, my friends. If I deny them for her, that is a sign of weakness—and she feels threatened. (For me, of course, it is a sign of strength—and evidence of my love.)

I must be strong, permissive, unreproachful, capable of joy (independently of her), able to take care of my own needs (but playing down my ability, or wish, to take care of hers). Remember what she said the other day about finding me so different from the way I appeared at first (autonomous, "cool")? It was that person she was originally attracted to. She must still sense that in me from time to time. I cannot ever show her all my weakness. I must limit my thirst for candor.

I cannot persuade her with words to love me, to trust me, to be with me. It must be done with actions. She must come to me freely. I must act as if I expect her to do that—but not say it, above all not ask her to confirm it. I must act as if ten days with her is as good as ten months.

I can tell her that I feel stronger (in myself, in my love for her) because of this past week—but not that "we" are stronger. That's already a demand for commitment.

I must not ask her to ask me to wait for her, to be patient, to have hope. I must simply show that I am, in fact, doing these things—without anxiety, without too much suffering.

Conversation with Eva [Berliner]:

The meaning of Carlotta's "collapse" this past week: You see, I would if I could, but I can't. For the behavior to be effective (i.e. self-exonerating) the collapse must be "total," which excludes even the slightest gesture of consolation or reassurance to me. For if she could make such a gesture, that would mean she was capable of concern for me (of feeling a sense of responsibility) and therefore that the collapse was not total, and if not total then demands could conceivably be made on her, etc. (That, not sadism—conscious or unconscious—explains why she couldn't give the smallest reassurance those last days.)

What I have to get over: the idea that the value of love rises as the self dwindles. What Carlotta doesn't want—should anyone want it?—is that I'm prepared to give up (disvalue) everything for her. What she was attracted to in me was that I was a person with interests, success, strength.

A bad lesson I learned from Irene, who did want me to give up everything for her, and did measure my love by the amount I was willing to give up.

The state that Carlotta was in last week: she has no "I." "It" was making her do things. That's her problem: not having a real "I." That is, hating herself. That is, believing that she's a killer—that she's fundamentally bad for people. (Hence, the meaninglessness of the notion of "responsibility" for a person without an "I.") But no person can give Carlotta an "I." Even if one could, it would feel threatening to her. A person who can give you an "I" can also take it away.

Eva said: I would be afraid of someone who was willing to give up everything for me.

Carlotta wants from me, first, the show of strength—the re-assurance that she can't destroy me. That, at this moment, much more than my reassurance that I still love her.

2/12/70

Conversation with Stephen [Koch]:

American	European
Analysis >>> inner modification	intuition >>> action
Psychoanalyis	astrology
Self-manipulation—goal of self-transcendence	one can't change one's nature
There must be something better than my nature	I have to be alone (everything shakes down—I see what I feel)
Incessant talking (talking it out)	everyone ultimately is alone
Help me	
What is the framework that explains why then I did X and now I did Y	It's vulgar (unnecessary, creates problems) to talk a lot; you either know or you don't know
I did it because . . .	Don't be so "logical"

I want to be better than I am	Take my latest words (actions) as me—why is it a problem for you that I said something different earlier? I felt differently then
Frontier thesis of America (let's move on—value of change for its own sake)	
How would you advise me? (What should I do?)	No one can advise anyone else (dangerous; meaningless)
Do you know how much I love you? (different kinds of love)	love = love
It's distinctive to be alone (unnatural)	Things happen—I control very little
I must take responsibility for everything I do; I am the author of my life	Meaninglessness of the idea of making oneself do what one doesn't want to do
Making plans What am I to do? i.e. what ought I to do?	Meaninglessness of question: what ought I to do?

I am a "decision head." I generalize from my experience. My principal source of self-esteem is that I can decide, and act (force myself) even when I don't want to do something. I am "in control" of myself. Function of intelligence: self-overcoming.

Carlotta an "occasionalist"—little connective causal tissue between acts (statements). She doesn't feel bound by her "intentions."

A month ago I said to Don [Eric Levine]: being in love means being willing to ruin yourself for the other person. But not now! I defined love in Paris as spectacular (total) generosity.

I have an anticipatory view of my life.

Carlotta would never say of an action of hers that it was a "mistake," because she doesn't see herself as acting on the basis of judgment made of calculations—but only on the basis of feelings and capabilities. Feelings can't be a mistake. Something she's done can be bad—or sad—but not a mistake.— I often speak of actions I've performed as mistakes because I assume an element of conscious judgment, evaluation (is this efficacious? What are its long-range consequences?) enters, properly so, into my decisive actions.

Carlotta not locked into an ambivalence problem—as Eva has often been. She operates through violent swings of the pendulum, but not because she has, say, ambivalent feelings towards Beatrice [*Carlotta's lover when SS met her*] which cause her to move toward me, then experience ambivalence toward me which causes her to return to Beatrice, then long for me, etc. She is not ambivalent about either one of us!

Carlotta doesn't take full credit (get the proper benefits in self-esteem) from her heroic quitting of heroin. Not: I stopped, therefore . . . but: it was possible for me to stop.

Beatrice's being "Chinese" made Carlotta feel safe. I'm loved, but not too much—not too expressively, too possessively, too inquisitively.

One of the strongest psychic factors in Beatrice's favor: C. feels grateful to her, indebted to her—for feeling more "well" in the past four years. Apparently, she is. Beatrice must really have been good to her. But it's also true that Beatrice subtly (not so subtly?) encourages—promotes—this sense of indebtedness in Carlotta. Her remarks to me at our summit conference in the Hotel Santa Lucia in Naples on August 1st: "I've given Carlotta four years of my life"—"Do you realize how fragile she is?"

In Milan once, I said to C. "Don't you see that you are the author of your life?" She replied that it wasn't true.

2/15/70

The functions of the seminar I've been having re C. this week with Stephen, Don, Eva, Joe [Chaikin], Florence [Malraux]: to erect a structure of understanding (comparative world-views, comparative consciousness) to transcend sorrow, anxiety, false hope—to plot strategy (have "realistic" hope, not make mistakes)—to experience mastery (through making an effort of intelligence) to counter-act emotional defeat, sense of impotence—to draw closer to my friends, experiencing the ways in which they are intelligent, sensitive, loving, and can therefore nourish me (the experience that I am not alone even if abandoned by C.)

Being in love (l'amour fou [*"crazy love"*]) a pathological variant of loving. Being in love = addiction, obsession, exclusion of others, insatiable demand for presence, paralysis of other interests and activities. A disease of love, a fever (therefore exalting). One "falls" in love. But this is one disease which, if one must have it, is better to have often rather than infrequently. It's less mad to fall in love often (less inaccurate for there are many wonderful people in the world) than only two or three times in one's life. Or maybe it's better always to be in love with several people at any given time.

Qualities that turn me on (someone I love must have at least two or three):

1. Intelligence
2. Beauty; elegance
3. Douceur [*"gentleness, sweetness"*]
4. Glamor; celebrity
5. Strength
6. Vitality; sexual enthusiasm; gaiety; charm
7. Emotional expressiveness, tenderness (verbal, physical), affectionateness

One great discovery in the last years (embarrassing) has been how much I respond to 4—Jasper—even Dick Goodwin, Warren Beatty—now C.

Intelligence means having a sensibility (articulatable, verbalizable) that if not really original has at least a definite personal signature. That I can be thrilled by things a person says. (Philip had it—Irene—Jasper—Eva)

Glamor requires a space between the person and an image (title) that preceeds the person. "This is X the—Jasper the painter. Carlotta the duchess. Warren the movie star." (But not Eva the German teacher—a role instead of an image. No space "between" a person and a role.)

Re: conversation with Ivan Illich:

Schools are an institution for the production of children. Cf. [Philippe] Ariès [*the author of* Centuries of Childhood]

Replacement of "learning" by "being taught." Now students demand not to learn but to be taught.

Assumption behind "modern," "Western" concept of the school:

1) universal and, ideally, compulsory
2) age-specific (for "children")
3) graded curriculum
4) testing >>> certification
5) role of teacher

Schooling a lottery, in which theoretically everyone has a chance at the Nobel Prize. Reinforces and institutionalizes class society, hierarchical relations.

Why not invoke 1st Amendment against schools (as there should not be "established" religion, there should be no other graded curricula); also the 5th Amendment (testing = self-incrimination); and the anti-trust laws (wish to establish uniform educational standard)? Instead of insisting that all people be schooled during "childhood," why not issue an Edu-card to every person at birth entitling the person to a minimum number of five years of schooling, to be cashed in (used) whenever the person elects—with dividends, perhaps, if one defers some schooling to the "adult" years.

With Ivan, after Bob Silvers [*a founding editor of* The New York Review of Books *and a lifelong friend of SS's*] left:

I make an "idol" of virtue, goodness, sanctity. I corrupt what goodness I have by lusting after it.— And I've always thought my idols were the best part of my consciousness! (My idol =

my moral aspirations; my private pantheon—Nietzsche, Beckett, etc.; my "standards" for myself.)

I neglect the convivium (many people) in the hunger for the kind of fullness of being only possible in the dialogue (verbal mostly, sometimes physical) with one other person.

Ivan says he is aware before he acts of the possibility of making a mistake, but never looking back on his actions. He is aware of committing sins—e.g. being cold, exploitative, cruel. One can be forgiven by a person against whom one has sinned. But one can't forgive oneself. What can you do with the awareness of having sinned? Nothing. Live with it. (Being forgiven doesn't cancel the sin.)

Process of dying (sterben) versus death (todt). Process of dying = one aims to "fall free." English doesn't have two words for death + dying (Sterben / Todt; nekros / thanatos) as it doesn't have two words for hope (l'espoir / l'espérance).

Every time a woman is raped (and murdered) in a big city, that's a lynching. Women's Lib. How the metaphor illuminates. What is sexual (i.e. "private" according to male-dominated society) becomes a political (i.e. public / social) crime—rooted in the public, ideological subjection of women.

Dialectic of the relation between conscious and consciousness:
—function of language (language promotes consciousness / an increase of consciousness is not only philosophically debilitating (cf. Dostoyevsky's *Notes from Underground*, Nietzsche), but, more importantly, morally debilitating)

Before the "school" there were collective forms of training consciousness in all traditional societies: ritual, pilgrimage, begging, silence, liturgy.

Ivan: There is no greater corruptor than the word of God

Isn't it spiritual arrogance on my part to feel corrupt (compromised) every time I am not present in the fullness of my being? A kind of moral hysteria? (Problem of [*Ingmar Bergman's 1966 film*] *Persona*—has Martin the answer?) Denial of creatural reality.

One doesn't speak language, one speaks (at any given moment) a particular language. One doesn't make music-in-general, but operates, at any given time, within a specific tonal system.

Kids now are open to death (todt—being killed) while dying as a (living) process is increasingly meaningless to them. Hence, it's no argument that cigarettes cause cancer or that heroin addiction is eventually fatal, for that's one of their points. The taste for apocalypse (being killed). At least death by, say, drugs is self-driven, individual, as opposed to death by nuclear holocaust.

After three months of silence in the desert, speaking is a violently physical act. (For how long?)

Ivan searching for a reply to something I said: "Wait . . . I can taste it but I can't yet find the words."

I make an idol of my moral consciousness. My pursuit of the good is corrupted by the sin of idolatry.

2/17/70

I'm in exile (America) from my exile (Europe).

Abandoned. Struggling not to feel abandoned.

Kleist (Puppet Theater): If you don't have your center of gravity within yourself, you have it somewhere else (in another person?) which sets up infinite possibilities of distortion. Carlotta's ambivalence—(unlike Eva) she doesn't project it on to persons (she's too gentle, too affectionate, essentially too uncritical of people) but she feels the profoundest ambivalence toward herself. Experiences herself as a deeply dependent person, and despises herself for that.

Re: her telegram: "Paris seems so far away."
—What I must understand is that nothing about Paris was a positive experience for C. It was for me: however painful, I was with her.

Importance, to C., of the notion of being "civilized." Being civilized means having self-control, being able to be gay and friendly when you feel despair. The ability to laugh on the phone with an acquaintance in the midst of great private suffering is "civilized" to her—dissociated and anxiety-provoking to me. [Being civilized] means keeping things separate—different states of being with people, different states of self-manifestation and self-revelation—with the standard of being pleasant for people to be with.

Carlotta thinks of herself as "decadent." How deep is this? Is it only aristocrats who can be decadent? She doesn't think of herself as either "compromised" ("self-compromised") or "corrupt"—epithets I might apply to myself (while I would never describe myself as decadent).

With C.'s telegram today, we're back in Square 1. Will she—and when—find the energy to make another move?

C. has become the first big intellectual event (this past week) since my trip to Hanoi. And [calls my] consciousness into question. As my trip to Hanoi made me re-appraise my identity, the forms of my consciousness, the psychic forms of my culture, the meaning of "sincerity," language, moral decision, psychological expressiveness, etc., so the trip to Paris—pain, loss, abandonment, the advent of anguish + insecurity—has made me re-appraise almost everything about the forms of my thinking and feeling. A shaft boring into my consciousness—deeper and deeper (as I talk to Don, Stephen, Eva—especially Don)—"the seminar." I feel a big gain in wisdom, in perceptiveness—if not in emotional maturity. The last 8 days have been like a year's worth of work with Diana. Better, richer in some ways than the psychoanalytic dialogue—this home analysis with friends—because I can analyze the cultural (Jewish, American, psychoanalytic, etc.) forms of my consciousness, not just their sources in my individual psychobiography.

I feel a sense of mastery, amid all the pain and anguish at being abandoned. A breakthrough of intelligence like this—perceptions not only verbalized, but spun out into a long, searching, open-ended discourse—makes me know I'm alive and growing. It's almost as great a source of vitality—of feeling palpably the sense of life in me—as being in love. I feel once again, and I rejoice, that I'm not busy dying—I'm still busy being born.

America vs. Europe again:

C. doesn't see herself as the product of her history, but the vehicle of her nature. For me, I am the product of my history. That's all my "nature" amounts to— And since I understand how arbitrary, in part, my history is—its result, my nature, logically seems modifiable, transcendable.

Psychoanalytic thinking sensitizes one to the contingent quality of the self—as the product of a history that is contingent, rather than the expression of a nature that is given. It persuades us that we are being "passive" if we merely accept our selves . . . Hence, the essential optimism of this culture. Psychoanalysis took root here, as it did nowhere in Europe, because it supports the feasibility of "the pursuit of happiness."

Carlotta is profoundly pessimistic about love, human relations, the possibility of happiness. Ultimately—whatever my melancholy and despair—I'm not. I think it is possible to make it, to break through, to avoid the traps (through grace, luck, intelligence, vigilance, passion, art, vitality—whatever.)

The biggest danger is that she will give me up.

I love C. just as much as ever, but my love is no longer innocent—and it never will be again. That makes me very sad—I feel an enormous sense of loss right there, quite apart from my anxiety that in the end I will lose her. But it was inevitable, I suppose; in the end, maybe better. Carlotta would have to be so exceptionally whole and sane to have not created situations which would have destroyed the innocence of my feeling for her. And that is too much to ask of her—of anyone.

It's no accident that I fall in love for the first time in so many years a year before David and I are separated. He's been too important to me in the last six years really to give myself to anyone. He's been safety, refuge; wall; security in being needed, and loved, and necessary, literally and morally. A relationship that needed no justification—self-justifying, fully functional, and limited. But no accident, too, that I've fallen in love with someone who invites me to exercise my parental talents, now losing the object on which they've been exercised (with David's growing up). To be "with" Carlotta even some of the time—I can no longer imagine living with her all the time, and I think I can settle for less (maybe it would prove to be better for me that way, not just better for her)—would still make great demands on my ability to give unselfishly, generously, undemandingly—to find my pleasure in pleasing her, my happiness in making her happy—to be permissive and strong. The sense in which C. plays the role of child with any lover is that one can't expect to be given to, to be supported, to be reassured by her. She offers her (unreliable) presence—the beauty of her person; her charm; her vitality; her pathos; her wit and intelligence. But she makes no promises (loyalty, fidelity, reliability, practical assistance)—about that she is extremely scrupulous and honest. It's other people, those who love her, who make promises to her. (Everyone who has loved Carlotta must have understood at least that much from the beginning.) And she tells them that she will not be surprised, or reproachful, if they can't keep the promises they make (or change their minds). She always thinks they are promising too much—and that she isn't worthy of their donation of self, and that they will, must ultimately become disappointed in her.

Carlotta is exceptionally free of rage, anger, rancor, hostility. She is a profoundly gentle person. I love this in her. (It reminds me of myself.) But this must be one reason for her terribly self-destructive history. She's rarely known how to defend herself, except by withdrawal (tuning out, running away). How come she never developed even a normal capacity for hostility? This can only be explained by things in her childhood. Too much insecurity to allow anger. But if there's no anger experienced, one feels so vulnerable—anxiety must then mount to intolerable levels. Thus, already at eighteen, she had to seek the extreme recourse of heroin to disconnect herself from the anxiety. (As she once told me, if she hadn't taken heroin, she would have committed suicide.)

I remember in August Robertino [*a friend of Carlotta's*] saying to me, "One gives up a lot when one loves Carlotta." And how surprised and moved I was when she replied quietly to both of us: "But I give up a lot too."

Can I love non-possessively, permissively—without withdrawing myself, setting up my own defenses and strategic retreats, on the one hand, or reducing the amount and intensity of my love, on the other? I would like to try, with Carlotta. Not just because I am so completely in love with her that I have no choice but to try anything that's possible— though that's true. But also because it might be very good for me. I have such strong tendencies to abandon myself to someone with whom I'm in love—to want to give up everything, to be possessed totally as well as to possess totally. What I envisage as perhaps possible with Carlotta is the contradiction of my symbiotic, Siamese-twin marriages in the past. I might have learned to love fully (as I really never have done) and to remain autonomous and be able to be alone without anguish—at the same time. That would be a tremendous victory, a great change in what C. would call my "nature" (but which I stubbornly insist on believing is less than that).

Telling Eva about speaking French so much (with Florence) makes my English deteriorate—I said, "It seems as if, ultimately, I have room for only one language"— She laughed and said, "Another example of your taste for monogamy."

I feel inauthentic at a party: Protestant-Jewish demand for unremitting "seriousness." Going to a party is a "low" activity—the authentic self is compromised, fragmented—one plays "roles." One isn't fully present, beyond role-playing. One doesn't (can't) tell the full truth, which means one is lying, even if one doesn't literally tell lies.

Carlotta has no share in this type of consciousness (typically Puritan). The convivium has its value, and standards of presence appropriate to itself. The fulfilling of these standards means one is "civilized." There is no guilt attached to the situation of being at a party as such for her, as there is for me. Rather, perhaps, some guilt attaches to unsociability, being uncompanionable. The lies, or partial truth-telling, that sociability requires are part of civiltà. No inner demand for complete authenticity in Catholic culture.

Mine is a second-class, truncated Puritanism. Parties depress me (I feel demeaned) while I don't usually feel depressed, corrupted, or demeaned if I go to a bad movie or play. As long as I am a spectator, a voyeur (however much response I may have inside) I haven't essentially violated or demeaned myself. I draw the line between participation and voyeurism. The only parties I go to where I feel clear (and usually not depressed) are those in which I behave like a spectator—the party becomes a movie—and I discuss it with the person I came with or the one person I already know who is there; and regard meeting new people as an intrusion on my essential activity. Or else I use the party as décor, backdrop to be in a different way privately with the person I came with (as when I used to go to parties with Irene, or go to parties to dance with Paul [Thek]).

If I were a full-fledged Puritan, I'd be worried about being corrupted by spectacles too. But I'm not.

I don't feel guilt at being unsociable, though I may sometimes regret it because my loneliness is painful. But when I move into the world, it feels like a moral fall—like seeking love in a whorehouse. Even more, I somewhere take my unsociability as evidence of my "seriousness," a quality which I take as necessary to my existence as a moral being. What a strange set of assumptions, as I now see by comparing them with those of Carlotta. Carlotta never seeks to establish, to herself or to others, that she is "serious." Indeed, the concept hardly makes sense to her. She has always been faintly amused (and, I suppose, somewhere alarmed) when I told her—as, God help me, I have repeatedly—that my love for her is "serious," that I'm a "serious" person. Now I see, for the first time, how it must seem funny to her.

For C., emotions—actions—are. Their quality and duration become self-evident. There's no need for advance certification of them as "serious," or for that kind of retrospective appraisal. It must seem to her like some pretentious, pointless kind of rhetoric.

Bigger gap for C. than for me between emotions and actions. I often use "will," the ethical ought, to make the jump. If you don't have the idea of laying down that kind of bridge (and pushing yourself across), it must be much easier to be indecisive. Protestants + Jews are much fonder of the will + the "ought" than Catholics. This must be very strong in her— bigger than Gemini character, neurotic patterns, etc.

Carlotta—Southern European, Catholic culture—uses the convivium (parties, dinners, etc.) to tune out. Protestant-Jewish culture uses work. One is allowed to tune out on the full authentic private self in work—in the fulfillment of the routines of a vocation, a profession, a job—because work itself is a moral imperative: satisfying the requirements of the discipline of the self and the necessity to relate communally to others. Work is experienced as discipline—the background of which is ascesis—even though it also gives pleasure. One is allowed to become "depersonalized" in work, to forget the self (to lose contact with its most intimate feelings and needs)—indeed all that is necessary if one is to give oneself fully to the work. The party and other forms of convivium are, of course, not at all ascetic—on the contrary. The depersonalization is hedonistic, non-utilitarian, not moralized.

Carlotta never asks herself if she has behaved "authentically," never scrutinizes herself to see if her actions really correspond to her feelings, never despairs of being in touch with her "real" feelings. She experiences her problem not as one of knowing what she really feels, but of living with—and not being torn to pieces by—the (contradictory) feelings she has.

Northern Europe, US:

Protestant culture proposed the self as a mystery to the self. Hence, the rise of introspection, the keeping of journals, silence in Protestant countries. (Cf. Sweden, especially for the latter.) Catholic culture doesn't propose the self as mysterious psychologically, only as complex, contradictory, and sinful. Carlotta doesn't experience her self as alienated (hidden) from herself, but rather as contradictory to the point of being almost intolerable. It's the problem of co-existence (peaceful co-existence) with her self that she hasn't solved, not the problem of contact with herself, which is what I feel is my problem (and task).

I see life as a set of projects / tasks. C. doesn't. This makes it much easier for me to make decisions, or at least to conclude that a decision must be made (and then force myself to take one—even if I have to invent it). Obviously, my set of mind corresponds much more to the conditions under which work in the world is performed. And everyone knows that much more work gets done in Protestant than in Catholic countries. This view is obviously exacerbated in a woman in a Catholic country—because there are strong positive pressures on every girl which discourage the mental set that creates a capacity to work. Intellectual skills, except those involving the development of sensibility, are not encouraged in girls. Executive or administrative force is disparaged as "aggressive," castrating, unbecoming, unfeminine. Women are encouraged to work, not only in Catholic countries but everywhere, only in situations where they take orders—or perform thoroughly routine tasks (as in housework). To be creative or to direct an enterprise, in a woman, is by cultural definition, aggressive. For a woman to function as an autonomous, independent, decision-making being is, by cultural definition, unfeminine—even though the culture allows, and even flatters, a small number of exceptional women who defy the prohibition and function this way anyway. So Carlotta's set [of mind] with respect to will, action, decision-making is not only furnished by her culture, but is heavily compounded by the fact of being a woman.

Women have traditionally represented the "Southern" values, men the Northern values—within any given country. Women are easier, softer, more amiable, less responsible, less intellectual, less serious about work, more spontaneous, more sensuous (though not more sexual—sexuality remains part of the masculine domain of will, force, decision-making, taking the initiative, exercising control, anticipatory behavior).

Simple (too simple?) thesis: the very burden of the project distracts—eventually cuts oneself off, promotes dissociation from—one's feelings. I conceive my life linearly, as a series of projects. Plans, the exercise of will, skill in judgment, and good instincts in decision-making make it possible for me to move along the line of my life, moving from one project to the next. In all this, is it any wonder that feelings—still, in my case (even in my old, most benighted days) a powerful motivating force in the choice and execution of every project—could get a little lost.

Carlotta has never conceived of her life as a series of projects—life is not a line, or a highway—it's basically a group of free-standing events. Those events are basically discussable separately. They can be compared with each other, and each can be understood as a reflection of (at least some partial aspect of) something all her actions share—as their underpinning—her "nature." Her actions all illustrate her nature. She discovers her nature through her actions. Indeed, she uses her actions to discover her nature—her actions, and her capacity for a particular action. Thus, she discovered her feeling about going to New York—the extent of her panic, fear of me, guilt toward Beatrice, etc., etc.—by her inability to leave Paris with me for New York. But there is no notion of a "key" action, more important and more self-revelatory than the others (even of a group of key actions). Hence, in a sense, no one action is irrevocable—or irrevocably self-defining. Thus, she doesn't define herself as brave—because of the action by which she freed herself of heroin. She doesn't (and this is my strongest source of hope) define our relationship as over because she abandoned us (our plans) and backed out of coming to New York.

She doesn't draw conclusions—in a general way—from her actions, though they do, of course, tell her the state of particular feelings and capacities at a specific time. This produces her belief in the openness (and unpredictability) of the future.

I know the future is open and unpredictable. My style, though, is to want to close it—to make it predictable—at least the immediate future (3 months, 6 months, a year) or the longer future with respect to my most intimate relations. A completely open, unpredictable future makes me horribly anxious. I can't imagine how I will function (because I assume functioning in an effective, creative—not blundering—way entails making plans). Of course, I'm fairly confident that I could function somehow—but on a lower level—even if I have no certainties before me. But it has never really occurred to me, I now realize, that this is anything but an undesirable (and, in the case of love, extremely painful and destructive) limitation. It's as if I'm supposed to walk through a forest without being allowed to inform myself whether or not it's full of wolves. Sure, I'll cross the forest anyway—but it seems just stupid, a pointless risk, that I wasn't allowed to inform myself first, when I know the information is available.

[*There are two vertical lines next to this sentence in the margin.*] Only now do I see the limits of my view of life—how carefully I limit surprise, risk-taking, unanticipated sources of change.

The fact is that I have been unusually loose and open to risk-taking in matters of work—tolerant and relatively anxiety-free in work situations that seem to arouse intolerable amounts of anxiety and insecurity in most other people. But I have been so damned cautious, self-protective, uninventive, anxiety-prone, and needful of reassurance in matters of love. I am so very much more cool, loose, adventurous in work than in love. So much more inventive. So easily convinced that if "this" doesn't work out, something else will—that there's always "more." Just what I don't feel about people—whether friends or lovers.

[*In the margin:*] "scarcity economy of love."

I relate my actions to each other. (I'm doing it now.) I draw conclusions from my actions, not just retrospectively, but at the time I perform them. I generalize from them easily. Of course, I often change my opinion—and revise my generalizations—but that form of thought remains habitual (I won't say "natural") with me.

Carlotta tends to particularize. Her generalizations are weak, vague (being "weak," "decadent," "dependent") and don't truly adhere to—or flow from a considered estimate of—her actions. Her generalizations aren't really thoughts as much as abstract words used as tokens of states of feeling. The abstract words are, notably, almost all put-downs of herself. (They are symptoms of when she's not feeling "well.") And when her state of feeling shifts—her feelings are very mobile—the use of the words (and the conviction) behind them shifts, fades.

I've operated with the unconscious aim of trying to lock my feelings into place. The goal of banishing or subduing bad feelings, promoting good feelings which—once installed—I could count on as remaining there, always available to me (to my will) to be used in an action. This is one of the things I mean when I assure C. my love for her is "serious"—that it's locked into place, that it isn't going to change (I guarantee myself). No wonder she reacts to that with uneasiness, as well as incomprehension. It must seem to her like such a mad thing to do.

I want to "promise" myself. One reason is anxiety (wanting to find a safe harbor, to be free of the debilitating fear of abandonment).

[*In the margin:*] Residue of childhood

That's the neurotic side. Another, healthy reason is my (unconscious, life-long) idea of a life of multiple projects, many levels of activity. If something—ideally, my most important private relations—are nailed down, reliable, I'm free to turn my attention to other things: mainly work, but also friends. If I'm not safe in the deepest relationship, I can't really give my attention to other things too. I'm always turning my head back, to look anxiously if the other person is still there.

Carlotta doesn't want to promise herself. The very thought of that arouses thoughts of being trapped with another person, becoming dependent, losing her liberty. Of course, she also wants to be safe somewhere. But she can only accept safety in a situation with a person where she can often test it, challenge it, refuse it.— C.'s problem is that she can't imagine safety as liberating, strengthening. Am I right in thinking that it can be—at least for me?

And C. doesn't have any notion of being safe with someone one loves in order to be freer (from anxiety, from love-starvation) to do something else specifically, to fulfill one's projects. (I'm sure Beatrice knows about this.) Once again, she doesn't have any projects. There is no activity of a public nature—except perhaps the creation of her personal appearance: her clothes, etc.—in which she feels herself competent, or even imagines that she typically, self-indulgently, irresponsibly becomes competent. Her lack of self-love, of self-esteem is so great that she probably wouldn't consider valuable any activity in which she was competent—and, certainly, it prevents her from trying responsibly to gain competence in any activity she does admire.

Back to the earlier point: for Carlotta, knowing her own feelings is not, at any given moment, an essential problem. It can become a problem, though, if she's asked to put her feelings into words—quite rightly, in a way—she feels when she talks about her feelings she is violating herself, because extended talk about or description of states of feelings always carries the taint, or temptation, of generalization. Talk about feelings itself locks feelings into place (at least it appears to do that). Her problem is not the identification of—or contact with—her feelings, but what to do about them—which of the several actions they could prompt she could take. She usually sees several possibilities of action, because she experiences her feelings as multiple, divided. The problem is easier only when action is experienced as a demand from outside her private life—Ken [*the fashion designer Ken Scott, whom Carlotta worked for intermittently*] expected her to do the show on Jan. 20—or from a sphere of her private life when she has explicitly placed responsibility over feeling— her mother wants her to come to Ischia for 10 days in August.

Since the problem is the selection among several feelings for the performance of an action, every action she performs is, au fond, tentative. She often hesitates before she does it—and while she's doing it she experiences waves of doubt as to whether it's right or whether she can go on with it (thereby increasing her sense of herself as weak, psychologically frail, vulnerable). Actions don't easily seem real—at least not until she's been doing them for a long time. Which is why, as she told me, she doesn't really love someone—fully believe in the reality of a love relationship—until at least a year of being "with" the person (in some form) has passed. She de-realizes her behavior by this sense of tentativeness, reversibility, contingency, arbitrariness of everything she does—and since situations only become real to her after a long time (perhaps never fully so) she has the space—of incomplete commitment, so to speak—to behave destructively, unreliably, erratically, self-indulgently, irresponsibly.

[*In the margin:*] None of these her words

Thereby she tests her own commitments to the action or the situation with the person—if it survives these tests, it deserves to (survival of the fittest); if it doesn't, it wasn't right. But thereby also she increases her burden of self-hatred, because somewhere she does know she behaves destructively with people she loves.

It must be partly because this burden of self-reproach and self-condemnation is so great that she views the events of her life mainly as "free-standing." The causal tissue between events, in C.'s view, is very thin. As much as possible, she minimizes it. It would probably be intolerable for her, as she is now, to see how many connections there are between the things she does. Bearing the whole (could she apprehend herself as a whole—intuitively or through the exercise of discursive intelligence)—herself as the sum of her parts—would be even more painful than bearing herself as a collection of disparaging epithets, loosely used, plus the separate parts.

Carlotta has a problem "bearing" herself at all. Therefore, she has an investment in a certain degree of inaccuracy—what she's doing when, her word, she "exaggerates" (e.g. "I'm desperate," "I wish I could disappear")—her feelings. Also a big investment in the ability to tune out—pleasures of the convivium, dolce vita, even the kind of chatter Beatrice provides which carefully skirts all real questions of feeling. (Those gay twice-daily phone calls to Milan in July + August.) Exaggeration—inaccuracy—obscure the exact contours of the burden of the self. Distraction temporarily suppresses the awareness of it.

How different from my procedures! I have found lucidity—and accuracy to the point of pedantry—offer me the only possibility I know of making some contact with my feelings. C.'s exaggerations always upset and confuse me. I can't understand why she would want to say something that isn't strictly true, when the subject is an important ("serious!") one. She finds that I lack a sense of humor, that I'm too literal-minded. I've agreed about that with her—and yet I know it's not true, or at least it's much more complicated. The explanation, of course, is that different problems—different anxieties—are at stake when I talk than when she talks. She's not hooked on talk as a creative dialogue, as I am.

[*In the margin:*] She isn't helped to know her feelings better by verbalizing them. It's a more purely creatural, convivial activity for her than for me. (For me, it's the principal medium of my salvation!)

The other procedure—finding distractions, tuning out—is also foreign to me. Of course, I can and do do it sometimes, but never without feeling I'm violating myself. If my health depends on my knowing—experiencing—my full intimate self, escaping into a "social" self feels simply bad. What I want is not to tune out, because the bad situation I started from was feeling tuned out.

I'm chasing myself (I have been for years). Now I'm chasing Carlotta, too. She's running away from confronting herself. She's running away from me.— This is, of course, the gloomiest way I can summarize the situation. It's much more than this.

2/18/70

I've told C. she can help me—being connected with her makes me grow, makes me more alive. These 4 pages I've written in the past few days are the concrete proof. I wish she could read them. But that's probably self-indulgent, my wish: I'm treating her—by that wish—as if she were like me. As if she needs words, thoughts, analysis, dialogue. She can't take it in this form.

Do I want to show what I've written because I think it would be good for her (help her feel better in herself) or because I want to force upon her the evidence of the fruitfulness and value (to me) of my love for her. Both, of course. But mainly the latter—which is why I must be very suspicious of this wish. It's self-serving: I imagine if she knew how much I'd gained from loving her, she would love herself more. Of course, I want that. But [in] the end don't I want her to love herself more than she can love me?

A lot of what I've written in criticism of my lust for virtue— my discovery that I've committed idolatry, making of the good an idol—is open to the charge of being still caught within the dialectic of idolatry. I've made a moral criticism of my moral consciousness. Meta-idolatry.

A similar charge could be made about my ideas of comparative consciousness re: Carlotta and me. I feel as if I've discovered the limits of my own unspontaneous, will-driven, decision-craving, anticipatory, linear, discourse-dependent style of feeling and acting. I profess to see the advantages (spiritual, psychological, practical) and validity of Carlotta's consciousness. (Stripped of its neurotic motivations and backlash of self-destructiveness, it offers an equally complete way of seeing things and of functioning in the world.) I profess to have detected the ravages of reason in myself. But am I not over-powering with the labor of reason the glimpse I've had of a more organic, less problematic, less consciousness-laden view of the world? The elements of Carlotta's view of the world I've sounded out exist in these pages only as packaged by my reason. It sounds as if I were not just proposing one more project for myself.

This entry seems to be devoted to self-criticism—I mean, meta-self-criticism.

I don't want to make my wisdom a product I'm packaging for my own use, and that of those I love. But how do I break free, let go?

I know I'm afraid of passivity (and dependence). Using my mind, something makes me feel active (autonomous). That's good.

What I want to fall away from the activity are my procedures of self-manipulation. I want to stop "aiming" myself, just aim. (There must be a lot of this in the Zen book on archery by [*the twentieth-century German philosopher and writer Eugen*] Herrigel.) But I can't do it yet. I'm too scared. [*There's a vertical line in the margin next to the last two sentences.*]

I think I must fear somewhere that spontaneity—following the lead of feelings much more than I do—will lead, at least in me, to passivity. This can't be so, but I won't really know until I have the experiences.

It's all a question of really feeling inside myself, so I don't always worry that I should get out, go behind, and push. And I must abandon the standards of efficiency (efficacity) in action. It's not necessary that an action necessarily leads to what one understands as a "result." If I were more inside my feelings—a whole range of feelings, not just my love for Carlotta—I wouldn't be so interested in results anyway. I wouldn't have the psychic room, at least not as much. I'd experience my feelings in a more imperative form, and satisfying them by acting on them would be a bigger, more gratifying experience—so that I wouldn't think so much about "what's going to happen after" (or "next") and I wouldn't even care so much if later consequences were, indeed, displeasing or frustrating to me.

I would be more loyal to myself, less loyal to my "life." I would stop treating my life as if its dimensions were already determined (or determinable) a vessel whose responsibility it's mine to fill with high-class goodies.

2/20/70

Conversation with Eva:
All pain enrages. Why am I not in contact with my anger? What do I feel? Depression. But that means I am "depressing" another emotion. Despair, then. But despair is a conclusion one draws from a history of pain (it's happening again).

Everyone who has had a bad childhood is angry. I must have felt angry at first (early). Then I "did" something with it. Turned it into—what? Self-hatred > Fear (of my own anger, of the retaliation of others). Despair. The ability to be just and fair—and to dissociate.

Eva says I talk about anger like someone who has never been psychoanalyzed.

Is Carlotta angry? Certainly, she must have had an awful childhood—though she knows consciously NOTHING about it—otherwise she wouldn't be as she is, wouldn't have started taking heroin at 18, etc. Only clue she has given me is when she said, "I feel about my mother as if she were my daughter"—she who is every lover's child! No wonder she fears separation from her mother—needs to visit her often (though only briefly): it's the one relationship in which she feels more adult. (To a lesser degree, she feels more adult than Giovanella [*Zannoni, a film producer and friend of Car-*

lotta's and SS's] + Robertino—is fond of, and very sensitive to, the childlike element in them.)

2/21/70

From a letter from Whittaker Chambers to William F. Buckley, Jr.—speaking of a man murdered meaninglessly: "This reality cuts across my mind like a wound whose edges crave to heal, but cannot. Thus, one of the great sins, perhaps the great sin, is to say: It will heal, it has healed, there is no wound, there is something more important than this wound."

. . .

2/22/70

My early childhood decision, "By God, they won't get me!" (absolute decision to survive, not to be done in) was executed principally [*next to this word, in the margin:* "No??"] in terms of my talent for emotional dissociation, for turning off feelings before they made me intolerably unhappy or confused—through doing things, being interested in other things. There's more to the world than just me, etc. Thus, one of the healthiest things about me—my capacity to "take it," to survive, to bounce back, to do, to prosper—is intimately connected with my biggest neurotic liability: my facility in disconnecting from my feelings. How to preserve the first while diminishing the second? It's hard. A risk. Did Diana know this?

When a small child, I felt abandoned and unloved. My response to this was to want to be very good. (If I'm tremendously good, they'll love me.) I could have responded quite differently: with self-hatred, with delinquency (revenge on others, calling attention to myself), with identifying with rebel-critic-outlaw-criminal role, as Eva did. Instead, I said, I will be enormously good—and deserve (attract) love—and seek responsibility, authority, control, fame, power.

When C. said at Orly [*Paris airport*] before I left, "You've been an angel," it wasn't entirely a compliment. I've assumed—my old idea—that I will win C. by being fantastically "good" (generous, patient, loving, never angry). But part of what attracts her to me is that I am tough, autonomous—not that I'm angelic, which must suggest (unconsciously) to her that I'm naïve, childish, innocent—and, as a result, not really strong, in the way she needs.

I musn't be afraid of showing anger to C.—afraid that I'll drive her away; indicate to her that I don't love her; show that I'm not "good." (Of course, I consider it precisely as not part of virtue—it's a fall, it's ignoble, it's demeaning.)

. . .

I can demand things from C. but not on the basis of needing her. That scares her

. . .

. . . an essay: Wittgenstein: Remarks on his influence on the contemporary arts

. . .

[For Wittgenstein] ethics and aesthetics are one (*Tractatus*)

. . .

2/22/70

... [Carlotta] fears that need is continual, insatiable—that she'll be trapped. Also, she doesn't believe she can satisfy anyone's needs—she's too weak and unworthy, she's a piece of shit, etc.

It's important to continue to indicate that she does satisfy needs of mine (that she's not *just* "a pole of erotic attraction," in Colette's words)—because that's true and it gives me pleasure to say it, and because it enhances her own self-esteem (something she needs so badly). But I must not plead with her to satisfy my needs—only indicate that she does in fact do that.

2/23/70

Could I write to C in several weeks: "I'm outraged, I'm hurt, I'm angry. I won't let you do this to me."?

The difficulty of contacting my anger (when it's aimed at people I love) is that it directly contradicts my notion of how to deserve love:—being good. No problem, of course, in getting angry with people I don't know, with people I don't know well, with people I don't love very much.

Being good! "I'm so good that it hurts"!

My idolatry: I've lusted after goodness. Wanting it here, now, absolutely, increasingly. Hence, built-in disvaluation of past work. It's good but it's not good enough ... There is always *more* (more goodness, more love). I suspect now that lusting after the good isn't what a really good person does.

3/2/70

Re conversation with Giovanella: cynicism of society in Rome (and south)—suspicion of idealism; fear of being ridiculous; demand that one be light, have a "sense of humor." The game of saying things that wound (not to be wounded is to win the game). Compulsive gregariousness—traveling in packs.

. . .

3/5/70

I think I am ready to learn how to write. Think with words, not with ideas.

. . .

3/7/70

[Luis] Buñuel's *La Voie Lactée*, which I resaw yesterday, is a "mannerist" film. (Cf. [*the twentieth-century German art historian Gustav René*] Hocke's book on mannerism, *Die Welt als Labyrinth*, esp[ecially] chapter on Arcimboldo, pp. 154–64). Mannerist art: dwarfs, dreams, giants, Siamese twins, mirrors, magic machines. Metamorphosis: animate < > inanimate, human < > animal; ordinary < > marvelous.

Emphasis on theatrical: costume, decors.

. . .

3/10/70

[In the margin:] "Lustra": five-year periods by which Romans marked out life's phases or stages

Read William Godwin's early anarchist novel, *Caleb Williams*.

"L'homme qui médite est un animal dépravé" [*"The man who meditates is a depraved animal"*] (Rousseau, *Discours sur* [. . .] *L'Inégalité*)! D H L[awrence] etc.

. . .

4/26/70

Novel about a doctor—trying to cure . . .

Enchiridion = handbook or survival manual

•

. . .

David's immense value in my life:

—someone I can love unconditionally, trustingly—because I know the relationship is authentic (society guarantees it + I make it)—because I *chose* him, because he loves me (I've never doubted that)—: my one whole-hearted experience of love, of generosity, of caring

—my guarantee of adulthood: —even when I experience my childishness, I know I'm an adult because I'm a mother. (Being a teacher, a writer etc. never has brought me this unequivocally)

—order, a structure, a limit to any tendency to self-destructiveness.

—endless delight in his company—having a companion, a friend, a brother. (Bad side: a chaperone, a shield against the world)

—what he has taught me, since he is as philosophically perceptive as he is and knows me so well

—appeasement of my fantasies of being a boy. I identify with David, he is the boy I wanted to be—I don't need to be a boy because he exists. (Bad consequence of this: it would upset me if he became homosexual. I'm sure he won't. But I shouldn't unconsciously forbid it.)

. . .

5/25/70

Art is the ultimate condition of everything.

. . .

Grotowski: "In life the first question is how to be armed; in art it is how to be disarmed."
Not true, but helpful.

. . .

Looked at [Edwin] Denby novel [*Mrs. W's Last Sandwich*]. Not promising. I'm more + more intrigued by [*Jack London's novel*] *The Iron Heel*. I need an American film. This is a propos (revolutionary sci-fi), could be cheap—Godardesque, etc. The two previous ideas I've had—[Melville's] "The Confidence Man" + [Dashiell Hammett's] *The Dain Curse*—would be more expensive + harder. (*Dain Curse* with Clint Eastwood?)

A philosophical dialogue: "Reasons for Being." A meditation on suicide, inspired by Susan [Taubes]'s death:

—Choice
—How do people find their lives endurable?
—Change, mobility
—The will (+ limits of)
—The tragic view of life
—The lunar perspective (Paul [Thek])
—Appetite (fastidiousness)
—Project of extending the self

[*In the margin:*] Am I my own property

. . .

6/22/70   Naples

More than ever—and once again—I experience life as a question of levels of energy. I've been drooping, waning these last eleven days, because of the unexpected sexual / affectional deprivation. I can't find another source of vitality—in my-self—because I expected to find it, these weeks, in my connection with C. That I didn't makes me heavy, stupid, reproachful. I humiliate myself asking blatantly for reassurance, and I further depress C. When will I learn *not* to ask her to reassure me?

Oh, to be rid of my fixed ideas of how things "ought" to be—

What I want: energy, energy, energy. Stop wanting nobility, serenity, wisdom—you idiot!

This isn't Paris, but I reacted—at least the first few days—as if it were. I felt rejected, I became desperate, etc. It's better now, but I'm still hoping to break through to C. Because I would never react to me as she is doing, were I in her situation. But she is different, and as I respect her, I must stop trying (covertly, partly unconsciously) to get her to behave as I would.

7/8/70 Naples

I'm loyal to my feelings. What does that mean? That if I've had a feeling I like I try to go on having it? What nonsense!

C. follows her feelings, but she isn't loyal to them.

C's face as a child (in the album of photos I saw at her house this afternoon): so much anger and belligerence. Ready to fight, ready to contradict. I look so vulnerable, sensitive, docile, in photographs from the same age. But which of us is really tougher, really more rebellious? C's boyishness in the photos meant that she had the right to fight, to be physically belligerent. My boyishness as a little girl meant something entirely different—I never fought, or wanted to fight; I wanted the right to be free, to run away. I didn't want to tell them off (I must have given up on that idea very, very early). I just wanted to turn my back on them, to go away.

7/9/70

C. says that she is always sorry after she has eaten—even if she enjoyed the meal—I understand that; I feel it now, too. But also that she's always, somewhere, sad after making love. She feels she's lost something, killed something (the desire), that she is now weaker, less. I don't understand that. I always feel glad after making love—unless, it's with someone I don't like really (in which case, I'm sad because sex is like playing at love and what I really want, miss is love). But even then I'm glad to feel alive, more alive as I always do when I'm in my body. I love anyone—at least a little—who touches me. Anyone who touches me gives me something in that instant: my body.

I musn't say to C: How could you think that *I* could do that, think that? Being hurt, insulted that she might think I'm less committed, serious, pure—etc. Tacitly assuming that we share the same standards—which, alas, we don't. I always protect her against my potential reproach that *she* is shallow or disconnected or insensitive, I take this potential reproach to her, and convert it into a reproach (inexplicable, unjustified) to *me*. I shouldn't. Rather, I must say: Would you really do that? Is that the way you would feel? How strange! I wouldn't, couldn't. E basta!

*Another title for the film: *Brother Carl* [*This became the title of SS's second film, made in Sweden in 1970.*]

7/11/70

Parameters of a film

[1] length of shot
[2] composition of shot
[3] camera movement/stasis
[4] shot changes

Rhythm of a film primarily determined by quality of (4). Any shot change should have more than *one* justification: polyphonic function, "double discourse" of film (continuity < > discontinuity)

Most people think (1) is the key to rhythm, but this isn't so. Duration of shot is too subjective—depends on lecture, readability of a shot. Follow a plan-fixe close-up of a face lasting 10 seconds with a plan-fixe long shot of a busy street lasting ten seconds, and most people will think the first shot lasted 20 seconds and the second shot lasted 5 seconds.

For (2) note the value of asymmetry. Cameramen usually, automatically, center the figures in a shot. Don't let them do this unless this is what you want.

*Advantages of 'Scope: all that extra space—poses formal problems that must be solved! Use it on this film? ($200 worth of special lenses—same raw stock; black-and-white 'Scope is unusual. Cf. Buñuel, *Journal d'une femme de chambre*)

Noël [Burch] says there are too many shot changes in *DFC* [*SS's first film*, Duet for Cannibals]. Instead of 400 shots there should only be about 200. Most of them, he says, serve *no* function. The only ideas I've had about shot changes have been a) dramaturgical, or b) promote some sense of spatial disorientation

a) = Now!   b) = Where are we?

Most of Godard's shot changes are cut-aways, not direct cuts (different shot of the same thing).

Bresson almost never uses anything except a 50 [mm] lens.

Potemkin has more shots (per foot) than any other film of Eisenstein. Each action is morcelized—mosaic of shots. Opposite is [*the Hungarian director Miklós*] Jancsó and [*the French director Jean-Marie*] Straub—all sequence shots (why cut?) For e.g. of morcellizaton final sequence of *Storm over Asia*.

[*A box is drawn around this:*] Movies

Naples:

[Vincent Sherman,] *The Young Philadelphians* (1959)—
Paul Newman, Barbara Rush
Mario Bava, *Il Rosso Segno della Follia* (1970)—Laura Betti

Paris   July 9 >:

Hitchcock, *Under Capricorn* (1949)—Ingrid Bergman,
Joseph Cotten, Michael Wilding, Margaret Leighton
Jean Eustache, *Le Cochon* (1970)
Michel Fano, *Le Territoire des Autres* (1970)

Stockholm   July 13 > Sept. 27

- *Terence Young, *Doctor No* (1962)
- Elliot Silverstein, *A Man Called Horse* (1970)
- Michael Wadleigh, *Woodstock* (1970)
- *Mai Zetterling, *Flickorna* (1968)
- **Bergman, *Tystnaden* (1963)
- Roman Polanski, *The Fearless Vampire Killers* (1967)
- René Clément, *Le Passager de la Pluie* (1970)— Charles Bronson, Marlène Joubert
- Roy Andersson, *En Kärlekshistoria* (1970)
- *Michael Curtiz + Wm. Keighley, *Robin Hood* (1938)—Errol Flynn, Olivia de Havilland, Basil Rathbone, Claude Rains
- Tony Richardson, *Ned Kelly* (1970)
- Alf Sjöberg, *Barabbas* (1953)—Ulf Palme
- Claude Chabrol, *La Route de Corinthe* (1967)

. . .

Rome   Sept. 27–Oct. 9

Buñuel, *Tristana* (1970)—[Catherine] Deneuve
[George Seaton,] *Airport* (1970)—B[urt] Lancaster, Dean Martin

New York   Oct 9–25

Mike Nichols, *Catch-22* (1970)
[Bob Rafelson,] *Five Easy Pieces* (1970)
[Donald Cammell and Nicolas Roeg,] *Performance*

•

What I did between sequences in *DFC* I must do between each shot in this film. The best shots in *DFC* are the "attacking shots" and the next one—i.e. the first two shots in each sequence. The "attacking shot" often poses a problem of spatial or dramaturgical orientation, the second shot answers it. Then the sequence runs down.

The longer the shot the more important (privileged) the shot change—the more justification you need for it.

. . .

Each shot change must either create tension or resolve it.

Noël says I'm like [*the French silent film director Louis*] Delluc, Bergman, Bellocchio.

. . .

Complicate (by shot changes) the spatial itinerary of the film.

. . .

Russians concentrated on shot changes—virtually eliminated camera movements.

[*In mid-July, SS went to Stockholm to begin work on* Brother Carl.]

7/16/70

. . . I'm working again on the script. I take things out, but then I add things. It does seem better with every change, but far too long. I'm afraid I'm going to make a three-hour movie that will be impossible to cut. Sometimes it seems to me too ambitious, too complicated. It's about suffering, sanctity, moral corruption, neurosis, health, love, sadism, masochism— in short, everything. The characters are so damned complex. I wonder if it's worth it. I wish I could make moral fairy-tales, like [*the Italian filmmaker Pier Paolo*] Pasolini.

From [Emanuel] Swedenborg to Zarah Leander, [August] Strindberg to Gunnar Myrdal. [Sweden is] a country of strong, obstinate personalities anyway.

Gamla Stan [*Stockholm's Old Town; SS lived in an apartment there during the shooting of* Brother Carl]: An artisanal world (crooked lines, weathered materials, uneven surfaces) is a human world.

7/26/70

. . . Habits of despair

10/3/70

It's over—just as suddenly, mysteriously, arbitrarily, unpredictably as it began.

I cry all the time—my chest, throat, eyes, the skin of my face are thick with tears, I have asthma: I want oxygen, I want the air to nourish me—and it doesn't.

I don't feel the big pain yet, That will come when I leave on Friday (the 9th). Now I rage at my own weakness. I can't *believe* in this situation which finds me so entirely impotent. I struggle to make some contact with C.—to instruct her or seduce her to make some affectionate contact with me—and everything fails. Whatever I do or say makes her more bitter or vague or remote or insensitive or unyielding or simply rude.

It's not like Paris, where I felt how much she suffered—even if she couldn't be loving to me. Now I feel something worse, more terrifying—a hardness in her, an incapacity of feeling and loving, an incredible selfishness. She said a few days ago that perhaps she has never loved anybody. That's not true, of course. But maybe it's true that she can *only* love intermittently—just as she can only "be" intermittently.

She doesn't want the kind of love I feel for her. She wants the intermittencies of D.D.'s love.

God help me—help me—to stop loving her if she doesn't love me any more.

I musn't hang on because I have loved her more than anyone in my life. I still have that victory of feeling—of *really* loving for the first time—even though it has ended in defeat.

It is an honorable defeat. I risked everything—I gave all that I had—for the first time. If I was naïve enough to imagine that it *must* work between us, because of the immensity and certainty of my feeling, it was an honorable naïveté and nothing to be ashamed of.

It will be a long labor of recovery. I must give up my love, I must give up my dream—*without* building up a wall again that prevented me from feeling fully until I met C.

[*In the margin:*] *I don't want to learn anything from the failure of this love.*

(What I could learn is to become cynical or guarded or even more afraid of loving than I was before.) I don't want to learn anything. I don't want to draw any conclusions.

Let me go on being naked. Let it hurt. But let me survive.

10/15/70

C: Hypnotized (?) into believing she is incapable of transformation ("sick," "confused")

Not capable of emotional generosity—she gives her golden radiance, but carefully, pointedly promises nothing

All the *timing* in our relationship has been hers

Bice is sage, a shelter; undemanding up to a point (me) because she is Chinese, undersexed, insecure, unpassionate, etc. I'm a risk. U demand, I promise—myself, the miracle of transformation. My generosity is heavy, oppressive. Bice's is light.

Joe's [Chaikin] fantasy of the man with the beast whom no one knows (names)—takes it into the cellar + tries to kill it, but it won't die—just keeps bleeding—gets weaker—doesn't recognize man any more. Man has to return periodically to cellar to reopen wound

Novel # # 9?): *Mutants*

Caspar Hauser—in a box until 17, no sense of distance; apoplectic fit when he saw the stars
Superman
The pig girl
Visitors from other planets
Dracula

A convention of mutants (Marvel comics)

10/17/70

It's dissolving. Blinded—looking away. The last image: bare legs in calf-length mauve socks.

10/19/70

I'm floating in an ocean of pain. Not floating—but swimming, badly—no style. But not sinking.

Like being run over by a truck. Lying in the street. And nobody comes.

I live inside a deep pain.

Being trapped in a small black box—that can't be set down anywhere.

An abortion. Scraping it out. Terrible ache—a bloody mess.

Standing in a wind tunnel. I feel dizzy. All my energy goes into bracing myself—not being blown over.

. . .

11/19/70   Stockholm

[*A box is drawn around this:*] NEW LIFE

Once again (how many times?) un petit effort [*"a little effort"*]

Fantasia—perfect example of fascist aesthetics

World divided into:

Good—Evil
Light—Dark
Fast—Slow   Types of movement:
                                   "flying" "dancing" "running"
Light—Heavy
Big—Small
Graceful—Clumsy

Masters   < >   "little" people

[Leopold] Stokowski   fairies
God who makes storm   baby animals
Devil in Mussorgsky   Mickey Mouse
Sorcerer in [Paul] Dukas

Image of conductor (Stokowski) outlined in light—drawing music from orchestra with his baton—on pedestal

Music an affair of the perfect master leading the ideal servants

All beings are clichés, types

> Male < > female (females bat eyelashes—males
>   bound forward)
> Master < > servant (cf. Negro servant / miniature
>   female centaurs in Beethoven Pastorale

Everyone is in his right place (or is quickly restored to it; world is correctly ordered)

Fantasia is a whole world-view; a morality, an aesthetics, a cosmogony ([Stravinsky's] *Sacre du Printemps*), a theology (devil of *Night on Bald Mountain* [*a version of the composition by the nineteenth-cenury Russian composer Modest Mussorgsky, orchestrated by Stokowski and used by Disney in* Fantasia] vanquished by *Ave Maria*)

Frame: idea of sound as visualized:

> the sound track—leaderless improvising
> the orchestra (playing Swing—relaxing, being
>   naughty—while waiting for Stokowski)

arrival of The Conductor—musicians fall into line

Beethoven's Pastorale

About sex (wooing), play, nature, ("lighting" the world), family life (Pegasus—mother—black child learning to fly[—] storm > peace)

[Tchaikovsky's] *Nutcracker Suite*—other races, their comedy mushrooms as Chinese

11/30/70

From [Saul] Bellow's *Mr. Sammler's Planet*, p. 136—"try[ing] to live with a civil heart"

Olaf Stapledon

Victor Hugo's maxim: "Concision in style, precision in thought, decision in life"

12/18/70   Paris

Film about Saint Theresa

Bernini statue
Sade visited it when in Rome

? black & white

. . .

Read H. G. Wells, *Mind at the End of Its Tether*

W[illia]m James's chapter on "The Sick Soul" [in] *Varieties of Religious Experience*

. . .

"Writing is only a substitute [*sic*] for living."—Florence Nightingale

1971

1/16/71   *[SS's thirty-eighth birthday]*

A crisis of self-respect.

What makes me feel strong? Being in love and work.

I must work.

I'm being wasted by self-pity and self-contempt.

. . .

I'm off balance.

I'm looking for my dignity. Don't laugh.

I'm very intolerant and very indulgent (of others). Toward myself, the intolerance predominates. I like myself, but I don't love myself. I'm indulgent—to an extreme—of those I love.

•

Idea for a fiction from one of Cioran's aphorisms: "Physical need for dishonor. I would like to have been the son of an executioner."
"The Executioner's Daughter" . . .

•

2/2/71

Is it possible I owe yet a second liberation to Simone de Beauvoir? Twenty years ago, I read *The Second Sex*. Last night, I read *L'Invitée*. No, of course. I still have much to live through to free myself. But, for the first time, I was able to laugh. Change the class (most important), age (20 years more experience!), country, and physique of Xavière, and it is a perfect portrait of C[arlotta]. I see the entrapment from the outside (the way that self-sacrificing, Christian love is provoked, alongside the sexual passion),—I didn't feel sorry for myself, I despised myself a little less. I ceased, a little more, to hope—and I felt lighter. I could laugh, tenderly, at myself.

4/11/71   New York

Joe: Two kinds of people—those who are interested in self-transformation and those who are not. Both require the same amount of energy—it takes as much energy to remain the same as to change.

I agree with the first—and I'm only interested in people engaged in a project of self-transformation. But the second: I wish I could believe something so optimistic. It seems to me to require much more energy to change.

Aphorism by [*the Polish writer, poet, and satirist*] Stanisław Jerzy Lec: "When you arrive at the very bottom, you will hear knocking from below."

What does sylleptic thinking mean?

. . . Stravinsky's death this week. I remember when [*SS's childhood friend*] Merrill and I used to debate whether we would sacrifice our lives to give Stravinsky one more year of life—or five. I was fourteen, maybe fifteen.

4/21/71

I'm suffering from a lack of intellectual stimulation. I've exaggerated, over-reacted against the academic milieu in which I was completely submerged in my youth. That was an exaggeration. Then, starting with Harriet, I began an equivalent exaggeration in the opposite direction. It has become more and more extreme, so that in recent years I have spent almost all my time with people with mediocre minds.— However [much] they pleased me (because they were warmer, more sensual, more sensitive, had more experience of "the world"), they didn't stimulate me. I thought less and less. My mind got lazy, passive. I gained a lot but I also paid a big price. And it's that price now that humiliates me. I find many books difficult to read! (Especially philosophy). I write badly, with difficulty.

My mind is stiff. (That's what's causing the trouble with the women's lib essay—more than my depression.)

. . .

Idea for a novella from [*the Yugoslav writer and dissident politician*] Vladimir Dedijer today. "The Suicide Club." A political story, set in Yugoslavia—imaginary small country. New social movement among students (high school, university): suicide clubs spring up. Young people charged with the project of committing "altruistic suicides" to awaken conscience, blackmail government. They have meetings, workshops, consciousness-raising groups to prepare themselves. Then do it. In all there are 24 who do—(some are murdered, lose courage at the end and are pushed by their comrades). Dedijer's son did it at 19—jumped off a cliff just over his father's house. Later, it's discovered that the clubs were organized by the secret police.

Dedijer had 3 sons. First committed suicide at 15, after being interrogated + beaten up by the police (about his father's activities) then sent home—he hanged himself. Second killed himself at 19 (suicide club). Third tried last year—failed—went on the road in US, took drugs, now in an athletic school in Switzerland.

Novella organized as a collection of "material" on the clubs. Like Oscar Lewis' anthropological studies of Puerto Rico + Cuba. Letters, taped interviews, report of researcher . . . Ends with researcher trying to leave the country and has his documents confiscated.

Read [*the French sociologist Émile*] Durkheim on altruistic suicide.

Use story Florence told me about her father [*the French writer and politician André Malraux*]—at the cemetery, following the interment of her brothers, they walked around and he delivered an impromptu lecture on the history of coffins from Sumerians to the present. Use that—father of one of the suicides; he is a professor or government minister.

4/24/71

The density of Ivan Illich comforts me—makes me more present to myself, stronger.

Jeanne [*the French actress Jeanne Moreau*] this weekend: all air. How depressed I was.

I believed in miracles—all my life. Finally, I decided to make one. I failed. I wanted to die.

I knew you have to put your life on the line to perform a miracle. There can be no holding back, no reserve. So I did. And I failed.

The assumption on which I'd based my whole life was finally tested. I—it—failed the test. My life fell down.

Do I build it up? The same way? A better way? Is there a better way? (Without believing in miracles?) Or is "building up" the wrong metaphor?

It was as if my whole life was growing toward that point I reached two years ago—to be open finally, to be wholly generous, to give myself. I did. I was rejected.

I was pure. (Was I?) And I was also grandiose? Was that wrong?

BC [*Brother Carl*] is about making a miracle. It is the testament of that faith I still had: my prayer, my confidence . . . I made the film. Carl succeeded. I failed.

The energy—and the pleasure, the reward—behind the miracle was the longing for symbiosis. A pure, generous dream. But a defective energy.

Am I through with the search for the perfect ideal symbiosis? Is one ever through with a longing so profound as that one?

I am alone. I know that now. Perhaps I always will be.

4/27/71

Solitude is endless. A whole new world. The desert.

I am thinking—talking—in images. I don't know how to write them down. Every feeling is physical.

Maybe that's why I can't write—or write so badly now. In the desert, all ideas are experimental in the body.

I touch a central place, where I have never lived before. I wrote from the margin, dipping down into the well but never fully gazing down. I drew up the words—books, essays. Now I'm down there: in the center. And I find, to my horror, that the center is mute.

I want to speak. I want to be a person who speaks. But, up to now, speech meant dealing in this left-handed, eyes averted way with myself.

I used myself as another person . . . Ivan says it's all in [*SS's essay*] "The Pornographic Imagination." (Or *Death Kit*, I would say.) But I didn't know it. I didn't look down, but rather marveled at those curious, morbid, extreme thoughts I had—and thought myself lucky in not having to pay (in madness, in thickening despair) for being their vehicle. Lucky!

I was afraid of going mad. Now I've looked—I'm there. I'm not mad. I'm not even depressed being alone night after night in the apartment.

•

[*The eighteenth-century German aphorist Georg C.*] Lichtenberg: "There is something in every person's character that cannot be broken—the bony structure of his character. Wanting to change it is the same as teaching a sheep to retrieve."

•

Trying to enlarge my inner space.

[Undated, June]

McLuhan: black people are more telegenic than white people—from the pov [point of view] of television, white people are already démodé.

Don't confuse *subject* (of a book, film) with its political character. [*The French writer and publicist Philippe*] Sollers thinks Céline is a radical culturally; his opinions are another matter.

Write a book about the body—but not a schizophrenic book. Is that possible? A book that is a sort of strip-tease, an elaborate minutely-detailed getting undressed in the course of which each bone-muscle-organ is tracked down, described, raped.

Greatest director? D. W. Griffith, hélas [*"alas"*]

Flora Tristan—French, early feminist (1803–1844)—praised by Breton

Fascist writers: Céline, [Luigi] Pirandello, [Gottfried] Benn, Pound, [Yukio] Mishima.

Valuable subjects:

> Destroy the bourgeois myth of the artist, the creator
> (anti-[Fellini's] *8½*)
> Political action by women
> That the enemy is human, but still the enemy
> (Stalingrad letters [*of German soldiers*])
> Spiritual action by a woman
> The *sacred*

[Undated, December]

"The sacred" + the bourgeois myth of the solitary alienated artist-creator are antithetical.

Experiencing the sacred is the opposite of being alienated. It is being integrated. Always implies relations to others— "a public."

"Sacred" always involved risk of death, annihilation.

Is it possible that the notion of the "sacred" is a mystification? (Most sophisticated form of universalism, denying class conflict and concrete struggle)

1972

[Undated, January]

Author's note for a thriller (Dick Francis, *Forfeit*): "is now, as a splendid thriller writer, exceeding his fame as a champion steeplechase jockey." Think about *that* idea of a writer.

Kindness, kindness, kindness.

I want to make a New Year's prayer, not a resolution. I'm praying for courage.

Right now, this moment. I'm not afraid. A tremendous weight that I feel almost all the time isn't there.

Why am I so afraid? Why do I feel so weak, so guilty? Why haven't I been able to write M[other] for a year now, or open her letters?

I must see C[arlotta], who has returned to Paris today with Gio[vanella Zannoni]. I must not be afraid . . . And call [Robert] Bresson, and Yuyi [Beringola] + Hugo [*Santiago, Argentine exiles in Paris with whom SS had become friendly*], and [*the French academic*] Violette [Morin], and Paul [Thek]. And write Roger [*Straus, SS's publisher and friend*] + [*the New York psychiatrist*] Lilly [Engler] + Joe [Chaikin]. Why have I been so afraid these last two months?

[*SS must have shown this entry to someone as, below it in another hand and underlined, is written:*] Please don't be afraid!

3/10/72

[*The Chilean filmmaker, theater director, and poet Alejandro*] Jodorowsky:

Grotowski the *end* of bourgeois psychological theatre, its final purification.
[Constantin] Stanislavski > Gordon Craig > Grotowski

"I used to ask [*the French mime*] Marcel Marceau, 'Why don't you talk?' You know why? Because he has a little squishy voice, like this—"

Can't do plays anymore—What?
Magic ceremonies. Rituals.

Three centers: belly, chest, head.
Play music for each [of the] three.
(Tibetan tapes.)
A meditation room.

Grotowski: an actor who trains as a monk does. Jodorowsky: a monk who can act.

Do comic strips. (His models: Little Nemo, Popeye before 1938, Flash Gordon.)

"G. likes a poor theatre. OK. So do I. (Mime, etc.) But I like a rich theatre too. (I like Cecil B. DeMille.)"

Buy:

> Goethe, *Elective Affinities*
> Paul de Man, *Blindness + Insight*
> Robert Coover, *Pricksongs and Descants*

Idea for a novel:

Look up Paris newspapers, late 1934—Galapagos adventure of baroness and three young men, recounted by [Paule] Thévenin . . .

Dr. Friedrich Ritter and Frau Dore Strauch von Koerwin arrived at the Galapagos Islands in 1929 to live there—both were Germans. Before coming there they had taken the precaution of having all their teeth extracted—replacing them by "râteliers" of steel. They wanted to create an Eden—which they called Friedo (first syllables of their first names). In 1924 (?) the famous Baroness Basquet von Wagner, accompanied by three very young men, arrived on the island. The total disappearance of the Baroness, who had herself called the Queen of the Galapagos, and two of her suitors; the fortuitous discovery of the third on the beach along with the corpse of a "pecheur de passage" [*"passing fisherman"*] made big headlines in the papers toward the end of 1934 . . .

3/13/72

[*The founder of* The New American Review, *Ted*] Solotaroff—our generation (Chicago, etc.): we knew all about values, but we didn't understand the connection between our values and our experience. We "evaluated" our experience, dismissing most of it as unworthy of our values.

The "Art Nouveau" appeal of smoking: manufacture your own pneuma, spirit. "I'm alive." "I'm decorative."

5/10/72   Cannes/Cap d'Antibes

Two films seen here I've learned from, admired. Herzog's TV-style documentary about blind-deaf people [*Land of Silence and Darkness*]. The new Jancsó "about" Attila [*La Tecnica e Il Rito*]—his obsessional meditation about war (armed struggle), power-domination—one of the most erotic films I've ever seen (the eroticism of men). A dream about how a charismatic world-conqueror is created: the psychological elements oneirically reconstituted. The opposite of the analysis made in [Roberto] Rossellini's *La Prise du Pouvoir par Louis XIV*, but equally valid.

Feminism: "GEDOK," an organization of feminist artists that began in Germany in 1926—was disbanded by Hitler in the 1930s

Romaine Brooks, [Dora] Carrington, [Gertrude] Stein

The Kurago—the black-clad men who handle the Bunraku doll puppets

[Masahiro] Shinoda film of Monzaemon Chikamatsu's 1720 doll drama, *The Double Suicide* [*Shinjû: Ten No Amijima (1969)*]

6/21/72

Idea for a fiction-meditation (in style of [*Kenneth Bernard's*] *King Kong* in *NAR* [*New American Review*] #14: "On Women Dying," or "Deaths of Women," or "How Women Die."

Material:

> death of Virginia Woolf
> death of [*the German soprano*] Henriette Sontag
>   (in Mexico—cholera—on tour—June 17, 1854)
> death of Alice James
> death of [*the Russian mathematician*] Sofia
>   Kovalevskaya (Stockholm, 1891)
> death of Marie Curie (July 4, 1934—pernicious
>   anemia due to radiation)
> death of Jeanne d'Arc
> death of Amelia Earhart
> death of Hélène Boucher ([French] aviator—d. 1934)
> death of Rosa Luxemburg
> death of [*the French playwright and political activist*]
>   Olympe de Gouges (d. 1793—guillotined)
> death of Carrington

another title: "Woman and Death"

Women don't die for each other. There is no "sororal" death as there is a fraternal death (*Beau Geste*)

. . .

Get *Cahiers de L'Herne* number on [*the twentieth-century American writer H. P.*] Lovecraft

Modern operas: Schoenberg, *Moses und Aron, Die Glückliche Hand*; [Bernd Alois] Zimmermann, *Die Soldaten*; [Luigi] Nono, *Intolleranza*; Luigi Dallapiccola, *Il Prigioniero, Ulisse*; [Franz] Schreker.

Forgotten writers:

> Georges Rodenbach (Fr[ench] "symbolist")
> Paul Nougé (Belgian Surrealist)

[Undated, July]

French, unlike English: a language that tends to break when you bend it—

7/5/72   Paris

A writer, like an athlete, must "train" every day. What did I do today to keep in "form"?

[*The American writer*] Leonard Michaels at the [Café] Flore: He said we looked alike (Russian-Polish-Jewish . . .), that what first turned him on to me was that I mentioned [*the Cuban-American torch singer*] La Lupe in the "camp" essay and he went to see her. He wants to write like La Lupe— writing for him is "musical"—the beat. He liked the fucking in the train at the beginning of *Death Kit*. He thinks [Samuel Richardson's] *Clarissa* is the greatest English novel. "Do you read? I mean do you read a lot?" He thinks the gauchistes are "barbarians." He can't speak French and he never heard of the Flore. He was born at the beginning of January 1933 on the

Lower East Side—his father immigrated in the early 20s, his mother at the beginning of the 30s—his first wife committed suicide (in the next room, 47 sleeping pills) while he was a graduate student—his second wife, naturally, is a DAR [Daughter of the American Revolution] (his words)—he has two sons, age 3 + 6 . . . He went to Music + Art [*public high school in New York City*] > Univ[ersity] of Michigan > Berkeley

7/20/72

. . .

I am invited to China for three weeks, starting Aug[ust] 25.

A China book? Not *Trip to Hanoi*—I can't do the "West meets East" sensibility trip again. And I certainly have no intention of recounting my actual trip. I'm not a journalist. Je ne suis pas raconteur. Je déteste raconter [*"I'm not a storyteller"*]. (Unless it is to use the story to illustrate a point—or to be able to analyze + discuss the story afterward + extract reflections from it.)

What book? Could I do now a "Notes Toward a Definition of Cultural Revolution"? Probably I'll get to see very little of the C[ultural] R[evolution]. (How could I? I'll never be alone. It will probably be mostly visits to factories, schools, museums). But the idea is there.

Another idea of the family—
An alternative to "société de consommation"
    [*"consumer society"*]
Against 4 Old's: Old Culture, Old Habits
Against art made by artists (people specializing in art)

Compare turn to East of non-political people ([*the French poet René*] Daumal, Hesse, Artaud)—for "wisdom"—with Maoist turn to East. *La Cina è vicina* [*a reference to the 1967 film* China Is Near *by Marco Bellocchio that SS greatly admired*].

Yunan lectures on art.

Recount story of film. My father. The China in my head as a child. The "book" on China for Miss Berken's 4th grade class that was the first long thing I ever wrote. The Chinese furniture in the house in Great Neck [New York]. Mr. Chen.

Opening: "I was, as far as I know, conceived in China (in Tientsin, in 1932), but since my parents returned to the United States for my birth (in New York, in 1933), I spent the first years of my life—in the United States—making up for their disappointing prudence by telling school friends that I was born in China. They had gone back to China soon after I was born in New York, and stayed there most of the first five years of my life. My father was a fur trader; he had an office in New York, in the fur district (231 W 31st St), at the head of which he put his kid brother Aaron—and he ran the main office of the company, in Tientsin, which is where he and my mother had lived most of the time since they married in 1930. My father died in Tientsin while the city was under bombardments (it was the time of the Japanese invasion) but of TB on Oct. 19, 1938. He had been born, the fourth of five children of a poor immigrant family on the Lower East Side in New York City on March 6, 1906—had started public school in 1912, at the age of 6, quit school in 1916, at the age of 10 to go to work as a delivery boy in the fur district, and made his first trip to China in 1932, by then a representative of the fur company he worked for at the age of 16. He went into the Gobi Desert on the back of a camel to buy fur skins from Mongolian nomads. He was eighteen when he had his first attack of TB."

Dedicate book to my father.
For Jack Rosenblatt (b. New York 1906—d. Tientsin 1938)—
"Daddy"—a set of photographs—a boy, as I think about him now—an unfinished pain, Death, the Great Disappearance. My son wears your ring. I don't know where you are buried. I weep when I think of you.— You keep getting younger. I wish I had known you.

Can use photographs:

> [Auguste and Louis] Lumière 1900 material
> Pudovkin, *Storm over Asia*
> Daddy's pictures
> Bataille photo of a man flayed to death
> Chinese-looking photo of Marx on *China News* cover

Biblio[graphy]:

> Ezra Pound on calligraphy
> [*The French sinologist*] Marcel Granet
> [*The British sinologist and historian of science*]
>   Joseph Needham
> 2 issues of *Tel Quel*
> Malraux
> Blue Columbia "China"
> Chinese pornography (Skira)

In *Tides in English Taste* (2. Vols.) on Chinoiserie
Look at Barthes on Japan

Perhaps it's something like a Broch-ish novel—a meditation on China. The opposite of Fred Tuten's book [*The Adventures of Mao on the Long March*] in tone, not a parody at all. But also mixed in form.

The everything book I've been trying to write. Remember what Richard Howard said 5 years ago when *Death Kit* came out? I have to find my own form—philosophic récit, reflections. Perhaps this is it, quite different from what he imagined but serving the purpose.

I can put my whole life into this book. It's about everything, and yet it's about the moon—the most exotic place—about nothing at all.

Another model for the book: John Cage, *A Year from Monday*. A collage. I can even photostat the cover and two pages from the China book I wrote when I was ten years old. Use cover—with Susan Rosenblatt—as faded cover design, over which the title of this book and Susan Sontag will be superimposed in heavy black print.

A collage: *The Shanghai Gesture*, *Turandot*, *The Bitter Tea of General Yen*, *The Good Earth*, *Shanghai Express* (Dietrich), Myrna Loy [*sic*] in Jules Verne's *Tribulations d'un Chinois en Chine*, Kafka, *The Great Wall*, *The East Is Red*, *La Cina è vicina*, *Storm over Asia*.

Themes:

> Search for dépaysement
> Vie Collective (fight individualism)
> Courtesans + cruelties

Situation of women
Sex—Chinese pornography

Can do a Brecht-type analysis of a speech of Mao Tse-Tung:
in two columns (like texts Barthes used)

. . . Idea of "the saying" in China
idea of wisdom

. . .

Calligraphy

Style of hagiography:

Confucius
Norman Bethune [*a Canadian doctor who was on the
Long March with Mao*]
Mao Tse-Tung

Possible book
Narratives / collages / discussions
Interspersed with 10 passages about my father + that Gatsby-
ish life—autobiographical

"If one out of every four persons born each second is Chinese,
does that mean that if I have four children, my fourth
baby . . ."

Importance of China landscape (Jesuit who painted)

Life of the concessions

II. Courtesies   On being good—style of hagiography

III. Chinese torture

"If white is the color of mourning, then black . . ." reversal of values

Twelve Travellers:

> Marco Polo
> [Matteo] Ricci
> Jesuit who painted
> Soulié de Morant
> Paul Claudel
> Malraux
> Teilhard de Chardin
> Edgar Snow
> Norman Bethune
> My father
> Richard Nixon
> Me

VI. "And besides the *I Ching*"
   Chinese religion Turn to East

"You have to finish your plate. Think of all the starving
   people of China."
Imperialism: *Storm over Asia*, Lumière
Imperialist imagery. Tell of British opium trade, the conces-
   sions
Lumière Bros. 1900 film

VIII. Not since Napoleon [—] Mao Tse-Tung [—] Long March

IX. Notes Toward a Definition of Cultural Revolution

X. To be a Maoist (ouside China)

Materials: jade, teak, bamboo

10 meditations (1 page each)
Chinese food
Chinese laundries
Mah Jongg
Chinese torture

I could write the book now. But I don't have the title, the permission, the credentials unless I go (even only for a short time, in which I'll see nothing).

. . .

Image of the monkey in Chinese mythology: wily, practical. Odysseus. Anti-heroic, "human."

The theatre of Mei Lanfang. (Idea of Chinese theatre chez Brecht + Artaud)

. . .

How did Kafka understand China—from Prague—in 1918–1919?

7/21/72

Telling Nicole [Stéphane] today how the whole story of *Death Kit* came in a minute—fell into my lap—the whole histoire: the train, Hester, Incardona, the business conference, the hospital, the return to New York—huis clos [*"closed hearing"*]—

the entry into the land of death.—everything, on the mention of that mysterious word "Diddy" by John Hollander at the beginning of our midnight coffee date at the Tant Mieux, that now-defunct coffee house on Bleecker Street where I used to go all the time. "What did you say?" "Diddy— Oh. Excuse me. I mean, Richard [Howard]. I always forget. That's what he was called in Cleveland, when he was a child." "Diddy?" "Yes." "How do you spell it?" "I don't know. D-i-d-d-y, I guess." And all the while, *Death Kit* was filling my head—and I asked John to excuse me, I couldn't stay. I had to go home. I was expecting a long-distance phone call—and I rushed home at 12:30 and began to write *Death Kit*—the opening part, Diddy & his life, his suicide attempt—in a fever until six in the morning . . .

Telling that story today to Nicole, the story of how the novel was given to me, intact, in a flash, all on the mention of the word "Diddy"—because Diddy has nothing to do with Richard Howard, is in no way even remotely based on him—it was just the word, a kind of "coup de foudre" [*"love at first sight"*] à la [*the French psychoanalyst Jacques*] Lacan for that word qui a tout déclenché [*"that unleashed everything"*]—but why? *Why* that word? I've never [understood]—telling Nicole that tale, as I've already told it thirty times in the last five years (remembering, as I told it, more my other tellings than the actual event)—suddenly, today, in a flash—again a flash—I understood. After five years, I understand. (And why today?)

Why Diddy? If John Hollander had said his nickname was Bubu or Toto—or Dig? No! Diddy, Diddy only. Those five letters. Why? I've never understood. Today [I] saw.

Diddy
Daddy

That's the source of the meditation on death I've carried in my heart all my life.

Diddy is 33 years old. So was Daddy when he died.

Did-he? Did he die? The theme of false death, la mort équivoque, la résurrection inattendue [*"unexpected"*] in all my work—

> Frau Anders (*The Benefactor*)
> The Bauers (*Duet for Cannibals*)
> Incardona (*Death Kit*)
> Lena (but it fails) in *Brother Carl*

An essay to write—on death.
The two deaths in my life.

1938: Daddy: far away, unassimilable.
1969: Susan [Taubes]: same name as me, ma sosie
  [*"my double"*], also unassimilable

It's finished. Daddy did die.

The resurrection of Lena fails because Susan did die. The manner of her death—and Karen's dream of her resurrection—are taken from that pain. (I ended by not shooting the actual suicide, and cutting the dream!) I had Karen's dream. I told it to Diana [Kemeny], who responded as Martin does.

. . .

In the first notebook for [Dostoyevsky's] *The Idiot*, it was Prince Mishkin who killed Natasya Filipovna, not Rogozhin.

. . .

Four days a year perhaps, I have "visits"—things come. Visitations, rather than inspirations. I live the rest of the year on that—executing the orders + sketches I've taken down . . . I turn myself into a commodity. The typewriter is my assembly-line. But what else could I do?

. . .

[William] Hogarth: everything is exteriorized. A person's face is his character *and* his social status *and* profession. Everyone is 100% what he is . . . Balzacian conception of his own work: paint (dissect, show the conflicts in, unmask the hypocrises of) a whole society. Painting that you have to "read" (a defect?). Cinema. Themes: conflict; hypocrisy; sensual excess.

Antonioni's *L'Eclisse*—his best film, a great film. All [*the French writer and filmmaker Marguerite*] Duras is there— but so much greater, richer. The Bourse scene is worthy of Eisenstein. Between [Alain] Delon + [Monica] Vitti, the second half of film: a huis clos ambulant, dehors [*"walking closed court, outdoors"*]. Delon (a really professional actor; opposite of [Jean-Paul] Belmondo, all charm) sets the rhythm—the way he moves, never stops moving.

A good listener: a physical presence that is warm, alert, intelligent—more important than any words.

Proust is not Balzac plus all the rest. Balzac was Balzac plus all the rest! The social portraiture plus the theories about society, love, genius, personality—pages and pages of stuff in Balzac just like Proust on time, Proust on recognition, Proust on the [connection] between homosexuals and Jews.

. . .

[*The twentieth-century French writer Pierre*] Drieu La Rochelle / Mishima [—] fascism < > virility cult < > suicide

a subject: the phenomenology of ideology

[On Wagner's] *Die Walküre*
. . . *Incest is instant eros* (like homosexuality)—the erotic couple of the first act are brother + sister, the erotic couple of the last act are father + daughter
Some of what is wonderful to listen to in *Walküre*—orchestral passages w[ith]o[ut] singing—becomes de-valued when one *sees* the opera. Then the music suddenly becomes just the accompaniment or illustration of the actor's gestures: like staring longingly.

7/28/72

It's not true that the ideal situation would be that *every* person be an artist (gauchiste-utopian cliché) [anymore] than it would be desirable that every person be a scientist.

What would the world do with all those *things*?

The universalization of art [would] be an ecological disaster. An idea of infinite productivity.

No better than the idea of infinite inventiveness (technology) or the infinite acquisition of knowledge. Concept of *limits*.

Fear of engaging in "élite" activities is what makes people say that, ideally, everyone should be [an] artist.

But some activities are possible *only* if a few people do them.

The only sense in which everybody could be an artist is if art were understood exclusively as *performance*—or throw-away art. Art would be something people did, and if it resulted in an object you wouldn't have to (perhaps even be able to) keep it, store it in a museum. Cage, therefore, has a right to say he wants everybody to be an artist. There's very little product-making in his notion of art. There's nothing to keep, monu-mentalize. It self-destructs.

To repeat: it's an ecological problem.

Essay on cemeteries (or film?)
> 20 min. (Franju)

1. "morbidity" as a form of sensibility
2. Cemetery as ideal *city*
   urban space
   "Streets," "garden"—flowers, "houses"
3. Cemetery as structures [—] cf. [*the twentieth-century Italian writer Umberto*] Eco
   bad taste
   kitsch
   "photographs"—Linguaglossa (Sicilia)
4. Cemetery & memory (time-effacement)
5. Individuality < > mass grave
6. Cemetery as literature [—] epitaphs [—]
   legibility
7. Cemetery + the family (love = the couple)
   Cemetery: artifice + reality
9) colors: white

Cemeteries:

> New one in Marseilles
> Haramont [*a village outside of Paris where Nicole*
>   *Stéphane had a house*]
> Linguaglossa (Sicilia)
> Long Island
> Highgate (London)
> Near Taroudant [Morocco]
> Panarea [island off Sicily]

9/3/72   NYC

Ego: Bobby Fischer, James Joyce, Norman Mailer, Richard Wagner, Mark Spitz, [Herman] Melville

Connection between male homosexuality and fascism, between Puritanism and communism: sex + politics

. . .

9/16/72

. . .

Best model for interview tone: Robert Lowell . . .

China book—cross between Hannah Arendt + [*the American writer Donald*] Barthelme, I told [*then editor of* The New Yorker] W[illia]m Shawn yesterday

Kinesics and Context, Essays on Body Motion Communication—
by Ray L. Birdwhistell (Ballantine pb, 1972)
Why is this book so reactionary and repulsive in tone?

its sexism ("appropriate mating," use of "he," etc.)
its assumptions of the rights of the scientist—
patient
layman // professional
amateur

its notion of the social e.g. universe / idioverse
the moral implications of its jargon

10/15/72   Paris

Model for noble tone in essay form—Arendt, *Men in Dark Times*

Re-read [Arendt's Gotthold Ephraim] Lessing + [Walter] Benjamin essays, often!

Hong Kong—the Lu Hu Bridge spanning the Sham Chun River, between China and Hong Kong. Walk across. Peaked cloth caps. [*SS used the first sentence virtually verbatim in her autobiographical story "Project for a Trip to China."*]

. . .

Modern idea of paradise: the place we don't understand (Katmandu, the Tarahumaras, Tahiti, etc.)

10/20/72

(theme of a novel) relationship between fascism and "the fantastic."
Lovecraft
Fantasia, Busby Berkeley's *The Gang's All Here*

mechanization of people
use of color

. . .

10/21/72

Two root metaphors of my life:

> trip to China
> the desert

Two-part book (prose poem à la Cendrars): Return to desert (Tucson); trip to China

Desert—statis, emptiness, stripped-down, too few people, being simple-minded, rinky-tink history

China—movement, superior culture, green landscape, grand history, too many people

. . .

10/28/72

Just learned that the China trip has been postponed until Feb. 15

Thank God I wrote "Project."

Instinct of self-preservation!

. . .

[Undated, November]

. . .

Recycling one's own life with books

11/6/72   Paris

Idea for a short story or novella (from a visit of [*the film producer*] Lise Fayolle and her husband Claude Breuer chez Nicole last night):

A man—handsome—42 years old—born in Brussels, brought up in Montreal. A writer. Drinks. Long hair. All the clothes he wears have been bought by women. A raté [*"failure"*]. Knows "everything." Doesn't keep anything—possessions, old manuscripts, journals. Has worked very little—occasional journalism, free-lance PR photography (John Lennon and Yoko at Colombe d'Or at Cannes Festival in 1970), script doctoring. Published his first novel two years ago; brought out by a small independent publisher in the Alpes-Maritimes, Robert Morel—a modern building in the middle of 180 hectares on the top of a hill . . . with one steel door "that closes like a safe"; printed 10,000 copies—all sold, but only in the South of France—not one copy in Paris (publisher refuses to send the books to Paris bookstores, even when they are ordered); [*Une Journée un peu chaude*]; won a small, prestigious literary prize, le Prix Roger-Nimier. Has finished second novel, started on third. Has quit Robert Morel—"it was painful"—"I love him"—letter: "Cher Robert, Je vous quitte. Claude." [*"Dear*

Robert, I am leaving you. Claude."] No explanation, no expression of regret. "He's pleasing himself. Why shouldn't I please myself?"—"It's for the most stupid of reasons. I want to be able to walk into a bookstore in Paris and see how my book is doing." Now he has an introduction (via [*the French novelist Françoise*] Sagan) to [*the Paris publishers*] Flammarion and to Grasset, one of whom will take his second novel. And he has 100 pp. of the third.

He has written all his life, but never had enough "confidence" to publish until 3 years ago. Plays, stories, novels. All the old stuff lost, thrown out, torn up.

Married twice—to a Canadian girl, when very young (she demanded fidelity), then after coming to Paris—in [his] late 20s, early 30s—Lise! Now lives in St. Tropez with a rich girl named Catherine. House in the pines.

Went to Cornell. Lived for a while in New York.

From a rich family. (What does father do?) One of four sons. (Is Claude the oldest?) One of his brothers is dead. The third? The fourth, Philippe, is 39 years old and is a Mongolian idiot.

Philippe didn't "speak" until age 6, didn't walk until age 9. "It was I who taught him to walk." The mother is 82 now. Has never left Philippe for one minute of her life. Is capable of tumbling in the garden now, age 82, to make Philippe laugh.

"My mother is a monster."

He calls Lise "Fayolle" [—] "Hey, Fayolle . . ."

Photograph of Philippe (5' 5", wears thick round glasses, receding hair, short-sleeved white shirt, grey slacks), mother (white-haired), and Claude—dirty, straggly-haired, unshaven.

1 in 50 children born to mothers age 45 and up are Mongolian; 1 in 2,000 to mothers under the age of 30.

"Mongolian idiot" called, properly, Down's Syndrome.

Claude: "Don't feel sorry for Mongolians. They're not unhappy. They're happy."

What do they want? "Nothing. They just want to be left alone. To be left in peace."

"C'est le contestataire dans l'état pur. Il *est* contestataire. C'est le refus total." [*"It's protest in its purest state. He* is *the protest. It's total refusal."*]

"Everything a Mongolian says is false." It's learned. It's an imitation.

"The refusal begins at conception. The sperm refuses the ovum, the ovum refuses the sperm."

Mongolians are less "affectionate" with each other than with normal people.

They often have a good memory.

"My mother doesn't understand Philippe. She is his reason for living, he is hers."

"If she dies, he would die the same day." Most Mongolians die young. He is one of the oldest alive in the world.

He [Claude] didn't see his mother for 17 years.

"They don't *want* to talk. They learn to talk because they are forced to." (Not True)

Says that his mother loved Philippe much more than her three other sons or her husband. "He is the strongest."

"One is never bored being with him."

"The novel I'm writing is not about my brother. It happens that I have a Mongolian brother, that's all."

The novel is in the 1st person. "I want to put myself inside the mind of a Mongolian. Describe the world that he sees— that I see as *him*." A world without "normal" assumptions and structures.

"My mother is not admirable. What she has done is completely egotistical. She should have let him die."

The claw-like grasp of a Mongolian—the spatulate nails— thick neck, raucous voice, rounded shoulders.

Shows rage and displeasure when he feels like it. A cup is to break as well as to drink from.

"I understand my brother."

Mother has founded a school—institution—for Mongolians. But Philippe has always been at home with her.

"Maybe I will imagine mental processes in the novel that *aren't* true of Mongolians, but I don't care. What's true is what I am capable of imagining."

Mother was 40 when Claude was born, 43 when Philippe (the youngest) was born.

How to transform this?

Journal of C.
 or
Letters between C. and S[agan].

In journal, could have the reflections he makes on his novel— his brother—his own life. But is he capable of commenting from the outside—e.g. to understand how this project of the third novel is a violent act of revenge against his mother and his brother?

in writing this novel, he becomes his brother—but he is more intelligent than his brother (that why he denies his character *is* his brother, or that it matters whether the mentality he will impersonate, render is in fact typical Mongolian mentality)

—in writing this novel, he becomes his mother—but more intelligent than his mother. He understands Philippe better than she does.

Becoming his mother and his brother, he becomes, finally, stronger than either of them.

He impersonates Philippe (but better than Philippe) thereby advancing his claim to his mother's love. He becomes, magically, the preferred son.

He replaces his mother in Philippe's love.

He becomes what he always wanted to be—in his sad, pathetic, "bohemian" style—the perfect contestataire.

(C. hates to eat or to sleep. Is very thin. Goes to bed usually between 5 and 7 a.m. Drinks, though. ????, all this, alongside the ideal contestation incarnated by Philippe.)

Letter form: could have a voice—a woman, former wife or lover of Claude, a successful novelist who lives in Paris, genre Sagan—say all this. She is lucid, cynical.

But the letter form makes the story too long. I want it to move fast—as condensed as possible.

Chute ("fall")? Mother dies, and it is Claude who dies right after—not Philippe.

. . .

Three themes I have been following all my life:

    China
    Women
    Freaks

And there is a fourth: the organization, the guru.

Three (or four) colonies which I administer—and can exploit. Three (or four) rooms that I can furnish.

*[In the margin:] Could write my autobiography in this way.
In four sections.*

. . .

11/7/72

Dedicate China book to D: For David
                              Beloved son, friend, comrade

. . .

11/16/72

Science fiction revisited. The misogyny of Jules Verne (+
Nietzsche)

. . .

1973

1/6/73

When I was an infant, I think, I already knew I only had two choices: intelligence or autism. Being intelligent isn't, for me, like doing something "better." It's the only way I exist. If I'm not [being] intelligent, I hover near being catatonic.

Film to be based on Raymond Roussel's *Impressions of Africa* (1910). He died in 1933. A funny, poetic, oneiric film (Story hinges on the fete of a theatrical character given on the occasion of a coronation).

Film on Gilles de Rais.

1/7/73

Perhaps I have begun to think again. It's too soon to tell. I had begun to believe I had lost my mind.— Or gave it away, because it was too heavy.

Can I love someone (N[icole]] and still think / fly?

Love is flying sown, floating. Thought is solitary flight, beating wings.

I have to think about what I think. And I'm afraid.

The terrible, numbing loss of self-confidence I've experienced in the last three years: the attacks on *Death Kit*, feeling myself a fraud politically, the disastrous reception of *Brother Carl*—and, of course, the maelstrom of C[arlotta]

Films (tentative hypotheses):

> The only kind of films I want to do are S[cience]
> > F[iction]: dreams, miracles, futurology. SF =
> > liberty.
> Any "period" film is reactionary in itself. Example:
> > Proust, *The Go-Between*, *Death in Venice*
> > Counter-example: Bresson's *Jeanne d'Arc*—Why?
> > Because there are no professional actors . . .
> > Hence [*SS's project to adapt de Beauvoir's novel*]
> > *L'Invitée* would have been a reactionary film . . .
> > Another counter-example: Rossellini's *La Prise*
> > *du Pouvoir* . . .
> What about stars? Conscious manipulation of
> > [Brigitte] Bardot-image in [Godard's] *Le Mépris*

Essay on violence in cinema:

Compare: 1) eye of woman in Odessa steps sequence ([of Eisenstein's] *Potemkin*); 2) eye being cut in [Buñuel's] *Un Chien Andalou*

(1) arouses compassion, doesn't brutalize; (2) brutalizes. Ken Russell's *The Devils* comes from (2). A steady progression

since *Psycho* in habituating audiences to endure sadistic assaults without flinching (*Psycho*, *Repulsion*, *The Music Lovers*, *The Devils*, [Sam] Peckinpah's *Straw Dogs*, Hitchcock's *Frenzy*). Where is [*Franju's*] *Le Sang des bêtes* in all this?

My position leads to censorship, if it leads to any public action at all. But I can't face up to that. I *can't* be for censorship.

•

[SS made a month-long trip to China and North Vietnam in mid-January 1973. I have not found a great many notes from the trip, but much of what was among her papers is reproduced here. Not all of it concerns China directly.]

Cultural imperialism is the key issue. No wonder the US is not xenophobic. It exports its culture—confident it will contaminate (seduce) anyone who touches it.

Current Chinese slogan: "China must make greater contributions to the world." The Chinese modesty about what it can export. China doesn't think it can be a model, not even to the Third World.

China wants to be left alone. To make a New Zion, need to be isolated. America had that chance. China doesn't, won't.

Calvinist base of American ideology: human nature is fundamentally dark, evil, sinful, selfish, will respond only to egotistical or material or competitive motives

Faces with China: either (1) it isn't real (it's a show, it's coerced); or (2) it can't last (wait until materialism gets *you* (!))

Belief that consumer society is the irrefutable seducer (corruptor). Have nostalgia for pristine past of US, but . . .

How *not* to use words like:

 regimentation
 catechism
 brain-washing
 conformity vs. individualism
 drab

[*The American sinologist John King*] Fairbank has pointed out (in 1971, testifying before [*the Senate Foreign Relations Committee chairman, Arkansas senator William*] Fulbright, p. 38) that American "individualism" translates as "ho-jen-chui," each man for himself, selfishness; "freedom" in Chinese is "tzu yu," means being out of control, doing as you wish, not following your responsible duties, licentiousness

Self-determination of small groups makes no sense—[the Chinese] believe people are one unit, must be unified.

Rituals of mutual aid

Eating: never help yourself, serve the person to the right + left of you. (Each course in big plate or bowl in the center of a round table.)

Chinese don't understand (deal with) a group that doesn't have a "Chairman."

"Culture" in the West, the bastion of the bourgeoisie

>   culture, a temple
>   an elite, its guardians

cf. Nizan book
In China, for the time being, only *one* culture—accessible to everyone

One iconography:

>   Mao
>   The "[Gang of] 4"
>   The rev[olutionary] ballets
>   Art mirrors daily life.

Same repertory—are likely to hear / see it everywhere: a.m. visiting a nursery, p.m. visiting a factory, eve[ning] professional Song + Dance ensemble in Sian, Shanghai, or Hangchow

Women's liberation

Women // blacks

important difference *not* degree or quantity of oppression (women through most of history have been slaves, chattel— from bound feet, clitoridectomy, immolation on husband's funeral pyre > no legal status, right to own property, vote, have own name > abortion laws, job discrimination, etc.) but the fact that they are integrated with their oppressors though in some societies—e.g. Arab, Chinese—women are almost ghettoized

Crucial question: integration or separatism

Separatism implies at least bisexuality (exclusive homosexuality a result of sexual polarizing—would decline with more integration, abolition of sex stereotyping).

N.B. Current tendency in movement toward separatism—Redstockings, Gay Liberation Front, Weatherwoman. *Aphra*, a feminist lit. magazine praised for "not trying to copy male literary standards."

My own view: pure integrationist.

Aim of women's lib should be the abolition of sex-specific standards for *all* activities—except child-bearing and, perhaps, a few jobs requiring great physical strength (like coal-mining—but these jobs are rapidly disappearing)

There may be a "black literature" with its own standards, but there is no "women's literature." Isn't this precisely the old male chauvinist slander. (Cf. treatment of Virginia Woolf) Women do not have—and should not seek to create—a separate "culture." The separate culture they do have is privative. It's just that they should be seeking to abolish.

Only function of caucusing—formation of separatist groups—is transition: to raise consciousness; to lobby.

Schools

Why not eliminate schooling between age 12–16? It's biologically + psychologically too turbulent a time to be cooped up inside, made to sit all the time. During these years, kids would live communally—doing some work, anyway being physically active, in the countryside; learning about sex—free of their parents. Those four "missing" years of school could be added on, at a much later age. At, say, age 50–54 everyone would have to go back to school. (One could get a deferment for a few years, in special cases, if one was in a special work or creative project that couldn't be broken off.) In this 50–54 schooling, have strong pressure to learn a new job or profession—plus liberal arts stuff, general science (ecology, biology), and language skills.

This simple change in the age specificity of schooling would a) reduce adolescent discontent, anomie, boredom, neurosis; b) radically modify the almost inevitable process by which people at 50 are psychologically and intellectually ossified— have become increasingly conservative, politically—and retrograde in their tastes (Neil Simon plays, etc.)

There would no longer be one huge generation gap (war), between the young and the not young—but 5 or 6 generation gaps, each much less severe.

After all, since most people from now on are going to live to be 70, 75, 80, why should all their schooling be bunched together in the first 1/3 or 1/4 of their lives—so that it's downhill all the way

Early schooling—age 6–12—would be intensive language skills, basic science, civics, the arts.

Back to school at 16: liberal arts for two years
Age 18–21: job training through apprenticeship, not schooling

[*Undated political note:*]

For [*the essay SS wanted to write*] "Notes Toward a Definition of Cultural Revolution"

Read, reread:

Sartre interview, *New Left Review* #58, Nov–Dec 1969

3/15/73

. . . Where does a writer's authority come from? Where does my authority come from?

Exemplary people, exemplary acts.

In "life," I don't want to be reduced to my work. In "work," I don't want to be reduced to my life.
My work is too austere
My life is a brutal anecdote

3/21/73

. . . Re-reading *The Magic Mountain* for the first time in 25 years, I discover today that a line from the Artaud essay, "Only the exhausting is truly interesting," is an unconscious parody of a line in the Foreword to *TMM*: "Only the exhaustive can be truly interesting."

[Undated, June]

. . . "When did the Ego begin to stink?" (*[the British critic]* Cyril Connolly, 30 years ago)

[*There is a question mark in the margin of this entry.*] Leni Riefenstahl's terrifying "Nietzschean" documentary, *Triumph of the Will*

Late June 1973   Venice

Flying low—approach to Marco Polo Airport—the landscape is "lunar"—poisoned by oil refineries at Mestre, range of wild colors—the bones of the earth lying under the shallow water.

The American novel as an imperialist project: Melville.

. . .

6/20/73   Haramont

. . . The only stories I want to write now are those to which I can feed a personal experience. That's why "China," "Debriefing," and "Baby" work. That's why the Fable I tried to write in Venice didn't work.

[Malcolm] Lowry story in *American Review*: one of the most beautiful examples of the writer's will: persisting, shaping

. . .

6/27/73   Paris

What matters, what eats me: What is usable from the past—

Philip
Sense of madness
America
Women
Freaks
The will
Cocktails & overdrive

A story is a voice.

Overdrive
[*In the margin, dated 2/13/74, is the added notation:*] This is
the name of the truck drivers' mag[azine]

The only story that seems worth writing is a cry, a shot, a
scream. A story should break the reader's heart

A beginning: "All my life I have been looking for someone
intelligent to talk to."

The story must strike a nerve—in me. My heart should start
pounding when I hear the first line in my head. I start trembling at the risk.

. . .

I know I "have" a story when the form (tone) comes, and
everything seems relevant to it—so it could be much longer
(more detailed) than it is.

. . .

Story called "Overdrive"

People in a car driving around the world make a tour of all the boring places: Bergen, Norway

Overdrive as title of the collection? *I, etcetera* too cerebral. [*In the end SS opted for* I, etcetera.]

7/31/73   Paris

Maybe I should go on writing stories for two years—fifteen, twenty stories—really clear the deck, explore new voices—before tackling the third novel. Can bring out two collections of stories in the next 2–3 years, re-establish myself (establish?!) as a fiction writer, and create interest—anticipation—in the forthcoming novel.

. . .

I'm now writing out of rage—and I feel a kind of Nietzschean elation. It's tonic. I roar with laughter. I want to denounce everybody, tell everybody off. I go to my typewriter as I might go to my machine gun. But I'm safe. I don't have to face the consequences of "real" aggressivity. I'm sending out colis piégés [*"booby-trapped packages"*] to the world.

That's why my voice is getting more American. Because I'm finally handling / touching autobiographical material directly. The Europeanized voice ("tranlatorese") of the earlier fiction was the just correlative of the fact that I had transposed—displaced—what I was writing about.

It started with the Paul Goodman essay—feeling grief, and having the courage (and interest) to advertize it. The second step was when I thought, in October, that the China trip was cancelled. I was so disappointed—and, above all I didn't want to waste (not have the opportunity to use) all the personal fantasies [*In the margin*: (Daddy, M. [*SS's mother*], my childhood)] that had been stirred up at the prospect of that trip. I wrote a story that started "I am going to China" precisely because I then thought I wasn't. I decided to let the four-year-old have her say, since the thirty-nine-year-old wasn't going to get to find out about Maoism and the Cultural Revolution. (Of course, when, in January, I did get to go—it was the 39-year-old who went; the 4-year-old, to my surprise, didn't even deign to come along. Was it because she'd gotten the load off her chest? No—probably she would never have come—because the real China has nothing, never had anything, to do with her China.)

The solution to a problem—a story that you are unable to finish—*is* the problem. It isn't as if the problem is one thing and the solution something else. The problem, properly understood = the solution. Instead of trying to hide or efface what limits the story, capitalize on that very limitation. State it, rail against it.

Freedom of using jump cuts.

8/14/73   Paris

Just re-read K[afka]'s "Investigations of a Dog"—for the first time in fifteen years (?) and realized that the opening line of *The Benefactor*—the argument of the first pages—indeed something of whole novel—comes directly from that.

Trashy life, rosy mythologies

. . .

All my life I've been looking for someone intelligent to talk to.

My mother lay in bed until four every afternoon in an alcoholic stupor, the blinds on the bedroom window firmly closed. I was brought up by a freckled elephant of Irish-German extraction who took me to Mass every Sunday and read me aloud stories in the evening paper about car accidents and loved Kate Smith. At seventeen, I met a thin, heavy-thighed, balding man who talked and talked, snobbishly, bookishly, and called me "Sweet." After a few days passed, I married him. We talked for seven years.

I did my homework with the radio on.

And Monday I reserved for Mahatma Gandhi.

Talking like touching
Writing like punching somebody

Talking in accents . . .

8/20/73

Story I'm finishing now called "Another Case of Dr. Jekyll"—using the material of story projected as "Walter and Aaron," built out of parts of "The Organization," written in 1962–63.

I find the old themes:

Young innocent (with "obsessions," a "problem" he's trying to solve) > older, cynical, fascist type

i.e. Thomas / Bauer [*Duet for Cannibals*]
    Hippolyte / Jean-Jacques [*The Benefactor*]

Reversing Diddy / Incardona relationship [*Death Kit*], it's the middle-class schmuck who has the good body, and the brute (working-class) who is frail physically.

But that's what fascinated me in the Stevenson novella when I read it several months ago . . . —that H[yde] is smaller, frailer, younger than J[ekyll]

And the "Gurdjieff" theme is finally treated openly, so perhaps I can finally purge myself of all that—not make a "Gurdjieff film"—and go on to newer, better obsessions.

The "fascist" sage—

> a theme in *The Benefactor*
> the main (unwritten) part of the novel started in
> > June 1965 and abandoned, "The Ordeal of
> > Thomas Faulk."
> Bauer in *Duet for Cannibals* [—] in first idea of film,
> > Bauer was a psychiatrist—Thomas was his young
> > assistant. The story took place in Bauer's private
> > clinic where Thomas come to work [*In the margin:*
> > Caligari, Mabuse.] (Most of "The Ordeal of
> > Thomas Faulk" was to take place in the clinic in
> > So[uth] Carolina where Thomas went after he
> > had his breakdown; in this earlier version . . .
> > Thomas was a patient, not a young doctor) [*In the
> > margin:* but in film still has the name of Thomas]

9/3/73

[*The German philosopher Karl*] Jaspers's concept of "the exception" in *The Philosophy of Existence* . . . (lectures delivered in 1937)

photography successor to Pop Art

The judgment of moral ambition

Buy: Valéry, *Cahiers*, vol. I (Pléiade)
　　　Leo Steinberg, *Other Criteria*

Herbert Johnson hats

Paraphasia—garbling, word-scrambling of speech caused by (among other things) a blood clot on the left side of the brain

Dysnomia—things called by their wrong names

Aphasia (loss of speech) of either

　　　the conduction type—word jumbling similar to paraphrasia, or

　　　Broca's type—implying inability to receive or produce verbal sounds correctly, combined with inability to read intelligently

9/14/73

Léger:

"You don't make a nail with a nail, but with an iron"

painting is piracy

"either a comfortable life and lousy work or a lousy life and beautiful work"

10/15/73

. . . Get up quickly—just switch on the white light of the will

Francine Gray's [*the contemporary American writer Francine du Plessix Gray*] great-great-aunt, a Carmelite nun in the 1880s (already in her 60s)—had never seen a train. Needed dispensation from the Vatican to look out the window.

. . .

For Adorno essay: look at Martin Jay, *The Dialectical Imagination*; Kostas Axelos essay on Adorno in *Arguments* III, 14 (1959); George Lichtheim, *TriQuarterly*, Spring 1968

For China book: look at [*the twentieth-century German-American sinologist*] Karl Wittfogel's book on China

Jasper quote in John Cage's last book: "I can imagine easily a world without art."

Morbidity a defense against sense of tragedy

I prance around cemeteries all over the world—gleeful, fascinated—because I don't know in what cemetery in Brooklyn Daddy is buried

•

SUSAN SONTAG

[At the time of the October 1973 Arab-Israeli war, SS made Prom-ised Lands, a documentary film shot in Israel and on the front lines (Suez, Golan Heights). I have found no notebooks on the film-ing, but believe these notes were entered during those weeks.]

Israel
Moshe Flinker—Jews / Germans
Yoram Kaniuk—Holocaust memory

Two myths [about] minorities

    revolutionary, secular, socialist
    orthodox, religious, conservative
    >> consumer society (rejected by both A + B)

Jews < > Israelis
Diaspora: envy, contempt

12/9/73   London

. . . The San Francisco earthquake; the San Andreas fault.

OK to be paranoid—that expands the imagination—but not to be schizophrenic (that shrinks it). Compare [Thomas Pyn-chon's] *Gravity's Rainbow* with *Death Kit.*

In the next novel: no one is catatonic; no one speculates, in self-blindness + dissociation (like Hippolyte + Diddy)

Gore Vidal's praise of Mary McCarthy—she is "uncorrupted by compassion." I am. That's my limit. In the next novel, I won't put at the center a protagonist who is "corrupted by compassion." No schmucks!

The hardness of Flaubert in Egypt.

Cupidity; a style of life based on ownership, possessions

. . . The guru theme—up front treat it honestly; make up your mind!

Too much ambivalence in [*SS's short story*] "Doctor Jekyll"—I am not sure how I feel about sublimation ([*the American literary critic*] Bill Mazzocco's criticism)

The autobiography of a guru?

The rape of culture—tourism—
(e.g. Samoa)

How *do* I feel about sublimation?

Story: "The San Francisco Earthquake"—Aunt Anne [*SS had a great-aunt who survived the earthquake*] in the brothel, standing in the doorway

The Marx Bro[ther]s—it should be funny.

12/10/73

[*The historian of Kabbalistic Judaism, adversary of Hannah Arendt, and friend of Walter Benjamin, Gershom*] Scholem said it was Jacob Taubes [*Scholem's student in Jerusalem in the late-1940s and Susan Taubes's husband*] who revealed to him the existence of moral evil. He paled when I mentioned Jacob's name. (The evening D[avid] + I spent with him in Jerusalem [in October 1973].)

Hannah Arendt said that Benjamin was the only person Scholem ever really loved. (The evening at Lizzy's [Elizabeth Hardwick] house last week in NY. Mary M[cCarthy], [*her brother the actor*] Kevin M[cCarthy], Barbara E [*Epstein, co-editor with Robert Silvers of* The New York Review of Books], Mme Stravinsky + [*the writer Robert*] Craft, [*the historian*] Arthur Schlesinger + [*his wife*] Alexandra Emmet also there.)

. . .

12/16/73   Milan

"Topoi" in letters of Resistance people on the eve of their execution:

> forgive me for the suffering I am about to inflict on you
> no regrets
> I am dying for . . . (Party / country / humanity / liberty)
> Thank you for all you've done for me
> I live on in x form
> Tell so-and-so that I . . .
> Once more, I . . .

Similarity, no matter what country + what class. (Thomas Mann, in preface to the book [*Lettere di Condannati a morte della Resistenza europea*]—pub[lished] by Einaudi in 1954—notes I[van] I[lyich]'s letter in Tolstoy story.)

Why?
Need to make a communication that is *efficacious*

: a) simple
clear
no point in subtlety, refinement

Such a letter is, pre-eminently, a *practical* communication. Its purpose is:

> to relieve (reduce) suffering
> to guarantee (shape) posthumous existence,
>   how one will be remembered

(Perfect text to illustrate Aristotle's *Rhetoric*)

Nevertheless, some differences:
difference of degree of [u], of personalization, of freedom to express "private" feelings, "sentiments" (least in Albania (+ generally in C[ommunist] P[arty] members), most in France, Norway, Italy, Holland)
difference between Prot[estant] + Catholic countries

Letters are mostly to mothers, not fathers—to wives—to children

. . .

12/23/73   Haramont

Two shattering reading experiences this year—the correspondence of Flaubert, and (yesterday) the two-volume biography by Simone Pétrement of SW [Simone Weil]

How depressed I am by both of them—at moments. I feel real hatred for them—because I understand them both so well, because they represent the two poles of my own temperament (longings, temptations). I could be "Flaubert" or "S.W."; I am neither of course—because one side corrects, inhibits, compromises the other.

"Flaubert": ambition; egotism; detachment; contempt for others; enslavement to work; pride; stubbornness; ruthlessness; lucidity; voyeurism; morbidity; sensuality; dishonesty.

"S.W.": ambition; egotism; neurosis; refusal of the body; hunger for purity; naïveté; awkwardness; asexuality; desire for sanctity; honesty.

What a painful demystification of S.W. this biography is!

Her death was a suicide—and she'd been trying to kill herself (notably, by starving herself) for many years.

"I am not a feminist," she said. Of course not. She never accepted the fact that she was a woman. Hence, her making herself ugly (she wasn't), her way of dressing, her incapacity to have any sexual life, her being dirty, unkempt, the disorder of any room she occupied, etc. If she could have slept with anyone, it could only have been with a woman—not because she was "really" au fond homosexual (she wasn't) but because at least with a woman she wouldn't have felt she was being raped. But, of course, that was impossible too—given the time she lived, her particular milieu; above all, the way she had survived implied a profound + irrevocable desexualization of herself.

(How lucky I am, since I could very well have made the same "saving" choice as S.W. But I was saved for sexuality—at least partially—by women. By the age of 16 on, women found me, sought me out, imposed themselves on me emotionally + sexually. I was raped by women and I found that not too threatening. How grateful I am to women—who gave me a body, who made it even possible for me to sleep with men.)

S.W. of course makes me think of Susan [Taubes]. Same hunger for purity, same refusal of the body, same unfitness to live. What was the difference between them? That S.W. had genius and Susan didn't. That S.W. assumed her own desexualization, affirmed it, drew energy from it—while Susan was "weak": she could never accept the love of women; she wanted to be hurt and dominated by men; she wanted to be beautiful, glamorous, mysterious. Susan's refusals only weakened her, they didn't give her energy. Her suicide was second-rate. S.W.'s was an exaltation—that's how, finally, she succeeded in imposing herself on the world, securing her own legend, blackmailing her contemporaries and posterity.

What is left of Susan? A novel nobody read and a manuscript on S.W. that I keep in a closet in NY (unread) whose existence nobody knows.

I remembered last night that in the story about Susan, "Debriefing," I had put in the voice of S.W. at one moment. Quite unconsciously—when I was writing the story in March of this year. Now I understand.

A lesson: purity and wisdom—one can't aspire to both— they're ultimately contradictory. Purity implies innocence, unselfconsciousness—(even) a certain stupidity. Wisdom implies lucidity, the overcoming of one's innocence—intelligence. One *must* be innocent in order to be pure. One *can't* be innocent in order to be wise.

My problem (and perhaps the most profound source of my mediocrity): I wanted to be both pure and wise.

I was too greedy.

The result: I am neither "S.W." nor "Flaubert." The hunger for purity checks the possibility of real wisdom. My lucidity checks my impulses to act with purity.

I am not attracted to suicide—and never have been.

I love to eat, even though it is easy for me not to eat (when no one feeds me, when there is no food around).

1974

1/20/74   Paris

short film (or long?) on l'habillement [*"dress"*]

    military dress
    wedding clothes (creation of mths / white + purity)
    actors
    transvestites

All dressing-up points [to] travesty, drag

Cf. scene of ecclesiastical fashion in Fellini's *Roma*. And to death . . .

2/6/74

. . .

"For me a sheet of paper is like the forest to a fugitive"— [*the twentieth-century Russian writer and dissident*] Andrei Sinyavsky

. . .

To be a great writer:

> know everything about adjectives and punctuation
> (rhythm)
> have moral intelligence—which creates true
> authority in a writer

2/9/74

"Live as you think, or you will think as you live." Valéry

A spy in the house of life.

7/25/74   Panarea [Italy]

"Idea" as method of instant transport *away* from direct experience, carrying a tiny suitcase.

"Idea" as a means of miniaturizing experience, rendering it portable. Someone who regularly has ideas is—by definition—homeless.

Intellectual is a refugee from experience. In Diaspora.

What's wrong with direct experience? Why would one ever want to flee it, by transforming it—into a brick?

Can something be too immediate?:
Imprisoning.: Too light.

Deficiency of sensuality? But that's a tautology.

[Undated]

Thinking about my own death the other day, as I often do, I made a discovery. I realized that my way of thinking has up to now been both too abstract and too concrete.
Too abstract: death
Too concrete: me

For there was a middle term, both abstract and concrete: women. I am a woman. And thereby, a whole new universe of death rose before my eyes.

I am not trying to control my own death.

. . .

All my life I have been thinking about death, + it is a subject I am now getting a little tired of. Not, I think, because I am closer to my own death—but because death has finally become real. (> Death of Susan [Taubes])

. . .

Women and courage. Not courage to do, but courage to endure / suffer.

Wife of my grandfather's brother Chaim—after the funeral she came home + put her head in the oven. Childhood image—kneeling down. But the oven is dirty.

Women + sleeping pills + water (not guns—[*the twentieth-century French author Henry de*] Montherlant, Hemingway)

. . .

1975

[Otherwise undated entries, marked only 1975:]

Stocking one's vocabulary—"Wortschatz," "word treasury"—
requires years, great effort, patience

Brecht's "Plumpes Denken" [*"crude thought"*]—thought +
language substantial enough to have its effect + not be
overlooked.

. . .

Jack London's story "To Build a Fire"—read aloud to Lenin
on his deathbed.

•

[*The Russian critic and writer Vasily*] Rozanov—another
member of the [*late-nineteenth-and-early-twentieth-century*]
Russian movement that includes [*the Russian writer Nikolai*]
Berdyaev + [*the Ukrainian-Russian author Lev*] Shestov

•

Poets: Cyprian Kamil Norwid (Polish, 19th century, friend
     of Chopin)
     Vladimír Holan [*the twentieth-century Czech poet*]

. . .

"This book is like a sophisticated rocket w[ith] an obsolete
warhead." (beginning of a review in the *TLS* [*Times Literary Supplement*])

. . .

Floyd Collins, who was trapped in a landslide in 1925—in a cave
in central Kentucky—and perished in slow motion, with much
of the world following by radio, newsreel, and newspapers.

. . .

"One photographs things in order to get them out of one's
mind."—Kafka

. . .

3/15/75   Haramont

Paul [Thek]: "not to try to be better than other people. Try to
be better than myself."

Brother Lawrence:—Born Nicolas Herman in French Lor-
raine—served briefly as footman + soldier, became a Lay
brother among the barefooted Carmelites in Paris in 1666
(known after that as "Brother Lawrence")—worked in a
monastery kitchen; died age 80

His conversion, at 18, was the result of the sight on a midwinter day of a dry and leafless tree standing in the snow, which stirred thoughts of the change the coming spring would bring

Cf. Chestnut tree in Sartre's *La Nausée*

Barthes now working on "le langage amoureux"—[Goethe's *Sorrows of Young] Werther*, opera texts

Photograph of Nietzsche and his mother taken in 1892—he was 48 [*This image was on the inside cover of the notebook begun in March 1975.*]

(3 years after collapse in Turin in 1889)—he looks at his mother, who holds his arm; she looks into the camera

Radio Play [*SS was collaborating with the Argentine writer and filmmaker Edgardo Cozarinsky on this project*]:

Career of Eva Perón as radio actress
Programs she did—great women in history (Jeanne d'Arc, Florence Nightingale, Mme Chiang Kai-shek)
Her mother
Ends with her being introduced to Perón (then a colonel) at a benefit given for flood victims in San Juan (the north)
Rivalry with another actress, a star of radio at the time, also named Eva

. . .

3/17/75

Consider the image of homosexuals in films where that is being subliminally suggested while at the same time being contradicted: for example, many of the roles of Clifton Webb, Edward Everett Horton, and George Sanders in films of the 30s and 40s. Seeing Preminger's *Laura* (1944) again, I was struck by the fact that the character played by Webb (who turns out to be the murderer) is clearly the portrait of a homosexual: sarcastic, cold, elegant, worldly, smart, an aesthete and art collector.

[Marked only as "Note from May 1975."]

Problematic essays from the 1960s for me—now—are "One Culture + The New Sensibility" and "On Style." Reread them, rethink the problems.

I don't want to go back on my public association with the new arts, the new politics. But how would I formulate those tastes / ideas today?

Sensibility vs morality?

Not that I have changed my point of view. Objective conditions have changed.

My role: the intellectual as adversary. (So now, must I be adversary to myself??)

In the early 1960s, the going ideas were conformity, middlebrow culture, certain kinds of inhibitions. So the aesthetic positions I took were good + necessary. Also, when the focus of political activity was (rightly) against the government + the war—the role of political adversary was right, indeed inevitable, if one had a conscience.

But, in the early 1970s, when the abuse is quite different—abuse of ideas of *liberation*. Now, ideas which came out of specific situations [of the 1960s] are junior high school norms . . . What status do those ideas have?

Genius of American capitalism is that anything that becomes known in this country becomes assimilated.

I was never taken in by the politics (pretensions to revolutionary potential) of the counter-culture. In the Cuban piece (1967) I already warned against that.

—political mistake of the New Left (ca. 1967) was to think you could invent gestures (styles, clothes, habits) that would really divide people. Like: long hair, Navajo jewelry, health food, dope, bell-bottomed trousers.

5/16/75   NYC

One has the feeling of having lived through an old script. Fellow-travellers of other people's revolutions: French, Russian, Chinese, Cuban, Vietnamese.

Cf. [*the American social critic Christopher*] Lasch's book, *The American Liberals and the Russian Revolution.*

Perhaps for the last time? "Right" and "left" are tired words.

The Movement harbored at least three different tendencies: the liberal one, the anarchist, and the radical one. And the radical one has as many themes in common with the extreme right as with the extreme left—so much that is New Left / gauchiste rhetoric being indistinguishable from fascist rhetoric of the 20s and early 30s, as so much that is right-wing (e.g. [*then Alabama governor George*] Wallace) sounds like potential left-wing populism.

Intellectuals played at crusaders and revolutionaries only to discover they were still patricians and liberals. (As kids played at being urban guerrillas and settled for being punks.) "Liberalism" seems a vast, obscure, swampy territory one never emerges from, no matter how one tries—and perhaps never should.

It is from liberalism that one gets one's passion for justice—and that longing for a juster order in which those freedoms guaranteed by liberalism probably couldn't survive. The problem with liberalism is that it can never have an unambivalent attitude toward revolutions. Finally, it must take a counter-revolutionary position. (The Maoists are correct.) Liberals can, ought to, support the right of national self-determination (the right of other peoples to have civil wars and make revolutions) and oppose our government's slaughtering them. But liberals can't survive under these governments—as we know from the history of every Communist regime, without exception, that has taken power.

To be an intellectual is to be attached to the inherent value of plurality, and to the right of critical space (space for critical opposition within society). Therefore, to be an intellectual supporting a revolutionary movement is to be assenting to one's own abolition. That's an arguable position: there is a good case to be made out that intellectuals are a luxury, and have no role in the only societies possible in the future. Cf. [*the American economist Robert*] Heilbroner.

But most intellectuals don't want to go that far, and will retreat from revolutionary fellow-travelling. Cf.: Lasch book;

[*the American editor and writer Melvin*] Lasky on English reactions to the French revolution.

The phenomenon of revolutionary tourism—cf. [*the German
writer Hans Magnus*] Enzensberger essay

. . .

Franz Hubmann, *The Jewish Family Album* (London: Rout-
ledge, 1975) 400 photographs

Writing at full voice

Paracelsus (1493?–1541)

5/20/75

. . . Already in Dostoyevsky, *Notes from Underground*—literary
space, the narrative that can't finish, that could go on forever,
that is potentially interminable

Cf. [*the German-American political philosopher and historian
Eric*] Voegelin comment to his Henry James letter in the
Southern Review

. . .

(Bob S[ilvers]:) The dense thicket of intuitions about people
in Faulkner's novels

Cf. Bellow, who has *not*, for all his talents, craft, intelligence,
produced a great body of work

5/21/75

My subject in all the fiction I've written, from *The Benefactor* on: the fiction of thought. The relation between thinking and power. That is, various forms of oppression and repression and liberation . . . I can't think of anyone else who has treated this subject fully, as fiction. Beckett, somewhat.

Conversation with Joe [Chaikin] tonight. When he thinks about the theatre, he said, he can't think of any reason to work in it, any meaning to what he's doing. Only when he doesn't think about it (i.e. ask himself the question about the meaning, value, importance of his work) can he enjoy the work— and he does. I replied that when one asks oneself a question for a long time without ever getting a satisfactory answer, there is usually something wrong with the question (rather than the answer). One didn't—until the late 19th century— ask for art to justify itself, to manifest its meaning. That was like asking art to be useful, practical. I made the distinction between activities which were slavish, practical—one knows why one performs them: they're useful, necessary, obliga- tory—and activities which were free, voluntary, gratuitous. If practicing an art belongs in the second type of activity, and that is what draws us to the arts, then it would seem a kind of mistake to be restless and demoralized because we were sub- sequently unable to justify that activity, because that activity failed to justify itself as belonging to the first type of activity. We would be in the situation of doubting the value (worth) of our activity—work—because of the very quality that drew us to it in the first place: its gratuitousness.

(Cf. Valéry—vagueness is not only the condition of literature, but of any life of the mind. "But perhaps vagueness is inde- structible, its existence necessary to psychic effulgence.")

. . .

5/22/75

Kafka on Tolstoy's *Resurrection*: "You cannot write about salvation, you can only live it."

I want to write a *Moby Dick* of thought. Melville is right: One needs a great subject.

Intelligence—beyond a certain point—is a liability to the artist. Leonardo da Vinci and Duchamp were too intelligent to be painters. They saw through it . . . And Valéry was too intelligent to be a poet.

A novel about the Jews: Sabbatai Zevi, Portnoy, Hyman Kaplan, Anne Frank, Mickey Cohen, Marx, Ethel + Julius Rosenberg, Trotsky, Heine, Erich von Stroheim, Gertrude Stein, Walter Benjamin, Fanny Brice, Kafka

5/25/75

. . . I must change my life. But how can I change my life when I have a broken back?

D[avid] said he wasn't fooled by my relentless cheerfulness—from the moment I wake up until the second I fall asleep—over the past two years. I read your fiction, he said. Nobody who wrote those stories could be that cheerful, genuinely.

But I don't want to fail, I said. I want to be one of the survivors. I don't want to be Susan Taubes. (Or Alfred [Chester]. Or

Diane Arbus [*the American photographer who committed suicide in 1971*].) I read aloud [to David] the passage from Kafka—his summary [*July 21, 1913*] for and against his marriage . . .

I feel like Kafka, I said to D., but I've found a system of safe harbors, to ward off terror—to resist, to survive.

. . .

I've constructed a life in which I *can't* be profoundly distressed or upset by anyone—except by D., of course. Nobody (except him) can get to me, get into my guts, topple me over the precipice. Everybody is certified "safe." The jewel and centerpiece of this system: Nicole.

I'm safe, yes, but I'm getting even weaker. I have more and more difficulty being alone, even for a few hours.— My panic on Saturdays this winter in Paris, when N[icole] leaves at 11 in the morning for the hunt and doesn't come back until after midnight. My inability to leave the rue de la Faisanderie [*where Nicole Stéphane then lived*] and go around Paris alone. I just stay there, those Saturdays, unable to work, unable to move . . .

The shadow of Carlotta panics me—most of all—because I don't want anything to make waves. I dread being in a state of conflict. Everything I do is designed to avoid conflict.

The price: no sex, a life devoted to work, to D., to my flagship N., and to bland maternalistic friendships (Joe [Chaikin], Barbara [Lawrence], Stephen [Koch], Edgardo [Cozarinsky], Monique [Lange], Colette, etc.). Becalmed, observant, doggedly productive, prudent, cheerful, dishonest, helpful to others.

Do I really want to have the rest of my life devoted to protecting my "work"? I've turned my life into [a] workshop. I'm managing myself.

reminds me that the safe harbor isn't going to be so safe for much longer. (N's bankruptcy, the inevitability of selling the rue de la Faisanderie.) Then it will be even harder to change anything.— My taste for custodial relationships. Propensity first developed in relation to my mother. (Weak, unhappy, confused, charming women.) Another argument against resuming any sort of connection with C., whom I found so pathetic, deteriorated in Rome this March.

6/7/75

Two texts which put "modernism" in perspective: Voegelin on his letter to [Robert] Heilman 20 years earlier re [Henry James's] *The Turn of the Screw*; Isaiah Berlin on Verdi (*Hudson Review*, 1968)

Talking about fascism, one thinks of the models of the past—the first half of this century (Italy, Germany, Spain, etc.). Most talk about the new variety of fascism that the second half of the century is spawning, which will be lighter, more efficient, less sentimental. Eco-fascism.

concern for a pure environment (air, water, etc.) will replace concern for a pure race; mobilize masses not on the basis of fighting racial pollution but of fighting environmental pollution

. . .

6/12/75

Read, for the first time, [Mary Shelley's] *Frankenstein*. Astonishing work by someone eighteen years old, much more astonishing than Radiguet [*who wrote* Le Diable au Corps *before he was twenty*].

It's an "education novel"—the dilemma of "l'enfant sauvage" (cf. [*the French filmmaker François*] Truffaut's *L'E.S.* [*L'Enfant sauvage*], Herzog's *Kaspar Hauser*) . . .

Victor Frankenstein, far from being the mad baron of the [James] Whale films, is a petit bourgeois scientist— . . . and Genevan: Smug, complacent, cowardly, vain, self-congratulatory. The hero is the monster—someone driven crazy for lack of love.

. . .

Theme of marriage + the family in [Goethe's] *Elective Affinities* + *Frankenstein*.

. . .

Life of [*the twentieth-century French poet*] Olivier Larronde—in *Art & Literature*, #10. His bedroom hung with astral maps. Monkey. Hermetic poems. Opium. Black curtains.

Connection between *The Benefactor* + *Death Kit*: Freud, at the end of *The Interpretation of Dreams*, seeking to integrate dream elaboration and its particular economy with the psyche as a whole: "Let us simply imagine the instrument which serves psychic productions as a sort of complicated microscope or camera."

. . .

"Man runs towards the grave,
  And rivers hasten to the great deep
  The end of all living is their death,
  And the palace in time becomes a heap.
  Nothing is further than the day gone by,
  And nothing nearer than the day to come,
  And both are far, far away
  From the man hidden in the heart of the tomb."

  —Samuel ha-Nagid
    (b[orn] Córdoba, 993, d[ied] Granada 1056)

. . .

6/30/75   [Paris]

Cioran (5:30 to midnight)—

The only acceptable life is a failure ("un échec")

The only interesting ideas are heresies

Sartre is a baby—I admire him and I despise him—he has no sense of tragedy, of suffering

A hubris, for which one will be punished, to give oneself more than one year

Après un certain age, tout craque [*"After you've reached a certain age, everything falls apart"*]

The only thing that makes life worth-while are moments of ecstasy

It's not what you do, it's what you *are*

Two kinds of conversation are interesting: about metaphysical *ideas* and gossip, anecdote

Writing as hygiene

The free intellectual: professors without students, priests without congregations, sages without communities

7/19/75   Paris

There is an essay—very general, aphoristic—to be written about *speed*, velocity. Perhaps the only new category in 20th century consciousness.

Speed is identified with the machine. With transport. With the light, slim, streamlined, male.

Speed annihilates boredom. (Solution to key 19th century problem: Boredom.)

Conservative	Revolutionary
Past	Future
Organic	Mechanical
Heavy	Light
Stone	Metal
Certainty	Unpredictability
Silence	Noise
Meaning	Pointlessness

From [*the Italian futurist Filippo Tommaso*] Marinetti to McLuhan. Contrast Ivan [Illich]'s critique of speed.

. . .

Seriousness	Irony
Memory	Forgetfulness
Repose	Energy
Habit	Novelty
Analysis	Intuition
Slowness	Speed
Sickliness	Hygiene

How does this fit with fascist aesthetics? Fascism? Riefenstahl?

Genealogy of this idea. Nietzsche, etc.

Nature	Life-as-theatre*
Pessimism	Optimism
Sentimentality	Virility
Peace	War
Family	Freedom

Relation of all this (Futurism, etc.) to Enzensberger's idea of the industrialization of consciousness. Does Fascism industrialize consciousness?

One point is that there . . . really is a "fascist aesthetics."

> Marinetti: "Everything of any value is theatrical."

And probably there is no such thing as a "communist aesthetics"—that's a contradiction in terms. Hence, the mediocrity and reactionary character of the art sanctioned in communist countries.

Official art in communist countries is, objectively, fascist. (E.g. hotels + palaces of culture of Stalinist era, [*the Mao-era Chinese propaganda film*] *The East Is Red*, etc.)

But what about Fascism's sentimentalizing of the past? The Nazis made Wagner their official music; Marinetti despised Wagner.

Ideal communist society is totally didactic (the whole society is a school); every consideration governed by a moral idea. Ideal fascist society is totally aesthetic (the whole society is a theatre); every consideration governed by an aesthetic idea.

This is another way in which aesthetics becomes a politics.

Re "Aesthetic Judgment." It always involves *preference* (implicit or explicit)

Is it understood that there are some categories upon which we must not exercise aesthetic judgment? That limitation is a constitutive part of the very idea of aesthetic judgment?

What happens if we decide we will judge *anything* aesthetically? Have we destroyed the idea?

N.B. Aesthetic judgment always involves preference, but preference doesn't always involve aesthetic judgment.

Some can say "I prefer my mother to my father" without suggesting any unseemly emotional distance, a "merely" aesthetic judgment.

But if we imagine someone saying "I prefer the First World War to the Second World War," we would think that wars were being treated improperly, heartlessly—that wars were being treated as spectacles.

. . .

7/22/75

Musical thinking. Magical thinking.

Elegiac.

Negative epiphany: Sartre's chestnut tree (*La Nausée*). Positive epiphany: Augustine's worm, Ruskin's leaf. Few writers now have a real contact with nature. The standard for writing is urban, psychological, cerebral—the bottom has dropped out of the world. Nature in a positive sense is anachronistic, unmodern.

Nuance, discretion, musicality—that's what I'm trying to get into my writing. What wasn't there before. No sensuality. I thought I had to say everything I thought.

Harold Rosenberg: "To be legitimate, a style in art must correct itself with a style outside of art, whether in palaces or dance halls or in the dreams of saints and courtesans."

It's the prose of goys [*non-Jews*] like Elizabeth H[ardwick], Bill Mazzocco, Wilfrid Sheed, [William H.] Gass, + Garry Wills that turns me on these days. No ideas, but what music. Poor Jews!

I'm irritated with images, often: they seem "crazy" to me. Why should X be like Y?

My exasperation when N[icole] wanted to play le jeu de la vérité [*the truth game—a variant of Truth or Dare*] the other night. The subject: Christiane. Let me guess, said N. If she were a food? (But she isn't a food.) If she were a car? (But she isn't a car.) If she were a hero? (But she isn't a hero.) Etc. I felt as if my mind were blowing a fuse.

Similes are something different.

8/7/75   Paris

(Cioran-like) essay: "Let the arts perish . . ."

Texts: [Henry James's] *The Princess Casamassima* (w[ith Lionel] Trilling introduction—Hyacinth Robinson as a "hero of civilization" . . .)

The Defense of Gracchus Babeuf [French Jacobin publicist tried under the Directory] (+ Morelly [*utopian writer of the French Enlightenment*])

Chinese material

Babeuf, quoting Morelly . . . : . . . "Society must be made to operate in such a way that it eradicates once and for all the desire of a man to become richer, or wiser, or more powerful than others."

N.B. "wiser" China

. . .

Or is this the subject for a novel? James wrote *The Princess C.* in the 1880s. Do we know any more than he knew then? Would Hyacinth Robinson kill himself a hundred years later?

There are two subjects for a noble novel:

    sanctity
    the "problem" of civilization

Who would a modern Hyacinth be? Is culture still a "value"— after its back has been broken in the 1920s by Dadaism, Surrealism, etc.

[*In a box at the top of the page:*] Cf. preface of [Théophile Gautier's] *Mademoiselle de Maupin*: attack on realist-utilitarian demands of republican journalism—". . . and thus royalty + poetry, the two greatest things in the world, become impossible . . ."

When Hyacinth goes to Paris, he doesn't have to deal with mass tourism—the degradation of all the objects he admires. His fellow-workers in the book-binding shop now take vacations in Europe, too.

(Christianity wasn't so good for art either—until it lowered its moral tone, got civilized, pluralistic.)

(What happened to great poets like [Pablo] Neruda + Brecht when they put their poetry at the service of the people, the demand for social justice.)

Little Red Book [*of Mao Tse-tung's sayings*] teaches that everyone can think but negates the (traditional Chinese) idea of wisdom.

Trilling on *The Princess C. . . .* : "Hyacinth recognizes what very few people wish to admit, that civilization has its price, and a high one."
—China!

8/8/75

Art Deco the last "international"—total—style. (From fine arts to furniture, everyday objects, clothes, etc.) All styles in the last 50 years have been comments on Art Deco. E.g. Art Deco straightened out, made rectilinear the vertiginous curves of Art Nouveau, the next to last international style; Bauhaus (Mies [van der Rohe], [Philip] Johnson, etc.) banned all ornament; but the structure remains the same.

Fascist architecture: parody + Art Deco ([Albert] Speer, "Mussolini")

Why has there been no new international style in 50 years? Because the new ideas, the new needs are not yet clear. (Hence, we content ourselves with variations + refinements on Art Deco and, for refreshment + fusions, parodistic—"pop"— revivals of older styles.)

A new style will emerge in the last decade of this century, with the ascendancy of the ecological crisis—and possibility of eco-fascism

> Low buildings
> Caves
> No windows
> Stone

The skyscraper will seem like hubris, + it will be impractical

Most influential "painter" of our century: Duchamp. Dissolves the idea of art

Most influential poet: Mallarmé. Advances the idea of the difficult writer. There have always been difficult writers (e.g. ancient distinction between esoteric and exoteric texts) but no one before had ever advanced difficulty—i.e. purity—i.e. elimination of content—as the criterion of value. Mallarmé invented the idea (not the practice) which has been influential in a way that no practice ever could be.

1910s—*art* inherited political rhetoric (that of Anarchism) cf. Marinetti

1960s—*feminism* inherited political rhetoric (that of gauchisme) against hierarchy, intellect (as bourgeois, phallocentric, repressive), the theoretical

rigged hopes, rigged despair

The "thou" which the self needs for its own fulfillment

Power of art = power to negate

. . .

fiction: schemes of enlightenment and redemption

obstacles:
    problem (temptation) of pessimism, grief
    break-up of cultural references
    temptation of catatonia

. . .

"Chaque atom de silence est la chance d'un fruit mûr." [*"Each atom of silence is the luck of a ripe fruit."*]—Valéry

versus

[Gertrude] Stein, "I cannot remember not talking all the time and all the same feeling that while I was talking . . . that I was not only hearing but seeing . . ."

versus

Jesuit silence; Trappist rule; Harpo Marx; Bucky Fuller

. . .

9/4/75   NC

. . .

PLEASURE—I have forgotten the rights of pleasure. Sexual pleasure. Getting pleasure out of my writing, and using pleasure as one criterion for what I choose to write.

I am an adversary writer, a polemical writer. I write to support what is attacked, to attack what is acclaimed. But thereby I put myself in an emotionally uncomfortable position. I don't, secretly, hope to convince, and can't help being dismayed when my minority taste (ideas) becomes majority taste (ideas): then I want to attack again. I can't help but be in an adversary relation to my own work.

The interesting writer is where there is an adversary, a problem. Why Stein is not, finally, a good or helpful writer. There is no problem. It's all affirmation. A rose is a rose is a rose.

Since Biblical times, to be connected with people sexually is a way of knowing them. In our century—for the first time—it is valued primarily as a way of knowing oneself. That's too much of a burden for the sexual act to carry.

. . .

PLEASURE   PURITY
           A conflict?

Pleasure wards off "apatheia," but is impure if not robust, is impure if willed

[*The English essayist William*] Hazlitt: "The American mind is deficient in natural imagination. The mind must be excited by overstraining, by pulleys and levers."

Films seen NYC

> Robert Altman, *Nashville* (1975)
> Norman Jewison, *Rollerball* (1975)
> [Nick Broomfield and Joan Churchill,] *Juvenile Liaison* (1976)
> John Ford, *Mary* [*of Scotland*] (1936)
> George Stevens, *Alice Adams* (1935)
> Woody Allen, *Love & Death* (1975)
> **** Eisenstein, *Ivan the Terrible, Part I*
> **   " " , *Part II*
> Renoir, *La Chienne* (1931)—Michel Simon
> Maysles brothers, *Grey Gardens* (1975)

Herzog, *Every Man for Himself + God Against All* (1974) —Bruno S.

Orson Welles, *Touch of Evil* (1958)

Bergman, *The Magic Flute*

[Howard Zieff,] *Hearts of the West* (1975)

Walter Hill, *Hard Times* (1975)—Charles Bronson, James Coburn

. . .

Kant the first to use the phrase "moral terrorism" (in a little book, published in 1798, called *The Disputation of the Faculties, Der Streit der Facultäten*)

Visit Paraguay for two weeks

"[*The twentieth-century American writer*] Iris Owens is like televison." (Stephen K[och])

. . .

1976

[Undated, February]

. . . Fits of lucidity

Grief can drive one mad

Foucault has wanted to do an essay on cemeteries—as utopias

. . . Every situation is defined by the amount of energy one puts into it—I put so much energy into my love, my hope—I am moved to put an equal amount into my grief, my sense of loss.

I must think about David—Yuyi [*an Argentine friend in Paris in the period*] said (rightly) that I don't describe him, I describe my relationship with him (us)—when she asked me to describe him, I felt blocked—embarrassed—as she were inviting me to describe the best part of myself. That's the key to the problem: I identify myself too much with him, him too much with myself. What a burden for him—all that admiraton, that confidence that I feel for (in) him.

I am convalescent—je [me] traîne—I'm looking for new sources of energy.

. . .

[*The German-American literary critic*] Erich Kahler wrote of [Thomas] Mann ten years before his death: "He is someone who feels a personal responsibility for the human condition."

•

. . . Yes, I am a Puritan. Twice over—American and Jew

•

It's not "natural" to speak well, eloquently, in an interesting articulate way. People living in groups, families, communes say little—have few verbal means. Eloquence—thinking in words—is a byproduct of solitude, deracination, a heightened painful individuality. In groups, it's more natural to sing, to dance, to pray: given, rather than invented (individual) speech.

•

. . .

2/18/76

The hot exaltations of the mind—

In youth, growing up, floated up by—with—the body; ageing or sick, the body drifting downwards, sinking or plummeting, leaving the self stranded, evaporating.

Half—or more—of all the human beings ever born are alive now, in this century.

Cioran: a Nietzschean Hazlitt.

•

2/22/76

. . . I need a mental gym.

. . .

6/1/76

Love affairs with their energy + hope [*SS means the doctors who were treating her for breast cancer.*]

When I can write letters, then . . .

•

Surgeon's green hospital shirt

•

[*This entry is emphasized by a horizontal line in the margin.*] Different kinds of texts, like a broken skyline.

Who, what do I get a boost from? Language, first of all. Among people, Joseph [Brodsky]. Books: Nietzsche, Lizzie's prose [*the fiction of Elizabeth Hardwick*]

Writing that is a grimace—virile, funny, shrewd. Not cynical. Malicious.

Beckett's subject: the poetry, the malice of senility.

. . .

6/14/76   Paris

The minimum utopia

Leaving time for meditating and grasping

—Are you faithful by temperament?
—Yes. I accumulate fidelities

Re: "The Dummy." It's a fable, a fairy-tale, rather than sci-fi. His choice (drop-out, clochard ["tramp"]) is that of a crippled person—is continuous with the dreary life he has rejected.

Models: [Virginia] Woolf, "An Unwritten Novel," [Robert] Walser, "Kleist in Thun," [Bruno] Schulz, "The Book."

•

. . .

Poets self-limited by some actual or mental regionalism, deliberately cultivated—so he / she will be seen to have [created] his / her "universe"

Weakness of American poetry—it's anti-intellectual. Great poetry has ideas.

6/19/76   New York

I returned Sunday night. Have been meditating helplessly, suffering compulsively. I squirm like a pinned insect. There is no help for it. I am afraid, paralyzed. I need:

Energy
Humility
Obstinacy
Discipline

All these together = courage.

Note that obstinacy + discipline are not the same. I have often been obstinate but I have no discipline at all.

. . .

Not only must I summon the courage to be a bad writer—I must dare to be truly unhappy. Desperate. And not save myself, short-circuit the despair.

By refusing to be as unhappy as I truly am, I deprive myself of subjects. I've nothing to write about. Every topic burns.

. . .

8/15/76

. . . Changes in the body, changes in language, changes in the sense of time. What does it mean for time to go faster, for it to seem to pass more slowly?

Jasper's observation that the reason time seems to go faster + faster as we get older is that we think in larger units. At forty, it's as easy to say "in five years" or "five years ago," as it was to say "in five months" or "five months ago" when one was fourteen.

Brodsky said there were two subjects: time and language.

. . .

8/30/76

[*Under a news photo of the former Black Panther leader Eldridge Cleaver:*] "Sceptical." Sceptical. Be sceptical.

(the key lesson of the 1970s)

"New" British novelists: B. S. Johnson, Ann Quin, David Plante, Christine Brooke-Rose, Brigid Brophy, Gabriel Josipovici

Saurian
Perplexed

Stendhal said he loved his mother "with a passion almost criminal"

9/3/76 Paris

Resemblance between J.-K. Huysmans' *Là-Bas* [*Down There*], published in 1891, and [J. G.] Ballard's *Crash*, published in 1973

Both are about Satanism; both describe and celebrate a Black Mass; both describe search for a metallic, transhuman sexuality;—but for Huysmans the tradition was already there, indeed it dated back to the Middle Ages, while for Ballard it is a "new" post-modern or futuristic sexuality or diabolism.

Both reject the modern.

Both acclaim the violation (self-violation) of the body.

Common sense (le bon sens) is always wrong. It is the dema- goguery of the bourgeois ideal. The function of common sense is to simplify, to reassure, to hide unpleasant truths and mysteries. I don't just mean that this is what common sense does, or ends up doing; I mean this is what it is designed to do. Of course, in order to be effective common sense must contain some part of the truth. But its main content is negative: To say (implicitly) that, this being so, that is not so.

Similarly, all polls of opinion must be superficial. They reveal the top of what people think, organized into common sense. What people really think is always partly hidden.

Only way to get at it is through a study of their language—a study in depth: its metaphors, structures, tone. And of their gestures, way of moving in space.

All orthodoxy, whether religious or political, is an enemy of language; all orthodoxy postulates "the usual expression."

Novalis' definition of Romanticism: to make the familiar appear strange, the marvelous appear commonplace

. . .

Beckett found a new subject for the drama:—what am I going to do in the next second? Weep, take out my comb, sigh, sit, be silent, tell a joke, die . . .

[Undated]

Duchamp: "There is no solution, because there is no problem." Cage, too. Stein.
Nonsense! Modernist-nihilist-wise-guy bullshit.

There are plenty of problems, everywhere you look.

[Undated]

(Conversation with Ted S[olotaroff])
1950s: Everyone wanted to be thirty—assume responsibility (marriage, kids, career), be serious.
We knew what our values were—we didn't know what our experience was
Trilling—the bad rabbi—made of bourgeois grief a tragic sense of life

11/5/76

[SS made remarkably few notes about her surgery and treatment for metastatic breast cancer between 1974 and 1977.]

Death is the opposite of everything.

Trying to race ahead of my death—to get in front of it, then turn around and face it, let it catch up with me, pass me, and *then* take my place behind it, walking in the right rhythm, stately, unsurprised.

Joseph B[rodsky]: Homosexuality ([*the Alexandrian poet Constatine P.*] Cavafy) a kind of maximalism.

The function of writing is to explode one's subject—transform it into something else. (Writing is a series of transformations.)

Writing means converting one's liabilities (limitations) into advantages. For example, I don't love what I'm writing. Okay, then—that's also a way to write, a way that can produce interesting results.

Writing like the five zig-zag lines of a [Oskar] Kokoschka [painting]—writing like the many different patterns of cross-hatching in [*an illustration by Gustave*] Doré.

The great American novels of the 20th century (that is, from 1920 on: post-James): [Dreiser's] *An American Tragedy*, [Dos Passos's] *USA*, [Faulkner's] *Light in August*.

Only thing Fitzgerald wrote that will last is *The Great Gatsby*—the rest (*Tender Is the Night, The Last Tycoon*) is midcult junk

Read [Robert] Frost's poem "Away"—

[Walt] Whitman > [Pablo] Neruda

Joyce, Thomas Wolfe ("Only the Dead Know Brooklyn") > [*the contemporary Colombian novelist Gabriel*] García Márquez Joseph: Latin American voice is a secondhand voice

An art of writing (that is, hearing): find the right tone of voice, the right *ennui*

Julian [*the last pagan Roman emperor, Julian the Apostate*], *Against the Galileans*

[*The early Christian historian*] Eusebius, "Eulogy on the Death of Constantine the Great"

Julian > Cavafy, Auden} theme of waning pluralist civ[ilization] vs. barbarian moralizing simplification

. . .

Terror incognita

Cavafy: "Ode to a Grecian Yearn" (Brodsky)

Protestant right-and-wrong vs. Catholic good-and-evil

Latin America has a tragic history, like Russia. The dictator, etc. A literature that writhes.

Misogyny in Barthes's writing

TB / cancer essay [*the book that became* Illness as Metaphor]

TB: consumed (dissolved) by passion—passion leads to dissolution of the body. It was tuberculosis but they called it love.

. . .

Intern at Memorial [*Memorial Sloan-Kettering Cancer Center in New York, where SS was operated on in 1974—a radical mastectomy and the removal of lymph nodes—and where she received chemotherapy and immunotherapy treatments for the following three years*]: "Cancer is a disease that doesn't knock at your door first." Disease as insidious, secret invasion.

Write aphoristically, with subheadings for sections (PASSION; INVASION; DEATH, etc.)—in form, midway between "Notes on Camp" and first essay on photography.

. . .

Patient at Memorial: "Physically I'm fine, medically I'm not."

. . .

(Read Gass essays when writing disease essay)

11/12/76

Technological reproduction not simply an "era," as Benjamin says. That's misleading. It has its history—rather, [it] is inserted into history. Its artifacts become "historical," not merely contemporary. Old litho[graphs], photos, comic books, movies, etc. are redolent of the past, not the present. B[enjamin] thought tech. rep[roduction] made everything into an eternal present—a Hegelian end-of-history (and abolition of history). Another four decades of living in this "era" has disproved this.

. . .

The range of recollection of a writer's work.

Poetry is the enunciation of universality—some poet said

Taste is contrapuntal, reactive (definition of taste)

Style comes into existence, only as it discovers a subject. True?

[*The Austrian art historian*] Alois Riegl (on form + design in industrial arts)

. . .

"This is *not* a subject: one delicate sensibility confronting the slimy, heartless, disappointing world. Go get yourself an agon." (me to Sigrid [*the American writer Sigrid Nunez*].)

. . .

[Rainer Maria Rilke's] *Malte Laurids Brigge*—the first "notational" novel. How important, premonitory, and underestimated it is.

Benjamin is neither a literary critic nor philosopher but an atheist theologian practicing his hermeneutical skills on culture.

Rivière's brilliant description of the Symbolist work of art— he describes what should be abandoned (as exhausted; too elitist; lazy; too life-denying) but I'm still in the grip of the Symbolist mentality . . . Proust included everything the Symbolists understood but still wrote a novel.

I'm looking for new forms of advocacy.

. . .

12/8/76

. . . "To think is to exaggerate."—Valéry

. . .

All orthodoxy, whether religious or political, is an enemy of language; all orthodoxy postulates "the usual expression."
Cf. China

. . .

12/12/76

. . . Voltaire's defense of Desfontaines. Saved from being burned alive, the penalty for homosexuality.

Mass suicide of ruling elite in Java (Bali?) in 1906

. . .

American culture is hospitable to the feminist revendications [*"claims, demands"*] (up to a point) in a way that European countries (e.g. France, Germany) are not because of the American cult of the individual—the right of the individual, of individual self-fulfillment.

1977

"If you want to be quoted, don't quote." (JB [Joseph Brodsky])

•

. . .

"All art aspires to the condition of music"—this utterly nihilistic statement rests at the foundation of every moving camera style in the history of the medium. But it is a cliché, a 19th c[entury] cliché, less an aesthetic than a projection of an exhausted state of mind, less a world view than a world weariness, less a statement of vital forms than an expression of sterile decadence. There is quite another pov [point of view] about what "all art aspires to"—that was Goethe's, who put the primary art, the most aristocratic one, + the one art that cannot be made by the plebes but only gaped at w[ith] awe, + that art is architecture. Really great directors have this sense of architecture in their work—always expressive of immense line of energy, unstable + vital conduits of force.

2/9/77

Title for cancer / TB essay:

"The Discourse of Illness"
    or
"Illness as Metaphor"

A good poem will have romantic form + modern content.
(Brodsky)

To think only about oneself is to think of death.

The egoism of modernism

    fantasies
    solipsism

The novel (19th century >) implies

    interest in the world (not solipsistic)
    ability to pass judgments on human behavior
        (moralistic)
    patience

Proust (the biggest, greatest work of prose fiction straddles
both worlds—is about the world and is about solipsism)

Novelist as moralist: Austen, [George] Eliot, Stendhal, Tolstoy, Dostoyevsky, Proust, DH L[awrence]

Modernist novel comes into being when no judgment seems
tenable (e.g. *Anna Karenina*: marriage is good, passion destroys). We always think of counter-examples.

Tolstoyan conception of the novel has been abandoned to the dummies (James Michener, etc.) at the apex of which is Gore Vidal. The track record of modernism—the "art novel"—is infinitely better. But it's at a dead end. What we have now is a codified orthodoxy of modernism (John Barth, *Lost in the Funhouse*; Sarraute; Coover, *Pricksongs & Descants*—they're not writing about anything.)

Problem of writing a novel now: No story seems that important to tell.
Why?
Because we are unable to draw any moral (meaning: judgment) from it.

Tolstoy has subjects: the nature of marriage (*Anna Karenina*); of history, etc. (*War + Peace*)

If no story[, no] narrative seems that important or necessary. The only material that seems to have any character of inevitability is the writer's own consciousness.

18th century:

> "reason" not motivational
> distinction between a sentiment and passion/
> emotion; sentiments are calm passions
> (e.g. benevolence, self-interest, sympathy)—
> see [the Earl of] Shaftesbury, [David] Hume,
> and Rousseau
> discovery of the plasticity of the emotions

[*In the margin:*] imagination as a moral faculty

Compare the Greeks:

> reason is motivational
> emotions are of two types—those expressing the
>   person + those understood as invasive, alien
>   (we don't make this distinction—everything
>   is "inner")
> little emphasis on the plasticity of the emotions.

[*In the margin:*] Cf. [Aristotle's] *Nic*[*omachean*] *Ethics*

. . .

2/20/77

Two experiences yesterday—lunch with [*the English–West Indian writer V. S.*] Naipaul and reading [*the Russian formalist Boris*] Eikhenbaum's *The Young Tolstoy*—remind me of how undisciplined and demoralized I am.

Starting tomorrow—if not today:

> I will get up every morning no later than eight.
>   (Can break this rule *once* a week.)
> I will have lunch only with Roger [Straus].
>   ("No, I don't go out for lunch." Can break
>   this rule once every two weeks.)
> I will write in the Notebook every day.
>   (Model: Lichtenberg's *Waste Books*.)
> I will tell people not to call in the morning,
>   or not answer the phone.

I will try to confine my reading to the evening.
(I read too much—as an escape from writing.)
I will answer letters once a week.
(Friday?—I have to go to the hospital anyway.)

. . .

2/21/77

Things I like: fires, Venice, tequila, sunsets, babies, silent films, heights, coarse salt, top hats, large long-haired dogs, ship models, cinnamon, goose down quilts, pocket watches, the smell of newly mown grass, linen, Bach, Louis XIII furniture, sushi, microscopes, large rooms, ups, boots, drinking water, maple sugar candy.

Things I dislike: sleeping in an apartment alone, cold weather, couples, football games, swimming, anchovies, mustaches, cats, umbrellas, being photographed, the taste of licorice, washing my hair (or having it washed), wearing a wristwatch, giving a lecture, cigars, writing letters, taking showers, Robert Frost, German food.

Things I like: ivory, sweaters, architectural drawings, urinating, pizza (the Roman bread), staying in hotels, paper clips, the color blue, leather belts, making lists, Wagon-Lits, paying bills, caves, watching ice-skating, asking questions, taking taxis, Benin art, green apples, office furniture, Jews, eucalyptus trees, pen knives, aphorisms, hands.

Things I dislike: Television, baked beans, hirsute men, paperback books, standing, card games, dirty or disorderly apartments, flat pillows, being in the sun, Ezra Pound, freckles, violence in movies, having drops put in my eyes, meatloaf, painted nails, suicide, licking envelopes, ketchup, traversins [*"bolsters"*], nose drops, Coca-Cola, alcoholics, taking photographs.

Things I like: drums, carnations, socks, raw peas, chewing on sugar cane, bridges, Dürer, escalators, hot weather, sturgeon, tall people, deserts, white walls, horses, electric typewriters, cherries, wicker / rattan furniture, sitting cross-legged, stripes, large windows, fresh dill, reading aloud, going to bookstores, under-furnished rooms, dancing, *Ariadne auf Naxos*.

2/22/77

. . .

I'm polite to too many people because I'm not angry enough. I'm not angry enough because I don't push my ideas far enough. The comfortable refuge of "pluralism," "dialogue," etc.

My refusal of intransigence. I lose energy thereby—every day.

The great intransigent arguments—SW [Simone Weil], Artaud, Adorno (in *The Philosophy of Modern Music*). I don't think I'm obliged to agree or disagree. They're my amphetamine, my points "de rigueur." I work in relation to those extremes, but, by self-definition—my own views are not extreme.

Too easy a way out? I'm not exerting myself.

The great question of pleasure. How "serious" a view is one to have of it? To what extent do moral criteria apply? Nobody wants to be known as a puritan, and yet . . .

Cf. Adorno's denunciation of pleasure in music as morally corrupt, historically reactionary

Didn't I feel this about [*the American theater director Robert Wilson's opera*] *Einstein on the Beach*— And yet I was pleased (glad) to be able to enjoy it.

Remember that Adorno is writing in 1940–41 (the awareness of Nazi horrors—and those unresolved; he is a refugee). The author of *The Philosophy of Modern Music* is the same person who wrote (in 1947) that there could be no poetry after Auschwitz. He would have said that in consumer society of Europe of the 60s.

. . .

For "aesthetic way of looking at the world"—see Hugo Ball's *Flight Out of Time: A Dada Diary* . . .

2/23/77

. . .

Story Irene told me about being robbed + raped four years ago. In her building: as she was returning home about 1 a.m. getting into the elevator, a black man forced it open. She screamed. "If you scream again, I'll kill you." Took her to the eighth (top) floor, then halfway up stairs leading to the roof. Then blindfolded her.

I asked, "Did you get excited sexually?" She said yes—then said I was the first person she'd ever told that story to who'd asked her that. "But it's such an obvious question," I said.

The next day (today) I called her. "I was saying how stupid your friends are," I said, "but I was thinking now that it was because you told me it happened four years ago—+ you obviously were OK, not traumatized, talked about it so coolly—that it was easy to ask that."

. . .

2/25/77

University of Chicago education: no idea of "the modern." Texts, ideas, arguments—exist in a timeless dialogue. The basic themes or questions are those stated by Plato and Aristotle (relation of theory and practice; one or many sciences; relation of virtue and knowledge, etc. etc.) and the moderns are interesting, valuable so far as they too discuss those themes. (We read Bentham, Mill, Dewey, [Rudolf] Carnap.)

The most radical opposite to the timeless, which starts with the category of "the modern." The basic themes or questions are those stated at the beginning of the modern era (by Rousseau; Hegel) and previous thinkers are interesting, valuable so far as they contrast with the moderns.

With historicist approach, you ask different questions. (Historicism *changes* the questions—and destroys the themes.) As N[ietzsche] saw, historicism is a fundamentally destructive pov [point of view]. For example, Foucault: the very subject of the human sciences ("man") is destroyed.

. . .

[Undated, March]

[The following is a series of notes on kitsch, dating from the mid- to late 1970s. Because of their interest, I have included them here, but I cannot be certain when SS wrote them.]

A word that has the power to hurt—e.g. kitsch—is still alive

Kitsch not just a quality of things—also a *process*
Things "become" kitsch

Kitsch as a historical category: when category of "authentic" becomes imp[ortant]—in 19th century

Japan as a theater of kitsch (Terry)

W B[enjamin]'s "aura" is a kitsch image.

Kitsch is not a stylistic but a meta-stylistic category
Relation of Russian "Poshlost" to "kitsch"

•

Is there a necessary role of kitsch in democratic politics / epistemology?

Cf. Tocqueville (*easy* to criticize totalitarian kitsch)

. . .

[Walter] Kaufmann: Kitsch is innocent

Bad art is *not* the same as kitsch—e.g. acres of bad paintings in Italian 15th + 16th c[enturies].

. . .

Pol[itical] religion is the natural world of kitsch

2 types

1) May Day parade ([Milan] Kundera)—"Long Live Life."
2) Burial of Horst Wessel ([Nazi] SA activist killed in a brawl with a Communist pimp in Hamburg [*sic*]; lay for a month dying in hospital: agony— Goebbels visited him every day (described by the American historian [Charles] Beard in journal article)

Burial at Berlin Nickolay cemetery depicted in *Hans Westmar* (Nazi movie of early 1930s)

Myth invented by *Goebbels*
Myth of resurrection + return

. . .

Disneyland + Nuremberg rallies are 2 diff[erent] types of kitsch

. . .

3/6/77

Essay to do: on Marxist (moralist) approach to art. (Complement to essay on "the aesthetic view of the world")

Texts:

> [*The Italian writer, politician, philosopher, and
>   linguist Antonio*] Gramsci
> [*The British Marxist art critic Christopher*] Cauldwell
>   (Stalinist, philistine)
> Benjamin

4/19/77

Clear = what one already knows
Obscure = a meaning one doesn't want to attend to

Copying out ten pages from [Proust's] *Le Temps Retrouvé* (to imprint them—like books one reads before the age of fifteen):

Proust didn't know he was writing the greatest novel ever written. (Neither did his contemporaries, even the most admiring, like Rivière.) And it wouldn't have done him any good if he had. But he did want to write something great.

I want to write something great.

I'm not ambitious enough. (It's not just a question of becoming truly intransigent.) I want to be good, liked, etc. I'm afraid of allowing real feeling, real arrogance, selfishness.

I want to sing.

I said it already, in the first thing I wrote for *PR* [*Partisan Review*] on [*the Yiddish-language writer Isaac Bashevis*] Singer. To hell with modern catatonia.

I have more than enough intelligence, learning, vision. The obstacle is character: boldness.

Ruthlessness

Duchamp: too smart to be a painter, like Leonardo; but destroys, parodies—instead of constructs. Leonardo, the great constructor; Duchamp, the great de-constructor. Same fascination with machines, but Duchamp's is entirely playful, nihilistic . . .

[Undated, July]

"The adjective is the enemy of the noun."—Flaubert

7/12/77

Project: convert my photographer's eye (mute) into a poet's eye, which hears—words. I see concretely; I write abstractly. The project: to have access, as a writer, to that concreteness. The clot of light on Bob S.'s [Robert Silvers] nose at dinner tonight in the Indian restaurant.

7/19/77

Story about a sorcerer (female)

What is most American about me (Emerson, etc.) is my faith in the possibility of radical change.

Joseph [Brodsky] said that when he began writing he consciously competed with other poets. Now I'll write a poem that will be better (more profound) than [Boris] Pasternak (or [Anna] Akhmatova—or Frost—or Yeats—or Lowell, etc.) And now? I asked. "Now I'm arguing with angels."

The importance of being envious, competitive. I don't try hard enough.

After THE LAST PHONE CALL FROM NICOLE, tonight

Let it hurt, let it hurt.

So this isn't my front door any longer. Then walk away.

Remember: this could be my one chance, and the last, to be a first-rate writer.

One can never be alone enough to write. To see better.

In a sense—in one sense—I was wasting my time the last three years w[ith] Nicole. I knew that—still wanted to do it. Now that that possibility is no longer available to me, though . . .

7/20/77

To be noble-minded. To be profound. Never to be "nice."

Stories (to write):

> [*Frank O'Hara's poem*] ~~"In Memories of My Feelings"~~
>   [*sic*]
> "Portrait of the Historian"
> "Speed"
> "Arguing with Angels"
> "And Mondays with Mahatma Gandhi."

DURCHHALTEN (hold fast)—D[avid] left me a note beside my bed

. . . The huge enrichment of the imagination and hence of language that comes with solitude.

8/4/77

Each cultural moment has zones of mystery:
—the island
—the scientist's laboratory

8/11/77

"Mais je t'aime" = "je ne veux pas te perdre complètement"
[*"But I love you"* = *"I don't want to lose you completely"*]

To say something is interesting—to postpone having to pass a more definite judgment: say that it's good or bad
A term that has its widest currency in the Duchamp-influenced art world. Cage, etc.

Or to make judgment irrelevant

. . .

8/21/77

. . .

Dinner w[ith] [*the American photographer Richard*] Avedon: "The past is completely unreal to me. I live only in the present + the future. Is that why I look young?"

Dorian Gay [*sic*]

. . .

9/8/77

. . .

4-page weekly newspaper I wrote and published (Hectograph) and sold for 5¢ a copy when I was 9, 10, 11 years old.

Fear of—irritation with—images in conversation. I'm already thinking, visualizing one thing; abruptly, I'm made to see something else. [*The American writer*] Walker Percy telling me how to get to his house from New Orleans. "Take the Pontchartrain Bridge—26 miles—straight as a string." I'm visualizing the bridge, the plantation house, the bayou, the moss-covered trees. Suddenly there's this damned string . . . Paul [Thek] today, talking about sexual attitudes. "And that's the bottom card." Later, slumping down, his arms dangling. "They cut my strings." (More strings!)

9/17/77

CONTEMPT, not indignation

> "There is only one thing I dread; not to be worthy of my sufferings."
>
> —Dostoyevsky

> "There is only one thing I dread; that my sufferings will not be worthy of me."
>
> —Sontag

Bresson, in *Notes on Cinematography*, quotes Leonardo as saying: in an artistic context all that matters is the end.

Athletes, dancers—having a romance with their bodies

Apollinaire compares Eiffel Tower + Paris roofs to a shepherd + sheep. Image that reduces things to their geography.

The cave of the self.

Emily Dickinson said that "Art is a house that tries to be haunted."
Now it doesn't have to try.

So it's a question of time—when the image comes. It should precede or be simultaneous w[ith] the picture. Otherwise, it's distracting.

9/20/77

Alcohol: to reverse a feeling.

Cal's [*Robert Lowell's*] poetry. How sad it is. All about loss. He was born old.

I, plus shell: child, adolescent, adult

"Let's see if I can produce a little theory."

Thoreau on his death bed—on being asked what were his feelings about the next world: "One world at a time."

There is no first-rate poet now writing in English.

The Russians didn't have an 18th century.

Joseph [Brodsky]:

His great love, the mother of his son: Marina (Marianne) [Basmanova]

He read Beckett when?

"Each time you find the line you're looking for it makes it harder next time."

Glory, glory, glory.

He likes prose writers who are failed poets. E.g. Nabokov

"If I look at anything longer than two seconds, it becomes absurd."

. . .

"Each thing pees on itself."

"Being with others—intimately—I'm deprived of a certain spiritual nutriment which I need for the work."

"The Other Land—language."

[Undated]

Joseph re: Derek [*the West Indian poet Derek Walcott*]
[You] have to shove him a little to get him in focus; then he
    can think.
For him everything is phenomenal, not cultural
Like flowers, no soil
He doesn't make connections
He can't learn anything
He's lazy

9/26/77

Conversation with [*the American painter R. B.*] Kitaj at Bob's [Robert Silvers]. Spoke of "transcendent" art. Not possible if one doesn't know how to draw (and that's no longer taught in art schools). Last great painters were Picasso + Matisse. Best living painter(s): Bacon (+ Balthus). Only interested in depictive painting, figure painting. Whole 19th century French tradition referred itself to Ingres—Impressionism not possible without him. And who can draw like that now? Among contemporaries like Lucien Freud, Frank Auerbach, David Hockney—in England; de Kooning only American painter he mentioned. "But what are we talking about if we think of Rembrandt? And that's the standard against which we should be measuring contemporary painters." Also: many painters did their best work when they were old—Michelangelo, Titian, Goya, Tintoretto, Rembrandt, Turner, Monet, Matisse, maybe (despite current view) Picasso.

Painting as craft.

Don Barthelme: "I don't need a rule to tell me that I musn't strangle swans . . ." After watching the thief from the Jeans Store being caught—"I hope they're not going to lynch him with tied-together jeans."

10/11/77

Story Sonia Orwell told me today about the daughter of a very minor Politburo member—about to be married—"I don't want another boring Moscow wedding!"—500 guests flown in gov[ernmen]t planes to a Caspian Sea villa where wedding was held—footmen in livery (breeches, stockings, etc.), a servant behind every guest's chair, maids in white caps—the regalia of the ancien régime in 1977. Were the servants cynical, or were they enjoying themselves.

. . .

11/23/77   Houston

[SS was the houseguest of the art collector and patron Dominique de Menil. Some of the artworks mentioned in the following entry were in the de Menil house.]

At the beginning, there was no abstract art. If it seems abstract to us (e.g. violin shape which is a female idol), it's because we are ignorant, + don't know how to read the object.

Celtic head (wood, from Ireland)—6th century?—which looks Maori.

Gold coins from pre-Merovingian (?) Gaul—or earlier??—which provide basis for Romanesque art.

Face of Alexander; Pegasus, etc.
Désamorcelé [*"taken apart"*] like a Picasso.

Bones (animals) from 30,000 BC with animals incised in them—imagery like Lascaux.

S.W. [Simone Weil] is profound, not just extremely intelligent. Compassion was general, for classes of people.
[*In the margin:*] *not* [George] Orwell.
Unlike Van Gogh: neurosis prevented her from living out her passionate compassion with individuals. But then, Van Gogh didn't have a mind anywhere as good as hers.

When the sun comes out, you don't see the moon any longer. (You don't solve the problem; it no longer exists.) I'm looking for the sun.

The letters of Van Gogh—like having the letters of Prince Mishkin

. . .

Promised Lands is a portrait of trauma . . .

[Evgeny] Baratinsky: Russian poet ("rather English," according to Joseph), friend of Pushkin

12/4/77   Venice [*SS had come to attend the Venice Biennale*]

Clear day, cleansing cold—the night comes early—I've never seen Venice more beautiful.

[*The Italian writer Alberto*] Moravia met me at the airport; [*the British poet and SS's friend*] Stephen Spender was just leaving. First dinner with [*the French poet and essayist*] Claude Roy + [*the French actress and playwright*] Loleh Bellon + Geörgy Konrád (Hungarian writer) in Do Pozzi Hotel, after an hour at Florian's [café]. Joseph's reading at the Teatro Ateneo from 9–11 p.m. I had shivers when he stood up and declaimed his poems. He chanted, he sobbed; he looked magnificent. Boris Godunov; Gregorian chant; Hebrew moan. After, 2nd dinner with Joseph and walk. Then to Hotel Europa for the first time, at 2 p.m. N[icole]'s call!

Nietzsche's main subject (?) was genius. He knew what genius was; he understood its pride, its euphoric states, its megalomania, its purity, its ruthlessness. He made it into a theory of history. (Subsequently the Germans made it into a politics.) He thought he was a genius, but, unlike Shakespeare and Michelangelo, he never wrote the Great Work. *Zarathustra* is his worst book; it's kitsch. The great N[ietzsche] is in the essays—mostly fragments.

Two kinds of writers. Those who think this life is all there is, and want to describe everything: the fall, the battle, the accouchement, the horse-race. That is, Tolstoy. And those who think this life is a kind of testing-ground (for what we don't know—to see how much pleasure + pain we can bear or what pleasure + pain are?) and want to describe only the essentials. That is, Dostoyevsky. The two alternatives. How can one write like T. after D.? The task is to be as good as D.—as serious spiritually, + then go on from there.

But, to give credit to Tolstoy, he knew something was wrong. Hence, he ended by repudiating his great novels. Couldn't meet his own spiritual demands as an *artist*. So he renounced art for action (a spiritual life). D. never could have repudiated his art, for moral reasons, because he knew how to reach a higher spiritual level with his art.

Only thing that counts are ideas. Behind ideas are [moral] principles. Either one is serious or one is not. Must be prepared to make sacrifices. I'm not a liberal.

Something wrong with the idea of "dissident" art. It's defined by the authorities. Abstract painting is dissident in the USSR, the art of large corporations in the US; in Poland it's been tolerated, even fashionable for twenty years. Nothing contestataire in itself about any content (?) or any style, e.g. abstract *or* figurative.

No panel discussions or debates here at the Biennale. Just papers—not coordinated with each other, mimeographed copies of which are distributed the minute after the speaker stops.

Solzhenitsyn is a genuinely epic writer; also completely eclectic in style (uses 19th c. language, Party language, etc.). Mixes genres: soc[ialist] realist novel, essay, satire, tirade, Dostoyevskian philosophical novel. His greatness depends on that scope.

Joke about Fidel [Castro] addressing rally right after Revolution, urging everyone to get to work + build socialism. "Trabajo si, rumba no." [*Work yes, rumba no.*] And the crowd roars back: "Trabajo si, rumba no. Tra-ba-jo si, rum-ba no. Tra-ba-jo-si, rum-ba-no."

Joseph: "Censorship is good for writers. For three reasons. One, it unites the whole nation as (or into) readers. Two, it gives the writer limits, something to push against. Three, it increases metaphoric powers of the language (the greater the censorship, the more Aesopian the writing must become)."

The status of the Jews in one brief joke. A. They're given an order to kill all the Jews + all the barbers. B. Why the barbers?

12/5/77

. . .

György Konrád looks so much like Jacob [Taubes]—as soon as I saw him yesterday afternoon, I was attracted + repelled; and this morning, late breakfast à deux at Florian's later joined by Joseph—I discover that, of course, he was the man with whom Susan [Taubes] had an affair when she was in Budapest in August 1969.

At 2 a.m. walking from the Locanda Montin to the Accademia, across the bridge, through the Campo Santo Stefano, back to the hotel: —light snow, silence, the empty streets, the fog, thrilling cold—so much beauty. Like breathing pure oxygen.

. . .

Italian expression for being groped: "la mano morta" [*"the dead hand"*].

Influence of [*the Russian-born French writer*] Boris Souvarine on Simone Weil. Souvarine wrote a book denouncing Stalin in 1934—was rejected by Malraux, the reader at Gallimard, with these words: "Vous et vos amis avez raison, Souvarine, et je serai de vos côtes quand vous êtes les plus forts." [*"You and your friends are right, Souvarine, and I will be on your side when you're the strongest."*] (Book not published in France until 1938.)

[*In the margin:*] *The three evils—misogyny (sexism), anti-Semitism, and anti-intellectualism—against which I struggle.*

Dissidence is a relationship (not relative) notion.

Joseph: "I feel like crying all the time."

Prisoners in the camps [*the Soviet Gulag*] speak a lot about absolutes—futile absolutes. The greatest fuck in the world. The metal that can cut through any prison bars (strip of metal in the soles of shoes issued in the 1950s). The other side of powerlessness.

[Pavel] Filonov—Russian artist of the 20s (continued until 1950s) whom Joseph considers greater than Tatlin, El Lissitzky, etc.

Russian Constructivists of 20s: good . . . and yet. Industrial narcissism.

An artist should be professional enough to be able to do anything well.

The exiled writer from Eastern Europe. Here, in the West, nothing menaces but everything is hostile.

Joseph: "Then I realized what I am. I am somebody who took the idea of individuality literally." His Eugene Onegin side again.

"Courage" is a word one can only use in the third person. Can't say "I am brave / courageous." Can say she or he is. It's a word about actions, a way of interpreting behavior. It does not describe any subjective state. "Fear," par contre, is a first person adjective. Can say / feel "I am afraid."

Many Russians get out now by marrying Jews. In the Soviet Union Jews are a means of transport.

12/6/77

The smell of wet stones. The rain. The lapping of the water against the "fondamenta" [*"a street parallel to a canal"*]. The peaceful groan of the vaporetto as it starts up. The fog. The sound of footsteps. Seven gondolas like black crows; parked in the narrow canal, waddling, lolling.

Only negative ideas are useful. "Ideas are a means of transport. Only ideas which a means of transport are my concern."

One feels "I wrote a bad story" but not "I wrote a good story." The latter is for the others. At most one feels, I didn't write a bad book . . . The same for courage. One doesn't feel "I was brave." One feels "I wasn't afraid." Or, at least it didn't show. I didn't act on my fear.

He [Claude Roy] is tired. He's known everybody.

The poet-in-exile [Brodsky], born in Leningrad, walking alone on the wet empty streets at two in the morning. It reminds him, "a little bit," of Leningrad.

Even though I feel like one, I'm not an only child. So my mother's narcissism, absences, inability to nurture was less damaging than it might have been. I saw she did it even more to my sister. I didn't take it "personally." I could say: I have *this* kind of mother. Not: she treats me badly, she doesn't love me because I'm not / don't have (these qualities). From an early age I learned to be "objective."

When I understand something completely, it goes dead. Hence, I am drawn to "exile." Being at home means knowing at each step what is possible. Events have an underpinning, a cushion of the possible. You turn the corner and you are not surprised.

Instead of "dissident" art, "non-authorized" or "unauthorized" art?

All political language is alienated. Political language as such is the enemy. (Joseph's position)

A world in which there are dissidents everywhere + they are free. Or a world in which dissidence is no longer necessary (i.e. a good society). These are the two ideals presumed here— entirely opposite.

. . .

12/7/77

What we call nihilism (now) I simply thought. What thinking doesn't lead to nihilism?

Everyone talks of rights (human rights, etc) . . .

. . . There is only social thinking (accepting "society") or individualism—a profoundly asocial view of the world.

The lonely figures everywhere—many of whom wouldn't have liked each other—who uphold the asocial position. Oscar Wilde. Benjamin. Adorno. Cioran.

True that Benjamin used a communist language in the last years of his life, so he looks different to us now. But that's because he died in 1940. Those last years were the ones in which communist language regained authority—seen as necessary to fight fascism (identified as The Enemy). Had Benjamin lived as long as Adorno [he] w[oul]d have become as a-social, as disillusioned with left as Adorno did.

(Dinner with Joseph + Roberto Calasso, head of Adelphi Publishers in Milan. Lunch was with [*the Polish theater critic*] Jan Kott + [*the scholar of Russian Literature*] Victor Erlich. Breakfast was with [*the Swiss journalist*] François + [his wife] Lillian Bondy.)
Roberto Calasso's story about John Cage's recent performance in Milan—2½ hours of nonsense syllables drawn from a Thoreau text—before an audience of 2000 people in the Lirico, biggest theater in Milan. Almost a lynching. It started after 20 minutes. At one point there were a hundred people on the stage—someone put a blindfold on Cage then took it off.

No one left. And throughout Cage never moved, went on reading at the table on the stage. Everyone cheered. It was a triumph.

Cage wants to put some emptiness in the middle of all the sense. [*In the margin, SS repeats "the sense" and adds an excla-mation point.*] He's not a musician but a genial destroyer. The empty cage.

•

When there is no censorship the writer has no importance.

So it's not so simple to be against censorship.

•

A lateral idea

•

The rhetorics of communism + nihilism. People who want to be good + [people] who want to be bad are both going in the same direction.

Both Marx + Freud were wrong. The one who was right is Malthus. Whatever happens, what's in front is a more repres-sive society . . . The 19th century wouldn't recognize the soci-ety we live in.

•

. . .

The fog. Standing in front of Museo Correr, looking across the Piazza San Marco and not seeing the Basilica. A new, surreal Venice in the fog: cut in segments, and then reassembled with the "far" parts missing (some of the parts missing).

12/8/77

Spiritual exercises: lowering the ideas into the body. Making it part of one's instincts. Can't be a Buddhist or Hindu without changing one's physiology.

•

The high water. Planks in the Piazza San Marco. The water is greener, more transparent in the canals. Staircases under water. The water tilts, rolls, laps, sways, slaps the stone.

Difference between cruelty and oppression. Nazis institutionalized cruelty—proclaimed evil (the SS death's-head insignia)—maimed and tortured bodies, killed as a matter of policy / principle. Nothing was ever as cruel, as heartless as Auschwitz. But a Stalinist regime is more oppressive because more politicized. Less space for the private. A rhetoric of the good rather than of evil.

"aria fritta" = fried air (confusion)

T. S. Eliot: to judge an art by religious standards + a religion by aesthetic standards may well be applying the best criteria we have
[*In the margin:*] "They become metaphors."

•

. . .

The sacred nature of the word

[*The Russian poet and writer Osip*] Mandelstam one of the great prose writers of the 20th century—w[ould] be one of the century's greatest writers even if he'd never written any poetry.

"Neither from the left nor from the right but from some extra-terrestrial place . . ."

•

[Inserted in the pages from the entries for 12/8/77.]

1713

André Breton in the early 1940s called up Meyer Schapiro to ask him if Newton's treatise on light was published in 1713; was exceedingly disappointed when Schapiro said it wasn't. Had wanted to put the date, as a signature, in painting.

Schapiro knew, collected the paintings of [*the German-American artist*] Jan Müller (d. 1958)

. . .

•

12/9/77

A great subject for a novel: the temptation (corruption) of the good. Communism. Who will be the Solzhenitsyn of the "clercs communisants" ["*communizing clerks*"] of the West?

Pound > Lowell. Poetry should be a record of everything that comes into your head.

•

Visit with Joseph to [*Ezra Pound's companion*] Olga Rudge between 5 + 8 pm—252 San Gregorio (near Salute)

Olga Rudge always referred to Eliot as "Possum . . ." Said that Pound was not contrite or penitent in the years between his release from St. Elizabeths and his death . . . With a hint of tears in her eyes, she paused (only once) and said: "You know, Ezra was right. He was right. There's too much democracy. There's too much free speech . . ." Said that [*the American writer*] Natalie Barney [*in the margin:* knew Djuna Barnes] spent most of the war in Rapallo, as Pound's guest . . . In the tiny living room she has [Henri] Gaudier-Brzeska's big bust of Pound (on the floor) + the Wyndham Lewis drawing of Pound . . . She insisted on the fact that Pound had a "Jewish first name" and didn't change it—"from the beginning—his first book—he signed himself 'Ezra Pound,' not 'E. Loomis Pound' or 'Loomis Pound'" and that the Loomises were a good family ("Look in the New York Social Register; you'll see many Loomises."). "A biblical name," I said. "That's right, a Jewish name. So if Ezra were an anti-Semite, as people say, he wouldn't have kept that Jewish name, now would he?"

She has an English accent. She says, "Capito?" after many sentences.

". . . I'm like the ancient mariner," she said at the door. Joseph + I, in our coats, had been standing there for fifteen minutes while she went on without a stop. "Now what was his story about? Oh, yes, wasn't it something about a dead bird?" A closing line she must have used many times.

Sinyavsky not only brought out his family from the Soviet Union but hundreds of books and his black poodle Matilda. His wife has been back several times. A deal was made.

An inscription in a copy of Cal's writing—a line drawn through "Robert Lowell" on the title page and underneath: "For Ezra, with love and admiration, more than for any other." CAL

•

New occupation: a free-lance drug designer.

Every century (era) invents its own noble savages. Ours are the Third World.

[*A vertical line is next to this entry:*] Joseph: "Akhmatova used to say, 'When I was young I loved architecture + water; now I love the earth and music.' "

Creaking of the vaporetto piers, audible at night, when the boat unloads. Cooing of gulls riding the water. The damp smells. The left side of the basilica, black and white, that is better + more sharply seen at night than in the daytime. One sees too much in the day. The senses are sharper at night.

Calvin was a spiritual aristocrat. I like his verticality. Luther was a slob. He didn't even see the point of what he was destroying.

[Carlo] Ripa di Meana [*the director of the Venice Biennale*] (smiling a little): "As you know, Italians don't drink lion juice for breakfast."

When I say that I hate stupidity what I really mean is that I can't stand spiritual vulgarity. But it would be vulgar to say *that.*

12/10/77

I'm reading [Beckett's] *Malone Dies.* That's prose that changes your life—that is, the way you write. How can anyone write the same in English after reading that?

György Konrád: "L'écrivain qui a des positions militantes est un masochiste: il se prive de ses propres dons." [*"The writer who takes militant (political) positions is a masochist. He deprives himself of his own gifts."*]

My political positions: all adversary. I am against (1) violence—+, in particular, colonialist wars and imperialist "interventions." Above all, against torture. (2) Sexual and racial discrimination. (3) The destruction of nature and the landscape (mental, architectural) of the past. (4) Whatever impedes or censors the {movement of people, art, ideas.

                    {transport

(If I'm for anything, it is—simply—the decentralization of power. Plurality.)

In short, the classic libertarian / conservative / radical position. I can be no more. I should not want to be more. I am not interested in "constructing" any new form of society, or joining any party. There is no reason for me to try to locate myself on either the left or the right—or to feel I should. That shouldn't be my language.

•

I feel guilty when I don't write, and that I don't write "enough." Why? What's this "guilt"? Joseph says the same of himself. Why should you feel guilty, I asked? "Because I used to write 20 good poems a year. Now I write only 7 or 10—though they're mostly better than what I used to write."

I accuse Joseph of doing his *Ninotchka* number [*Ernst Lubitsch's 1939 comedy starring Greta Garbo as a Soviet agent*]. (Which corner of the room is mine? [*a paraphrased line from the film*] etc.)

Ripa de Meana: "Intellectuals in Europe have a Tabasco role." Are, inevitably, drawn to extreme positions.

The enemy is the thought: All problems are, finally, political problems. And, therefore, to be solved by political means.

•

"Nothing survives in the same form" ([*the French Marxist literary critic*] Pierre Macherey). Until recently the main form in which G[ree]k art survived in Western society was as a hegemonic ideal, through what Marx refers to as its capacity to "count as a norm and as an unattainable model."

[*The following entry has a box drawn around it:*] Art in the West: this once unwanted, but now accepted, telescope into ourselves.

•

In 17th + 18th century, Greek art functioned as essentially an attainable model. With the industrial revolution it begins to acquire attributes as unattainable (an "ideal"). Now the classics have been replaced by the study of national literatures. "The home of the totality has become literary criticism." ([*The contemporary English critic and historian*] Perry Anderson)

•

The formalist method: suitable for those ignorant of, or indifferent to, history. This, surely, is part of its appeal now. One doesn't need to be "learned" to understand a literary text or a painting, only intelligent. One doesn't need more than the work itself.

12/12/77

Churches: San Silvestro (in Piazza San S[ilvestro]). And Sant'Ignazio (in Piazza Sant'I[gnazio]. [Rome]): Baroque (Counter-Reformation, Jesuit) folie. The ceiling that is too high—the vertiginous scene—the false cupola (trompe l'oeil) that's right only from the center of the church! And now you have to pay 100 lire to see it!

•

Beckett the opposite of Joyce. Get smaller, more precise, fuss-
ier, bleaker . . . smaller and briefer. Could one be the opposite
of Beckett now? That is, not Joyce. But not only bleak; and
larger, and less *old*—

[Dated only "Note from 1977"]

So far as it is really denied, death becomes the most important
thing. (Like anything which is denied.) It is nowhere, and it is
everywhere. While we deny death, the morbid has a supreme
attraction for us. Perhaps because no transcendent source of
values can anymore be detected, death (the extinction of consciousness) becomes a seal of value, of importance. (In a sense,
only what concerns death has value.) This leads to both a pro-
motion and a trivialization of the concept of death, which
gives perhaps the deepest stimulus to the persistent iconography of violence + violent death in the artifacts of our culture.
(The extraordinary frequency with which the plot of a serious contemporary novel turns on, or resolves itself, by a murder—compared with the extreme unlikelihood that the
educated writers of vanguard fiction have ever been anywhere near a murder in their lives.)

•

Best films (not in order)

1. Bresson, *Pickpocket*
2. Kubrick, *2001*
3. Vidor, *The Big Parade*
4. Visconti, *Ossessione*
5. Kurosawa, *High and Low*
6. [Hans-Jürgen] Syberberg, *Hitler*

7. Godard, *2 ou 3 Choses* ...
8. Rossellini, *Louis XIV*
9. Renoir, *La Règle du Jeu*
10. Ozu, *Tokyo Story*
11. Dreyer, *Gertrud*
12. Eisenstein, *Potemkin*
13. Von Sternberg, *The Blue Angel*
14. Lang, *Dr. Mabuse*
15. Antonioni, *L'Eclisse*
16. Bresson, *Un Condamné à Mort* ...
17. Gance, *Napoléon*
18. Vertov, *The Man with the [Movie] Camera*
19. [Louis] Feuillade, *Judex*
20. Anger, *Inauguration of the Pleasure Dome*
21. Godard, *Vivre Sa Vie*
22. Bellocchio, *Pugni in Tasca*
23. [Marcel] Carné, *Les Enfants du Pradis*
24. Kurosawa, *The Seven Samurai*
25. [Jacques] Tati, *Playtime*
26. Truffaut, *L'Enfant Sauvage*
27. [Jacques] Rivette, *L'Amour Fou*
28. Eisenstein, *Strike*
29. Von Stroheim, *Greed*
30. Straub, ... *Anna Magdalena Bach*
31. Taviani bro[ther]s, *Padre Padrone*
32. Resnais, *Muriel*
33. [Jacques] Becker, *Le Trou*
34. Cocteau, *La Belle et la Bête*
35. Bergman, *Persona*
36. [Rainer Werner] Fassbinder, ... *Petra von Kant*
37. Griffith, *Intolerance*
38. Godard, *Contempt*
39. [Chris] Marker, *La Jetée*
40. Conner, *Crossroads*

41. Fassbinder, *Chinese Roulette*
42. Renoir, *La Grande Illusion*
43. [Max] Ophüls, *The Earrings of Madame de . . .*
44. [Iosif] Kheifits, *The Lady with the Little Dog*
45. Godard, *Les Carabiniers*
46. Bresson, *Lancelot du Lac*
47. Ford, *The Searchers*
48. Bertolucci, *Prima della Rivoluzione*
49. Pasolini, *Teorema*
50. [Leontine] Sagan, *Mädchen in Uniform*

[The list continues up to number 228, where SS abandons it.]

1978

1/17/78   NYC

Tannhäuser tonight at the Met [*the Metropolitan Opera*] (with [*the American literary critic*] Walter Clemons). The music is about sex—eroticism—voluptuousness. That's why one goes on loving Wagner. The stories of the operas, alas, are something else: the vulgarity; the kitsch problems (sex vs. soulfulness); the martial proto-Nazi volkishness. Nietzsche was right about Wagner—more right than he knew. And yet, and yet—that voluptuousness . . .

The Hebrew word for life, "chai," is spelled with two letters, chet and yod. These letters have numerical equivalents, chet, 8, and yod, 10, which add up to 18. Tradition of giving $18 as a charitable donation. (To give a "chai" for . . . to give a "triple chai" ($54), one chai for my family, one chai for my friends, . . . etc.) . . .

The need to find patterns, the need to pattern . . .

. . .

1/21/78

Sex is getting a bad reputation. The 1960s—seemed like energy, joy, freedom from stuffy taboos, adventure. Now seems to many people more trouble than it's worth. A disappointment. Sex a sublimation of the desire to work. Sexual drive took them, into a wall . . . Male homosexual "world" abandoned the gentle / bitchy homosexual (the "fairy," "fag," "fruit"—compulsively attending to his sexual needs)—+ gave itself over to lechery, vice, and sexual manias.

•

Distinction of "novel" from "romance" important through 19th c[entury] ([Samuel] Johnson's *Dictionary* defines a novel as "a small tale, generally of love"). Only rather recently did the term "novel" spread imperialistically to cover any long prose fiction.

Another way of thinking about why the questions, "Is this a novel?," "Is the novel dead?" are stupid.

—Scrim (transparent curtain)

3/1/78 [or 3/9/78—the date is unclear in the notebook]

I'm not thrilled anymore by literary criticism as autocritique—the construction of methodologies, the deconstruction of texts. Criticism that is about itself.

Illness as Metaphor is an attempt to "do" literary criticism in a new way but for a pre-modern purpose: to criticize the world.

It's also "against interpretation"—once again. With a subject, instead of a text.

I AM against turning illness into a "spiritual condition."

About how the metaphoric understanding, and the moralization of a disease, belies the medical realities.

•

So many modern ideas thought to be liberating to some class or relationship or just aspiration have turned out to be more enslaving than not.

Don B[arthelme]: "I know you have a lot on your plate right now."

Sci-fi: heartless apocalypse.

Furies and demons with electric guitars, narrow shirts, and back-lit hair.

3/16/78

... "A plot so thin you could thread a needle with it." [*Film critic Janet Maslin*, The New York Times, *on* American Hot Wax]

•

"Never mind. No matter ..."

3/24/78

[*The American choreographer*] Merce Cunningham said in an interview the other day (*NY Times*) that his dance (events) were constructed so that there is no particular focus of attention (de-centered?), + the viewers can choose what they want to look at: "like television—where we switch from one channel to another." !

. . .

I want to fight my resignation—but I have only the tools of resignation to fight with.

. . .

Spelling went out when reading went out.

5/10/78

Pulse of red on the horizon for the ten minutes after the sun has set

. . . the rim of the mountain behind which the sun has just set

like the top of a volcano—

5/14/78   Madrid

Reading Benjamin—the new volume—and finding him less extraordinary, less mysterious. I wish he hadn't written the autobiographical works.

A story about the city. Two people traverse it, wander about— one looking for sexual adventure (prostitutes?), the other looking for an apartment. A. looks forward: desire. B. looks backward: regret, nostalgia for the lost space. Two experiences of time, two experiences of space (the labyrinth).

5/20/78   Paris

In 1874, Mallarmé started—and edited—a fashion magazine: *La Dernière Mode*. There he discovered (?), made his first experiments with layout and typography.

5/23/78

Old [*German publisher*] Carl Hanser: He lives in a Biedermeier bunker.

Lots of emotion, but only five channels.

Benjamin wrote radio dialogues in the early 20s—+ hundreds of reviews. Spent a lot of his time chasing women; frequented prostitutes—bourgeois romance about crossing into forbidden class-territory through sex.

Novels of [*the contemporary Swedish writer*] Lars Gustafsson + essays. Novels of [Siegfried] Kracauer.

This is a time for inventing new things, not new ideas. True?

Enzensberger writing a two-hundred-page poem about the sinking of the *Titanic*—an epic subject—how people face death. No more politics!

[*The Italian writer Italo*] Calvino is writing stories set in 19th c[entury] Paris.

•

The fact that I now wear two pairs of glasses, one for seeing far, one for seeing close. It doesn't really work, for example, in a bookstore—or sitting in a café, where I want both to read and to look at people.

The language of a consumer society: the jargon of satiety.

. . .

5/24/78   Venice

Venice makes me weep. Walking alone in the Piazza San Marco in the early morning. So I went into the cathedral, sat among the five or six faithful, heard the mass, and took communion.

Puritanism: a variety of moral kitsch. ([*The Bulgarian-British writer Elias*] Canetti)

One sign of a strong personality is the love of the impersonal.

5/25/78

Benjamin essay—the theme of the city. Benjamn as writer. Proust; the shock of [Louis] Aragon's "Le Paysan de Paris" (letter to Adorno, May 31, 1935)

Structure
Labyrinth
The book

Compare with Canetti.

Importance of [*the Austrian critic* Karl] Kraus essay.

Flâneur. Hidden theme of prostitution. Crossing class barriers.

Surrealist sensibility.

Attraction to Marxism. Servility w[ith] Brecht.

Making a living as a literary journalist. If he had become a professor (like Scholem, Adorno, Marcuse, [Max] Horkheimer!)

Figure of bookish wanderer—Steppenwolf; Kien in [Canetti's novel,] *Auto-da-Fé*.

Situation of the exile. Theme of the death of Europe. But he could not support that ultimate exile: America.

Says in a letter that one should weep for the murder of German culture but that it is obscene to be nostalgic over the Weimar Republic.

Benjamin thought of himself as the last European. Not just an intellectual but a German intellectural.

Kant not Hegel (or Nietzsche)
"dialectic" conceived as ambiguity, complexity untouched by Wagner–Nietzsche, etc.

Description of Moscow: banality, clarity

5/27/78   Venice

My ninth stay in Venice:

1961—with M[other], I[rene] ([Hotel] Luna; Hotel des Bains)
1964—with D[avid] (Bob + Guido)—Luna
1967—with D[avid] (Film Festival—Hotel Excelsior)
1969—with C[arlotta] ([Hotel] Fenice)
1972—with N[icole] ([Hotel] Gritti)
1974—with N[icole] (Gossens apartment)
1975—with N[icole] (Gritti)
1977, Dec.—Joseph [Brodsky] ([Hotel] Europa)

And he retired to Venice, to write a two-hundred-page poem on the sinking of the *Titanic*.

Imagination: —having many voices in one's head. The freedom for that.

In every era, there are three teams of writers. The first team: those who have become known, gain "stature," become reference points for their contemporaries writing in the same language. (e.g. Emil Staiger, Edmund Wilson, V. S. Pritchett). The second team: international—those who become reference points for their contemporaries throughout Europe, the Americas, Japan, etc. (e.g. Benjamin). The third team: those who become reference points for successive generations in many languages (e.g. Kafka). I'm already on the first team, on the verge of being admitted to the second—want only to play on the third.

•

Dionysus was bisexual. (cf. [*the Austrian-American psycho-analyst and writer*] Helene Deutsch lecture)

. . .

•

6/21/78   NYC

Crisis of Leninist ideology in the 1970s

Judge a regime by what it does with its opponents

. . .

7/2/78

. . . Woman in Chicago (Jory Graham—columnist for *Sun-Times* ("A Time to Live")—sidekick in my cancer minstrel show—telling (on [Irv] Kup[cinet]'s show) how she was recently on a plane that lost an engine—how she panicked, though she tried to convince herself she was better off dying now, in 5 minutes, than going through the smelly, slow, agonizing hideous cancer death that awaits her soon—she wanted not to crash—she wanted her own death, the one she'd been working on, living with, getting reconciled (accustomed) to.

7/8/78   Paris

Modern eroticism—theme of reflections on the erotic:
Foucault on sexuality
Kenneth Anger, *Inauguration of the Pleaure Dome*
[Nagisa] Oshima, *In the Realm of the Senses* (?)
Pasolini, *Salò*
Syberberg, *Ludwig + Hitler*

The homosexual baroque

•

Neo-kitsch

The great contribution of the modern homosexual sensibility
to eroticism.

•

Men never forgive women for being their mothers . . . (>>>
Wagner)

[*This text has a rectangle drawn around it:*] The next ten years
must be the best, strongest, boldest

Re: [*the Russian writer Andrei*] Biely:

Modernism invented several times—once in Soviet Union. Important for us because it was suppressed.

Compare [Biely's novel] *St. Petersburg* + [Henry James's] *The Princess Casamassima*—ordered to kill a duke, kills himself. Classic plot of revolutionary tragedy: orders to kill. Cf. Conrad, *The Secret Agent*

•

I like films with voice "off" narration or commentary—it re-introduces (allows) the virtues of *muet* [*"silent film"*].

[Sacha] Guitry, *Roman d'un Tricheur*
[Marcel] Hanoun, *Un Simple Histoire*
Melville, *Les Enfants Terribles*
Godard, *2 ou 3 Choses . . .*
Straub, . . . *Anna Magdalena Bach*
[Michel] Deville, *Dossier 51*
Bresson, *Un Condamné à Mort . . .*

And films that mix genres:

[Benjamin] Christensen, *Häxan*
[Dušan] Makavejev, *WR*

>>>>>> [Syberberg's] *Hitler, A Film from Germany*

7/17/78   Paris

. . .

Eisenstein directed a production of *Die Walküre* in Moscow in 1940. After the [Hitler–Stalin] Pact + before the invasion—pro-German period, officially. Are there production notes?

7/21/78

A "Wagner" essay? The Syberberg film and the [*the French opera director Patrice*] Chéreau / [Pierre] Boulez production of *Ring*.

. . .

Berlioz didn't have an ideology—didn't seek to institutionalize himself.

. . . *Siegfried*—the problem: first two acts composed earlier —new conception in third act. *Ring* breaks in two parts.

. . .

7/25/78   London

Jonathan Miller has metaphoria—metaeuphoria.

"I think I've beached my boat in the theater." (Jonathan)

Only by understanding body as a machine do we give human beings their humanity.

Metaphors for understanding body (e.g. heart = pump) come from machines

. . .

Two basic tools of modern medicine: salt water (saline solution) + other people's blood

. . .

8/7/78   Paris

. . . The novel as a "technique of trouble" ([*the twentieth-century American critic and poet*] R. P. Blackmur), a means of exposing predicaments. Insoluble predicaments of modern existence. (!)

Dec. 31, 1999. I would like to be there. It will be one of the great kitsch moments of world history.

Modernism. Restore the historical view (reference points: French Revolution, Romantic poets). Anti-intellectualism. The project of the intellectual.

. . .

Jonathan made a BBC film of Plato's *Symposium* called *The Drinking Party*

8/11/78   Paris

Remember the exemplary career of Herwarth Walden . . . Founded *Der Sturm* (published Kokoschka, Futurists, Kandinsky, Apollinaire) in 1910; married [*the German Jewish poet and playwright*] Else Lasker-Schüler [in 1903]. In 1932 stopped publication of *Der Sturm* + emigrated to USSR. Wrote novel there, "Neutral": never published. Arrested 31 March 1941 at the Hotel Metropol in Moscow; died in the hospital of the camp at Saratov.

8/12/78

334 miles between Odessa and Istanbul, across the Black Sea

Get a large schoolroom map.

Stick white, fluorescent stars on the bedroom ceiling.

Notional Rome in Shakespeare . . .

. . . doesn't have a representation in consciousness. (Of some bodily process)

"Fait Divers" [*"news item"*] of 1920s (?) in England: the fate of the Vicar of Stiffkey (pronounced Stukey): frequented prostitutes; was defrocked; ended in a circus, exhibited in a barrel; was eaten by a lion.

. . .

[*In the margin:*] aristos

aristo talk (English):
"inties" (for intellectuals)—
Duchess of Devonshire, overheard on the phone by [*the English novelist*] Angus Wilson—Wilson + friend had been

invited to tea: during tea, D. of D. got a call from a friend inviting her to her lunch tomorrow with Cyril Connolly. "I'd rather not. I already have two inties for tea today."

To be older: to find everyone else pathetic.

. . .

No such thing as an "experimental" writer, director, artist. A philistine notion! It assumes an option, a choice. No. You either are original or not.

Play: Original production
     Satellite productions

Heretical production (reverses or contradicts original staging)

Only a great work can survive this process
Wagner > [Adolphe] Appia [*the Swiss architect who designed the sets and lit many Wagner operas*] > [*Wagner's grandson*] Wieland > Chéreau

Cf. Benjamin on the after-life of a woa [work of art]—in essay on the translator

8/13/78

[*SS adored Wagner's music and went to the Bayreuth Festival a number of times.*]

Bayreuth notes:

You have been touched by two other models—the bohemian and the aristocratic, I said to Bob [Silvers]. Alternative to middle-class life and concerns. Bohemia: Alfred [Chester]. And look what that led to. Whereas, the discreet charm of the aristocracy . . .

The code of the nobleman: never complain

Someone could be virtuous, decent, not corrupt through passivity or timidity.

Futurism the source for constructivism and much else

Thesis (?): fascism in Italy was special > [Giulio Carlo] Argan, present C[ommunist] P[arty] Mayor of Rome, was a fascist cultural bureaucrat in the late 30s. Sponsored good artists, protected Jews, gave jobs to many. Got [*the Italian classical historian Arnaldo*] Momigliano [a] job on Encyclopedia)

May Taback, coming home, stepping over naked one-legged Harold Rosenberg [*her husband*] fucking girl on living room floor, to HR: "Dinner in one hour."

8/20/78 NYC

Joseph B[rodsky] says he decides to write a poem—picks a subject and / or a model (a poet he admires); says to himself "I will write an Akhmatova poem" or ". . . a Frost poem" or "an Auden poem" or a "[*the Italian poet Eugenio*] Montale poem" or a "Cavafy poem." The idea is to do it like the poet, only better. Of course, it never is like the model poet—that's a game one plays with oneself—if one is a real poet one can only write of one's own world.

A possible practice for the next year: a Borges story (the discovery of a play of Agathon [*the classical Greek playwright whose works were supposedly lost when the great library of Alexandria burned in 48 BC*]; a Calvino story; a Walser story; a Konrád story; a García Márquez story.

I've already done my Barthelme story—[*SS's autobiographical short story*] "Unguided Tour"—that is, written a better story than Barthelme. I should have admitted to myself that's what I was doing.

An Ideal Story Anthology:

V Woolf, "The Moment" or "The Unwritten Novel"
Robert Walser, "Kleist in Thun"
Paul Goodman, "Minutes Are Flying"
Laura Riding, "Last Lesson in Geography"
[*In the margin: the German writer Wolfgang*] Borchert, [*the Jewish Serbian-Hungarian writer Danilo*] Kiš
[Tommaso] Landolfi, "W.C."
Calvino, "[The Distance of the] Moon" (from *Cosmicomics*)
Beckett, "The Expelled"
Barthelme, "The Balloon"
Philip Roth, "On the Air" [*Roth's story published in* New American Review *in 1970*]
John Ashbery, "Prose Poem"
John Barth, "Title" or "Life-Story"
Elizabeth Hardwick, "Prologue"
John McPhee, "Boardwalk"

Bruno Schulz, "Hourglass" or "The Book"
[Elisabeth] Langgässer, "Mars"
des Forêts,
Sinyavsky,
[Peter] Handke,
[*the Austrian poet Ingeborg*] Bachmann,
Borges, "Pierre Menard"
Gadda,
García Márquez,
[Stanisław] Lem, "Probablaism..." [*likely means "The Third
Sally" or "The Dragons of Probability"*]
Ballard,

Essay anthology:

Gass,
Benjamin,
Rivière,
Sinyavsky,
Enzensberger,
Trilling,
[Alfred] Döblin, preface to [Face of Our Time, *a book of
photographs by August*] Sander
Goodman,
Sartre, "Nizan"or "Tintoretto"
Benn, "Artists + Old Age"
Broch, Introduction to [*the Ukrainian-Jewish philosopher
and critic Rachel*] Bespaloff['s On the Iliad]
Adorno

avant-garde: shallow enigmas

Cioran's work teaches one how to die

Brecht advised his pupils "to live in the third person"

Nihilistic attitudinizing

Late 18th [century] to now: recurrent walking statues, haunted portraits, and magic mirrors

A constant theme in my writing / imagination (how central): [*in French*] the vision of an encumbered world, supersaturated by objects, things! In *Death Kit* (the lists, inventory at the end), in *On Photography*, in "Unguided Tour" (+ "Debriefing"). The antonym: silence.

. . .

[*In the margin and underlined:*] "It's a question of being alone, in writing." V Woolf (letter to Vita [Sackville-West], Nov. 1925)

"Cheyne-Stokes breathing": sign of the end [of life]— irregular

Post-[*the mass killer Charles*] Manson sensibility:

Texas Chainsaw Massacre a new threshold; most imp[ortant] Am[erican] film of the 70s.

punk Grand Guignol—the walking dead—vampire make-up

"danger"

Sex Pistols inspired by a young couple, art school graduates + admirers of the Situationists, who ran a boutique in Chelsea ca. 1975–6, called, successively, "Rock and Roll" > "Too Fast to Live, Too Young to Die" > "Sex" > "Seditionaries"

. . .

shy nihilism
a kind of motiveless sorrow
fanned with strange feelings
geography of pleasure

11/1/78

Dinner yesterday late with Joseph. He's trying to admire [*the English poet John*] Betjeman—for his "lightness of touch." The poet he's trying to beat now—it's no longer Mandelstam— is Montale. (Clever Joseph.) "And, Susan, I think I already have."

Literature and the national echo.

11/17/78

After the party at Roger [Straus]'s for *I, etcetera*, published today—with Joseph at the coffee shop on the corner of 3rd Ave and 17th at midnight. "I realize that I've become a simpleton in the six years I've been in America. I'm no longer subtle, as I was in Russia. It's the American straightforwardness . . . Everyone is positive here . . . people trying to be helpful, kind, supportive . . . explaining, making things clear."

"You don't want a last line that's not an effect." Joseph's criticism of the last line of [*SS's story*] "Baby." I think he's wrong.

I get boosted by reading. But does this help to be subtle? Joseph: that comes only from other people.

11/21/78

The Beckett manner has no use for allusiveness. You can't say "a Gioconda smile" in his idiom. [*The Canadian literary critic Hugh*] Kenner

Napoleon's wet, chubby back (Tolstoy)

Beyond compassion? Don't give advice. I ignore the difference between me + the other person.

A tribe in the Sudan, with a complex theology in which the middle-aged are initiated. Old people laugh continually.

The unity of the eight fictions in *I, etcetera.* Meaning that circulates. Stories like prisms. They are "about" narration. Unity of the ethical project.

I'm making it impossible for myself to write essays any longer.

I disregard the separation (a dogma) betw[een] the essay + fiction. In fiction I can do what I've done in essays, but not vice versa.

12/5/78

Joseph's operation [for open heart surgery]

. . .

Italian Futurists were self-styled "primitives of a new sensibility"

. . .

STOP HECTORING

. . .

Canetti essay—

Should be on the idea, the project, of the writer (the great writer)

The European model—how it seems dated—its grandeur, its pathos

Start from C[anetti]'s essay on Broch
Broch, Kraus, Kafka—models for C.

C's idea about death—dread—his desire for immortality

Condescension to women

Essay on Hitler—his crowd is the dead

[Canetti's] *Crowds + Power*: History into biology (biological metaphors)

cf. *Ring*: a biological epic (begins in water, ends in fire)

[Canetti] has stayed free of the temptation of the left. How?

12/27/78   Venice

Venice in December, a photographic negative of the sun-lit summer Venice. A kind of seeing-for-the-first-time.

Abstract Piazza San Marco—geometric—defined by borders of lights—space defined by thickness of light. Every figure is a silhouette.

In the vaporetto coming up from the Casino (Palazzo Vendramin . . .): seeing nothing on either side of the boat. Looking into a brown-grey void.

The basilica from the top of the campanile—barely visible— The Doge's Palace like a Monet or a [Georges] Seurat drawing in the fog.

Winter Venice is metaphysical, structural, geometrical. Drained of color.

I've re-read [Henry James's] *The Golden Bowl*.

To feel the pressures of consciousness, to be informed, to understand anything, one must be alone. Being with people, being alone—like breathing in and breathing out, systole and diastole. As long as I'm so afraid of being alone, I'll never be real. I'm in hiding from myself.

I act in haste—I reason for results—my intelligence is facile.

The depression I feel when I'm alone is only the first layer. I can get beyond it if I don't panic. Sink down—let it happen. Listen to the words.

. . .

(Talking to Bob [*SS had by then made several trips to Japan and was contemplating a short book of her impressions*] on the phone) Japan:

Feudal society that has been modernized. Full of Western "signs" that don't signify anything in particular except modernity. Parody of Western "culture." National project: To "transcribe" (adapt, transmogrify) modern Western capitalism . . . No law in our sense, but rather an immense system of accomodations, deferences, hierarchies. Consensus society— everyone is recuperable (leaders of [*the extreme left student movement*] Zengakuren in the late 60s are now important business executives) except for criminal underclass. Ritualized violence—in strikes, demonstrations against Narita [*the construction of an airport there*], etc.—which provide signs for new accommodations. Much energy, many signs—little substance. Big homosexual culture, 1000 gay bars, see Don [*SS's friend in Tokyo, the American writer Donald Richie*] and his German friend [Eric Klestadt]. In the green room of the Kabuki Theatre—prize is to know transvestite actors: —like ballet dancers or opera singers in the 19th c. Twelve department stores in Tokyo like Bloomingdale's: everything looks the same but it's really endlessly different.

. . .

1979

1/1/79   Asolo

Syberberg essay [*SS had discovered the films of Hans-Jürgen Syberberg some years earlier, helped arrange of the U.S. distribution of* Hitler: A Film from Germany, *and by the beginning of 1979 had been planning this essay for several months.*]
Begin with the idea of "Trauerarbeit" [*"work of mourning"*]

"It's worse than being a child."

The statue of St. Sebastian in the Duomo of Vicenza. (Altar nearest entrance on the left). The tradition of the beautiful nude youth transported from G[reco]-Rom[an] art into Christianity—was homoerotic—now an object of erotic contemplation by women mostly and men. The first three-dimensional St. Sebastian I've seen. The eroticism of this figure even more flagrant as a sculpture than as a painting . . . The number of arrows (I've seen as few as two, as many as ten) and their placement.

Again and again, I'm struck by the erotic obsessions that are so much in the foreground in Christianity. The Virgin—the breast of the Virgin / mother—the swooning woman—the beloved disciple leaning into Jesus' lap—the tortured male body, almost naked (Jesus, Sebastian)

[*The poet Robert*] Browning's word "asolare"

How modern were Ruskin's pleasures? Not our mix of enthusiasm and nostalgia (almost mourning) when we see Venice, Florence, Verona, etc. He was a discoverer. For whom? What does it mean to discover something already known? Known by whom?

The circle of removable plastic set in each of the two windows (Cipriani Hotel—Asolo). Like the removeable glass carreau in mullioned windows in the 19th century—but this is ugly, because it's an unbroken piece of glass—not mullioned.

1/5/79   Paris

One to six with [György] Konrád (Scossa > Stella [*two cafés*]). Stories about Eastern Europe. "L'étatisation des écrivains" [*"the subsuming of writers into the state"*]. What it means to receive a prize . . .

A story in this—about getting a prize?

When I say, how can you compare the Russian empire with the American empire ("it's the same if I die from capitalist bombs or from communist bombs"—his Venice speech last December), he reminds me that I forget the periphery, the colonies of the American empire. Of course, if one compares New York with Moscow, there is no doubt that one is infinitely freer in New York—one is free, "tout court" [*"and that's that"*]. But, Cambodia apart, there is nothing as cruel, as bloody in the Communist countries as what went on in Iran (the Shah's SAVAK [*secret police*]), in Nicaragua, + in Argentina right now. Intellectuals are not being murdered in Hungary, Poland, Czechoslovakia, etc. They are being wooed—or expelled.

. . .

[Wagner's] *The Flying Dutchman* is a vampire story

anoxia = lack of oxygen

1/13/79   Paris

A novella based on the idea of "the portrait game" [*a book by Ivan Turgenev and his lover Pauline Viardot-García*]—+ the triangle Viardot, husband, Turgenev. A Jamesian story. A Resnais film (*Last Year in Baden-Baden*). A García Márquez–ish fantasy. A Borges retrouvaille [*"rediscovery"*] in the World Library.

1/14/79   London

Jonathan: "I wrote the medical book to make money and staple-gunned a few ideas in the middle."

I was praising [Henry James's] *The Golden Bowl*. J[onathan] said, "if you could have bolted Henry + William together you would get Proust."

J. talks of his long-projected book on 19th c. spiritualism. Description of cataleptic trance in "Maud" comes from Tennyson having read Harriet Martineau's *Letters on Mesmerism* (1845).

. . .

[Henry] James consulted [*the British neurologist John*] Hughlings Jackson in the 1890s in London for his migraines; Jackson told him about "temporal lobe epilepsy," during whose aura all sounds seem to stop, there is a strange smell, + one is overwhelmed by an awareness of unbearable evil. This is the origin of James's description of the governess' "hallucination" (?) in *The Turn of the Screw* . . . *The Golden Bowl* is about observation, about seeing, about how one really never knows what another person feels.

Fascination in 19th c. with altered states of consciousness. Two traditions of interpreting these. (1) An alter ego—another state, side, aspect of me; exalted states (cf. Wordsworth, Dostoyevsky)—the egotistical interpretation. (2) An other world—the supernatural—spirits. (cf. Poe, [E.T.A.] Hoffmann)

1/15/79   London

V. Woolf lost, Arnold Bennett won—here

Madness is single-mindedness

1/27/79   Rome

Carmelo Bene's [*production of Verdi's*] *Otello*. The action is
mostly played on a huge bed—begins with O[tello] strangling
D[esdemona]. It is played inside the handkerchief. Everyone
wears white. O. in brownface. People pass their hands over
each other's faces, leaving them black. Voices are miked.
Music of Verdi, Wagner, etc.

[Undated]

Conversation with Jacob [Taubes]

"ideas with broken wings" (Adorno)

[*In the margin:*] Jacob's right hand as he talks. "Turning the
celestial screw," I called it in 1954.

Adorno to Jacob in 1968: "If they [*the students*] invade the
Institute, I'll put on a yellow star."

[*The Marxist philosopher and SS's friend in the 1950s in Cambridge, Herbert*] Marcuse's position in 1956, for Soviet repression of Hungarian revolution; his complicity with students in
1968 (cf. Adorno)—because he comes from Heidegger

2/1/79

[*The early French filmmaker Georges*] Méliès > Syberberg.
Méliès filmed imaginary newsreels (*The Emperor of China
at the Court of St. James*) in his back yard in Paris.

[*Méliès's contemporaries Auguste and Louis*] Lumière > Godard?

Language as a found object: [*the Argentine writer Manuel*] Puig. He can't create his own language. It's all found. He's an extraordinary mime—has converted his liability as a writer into a system.

[*The Belgian surrealist René*] Magritte show at Beaubourg. *L'Empire des lumières* ([1953–54])—named something, as an image, that now everyone sees: blue sky, dark trees, the street lights on.

An imperial mind. Writers like Joyce, Gadda, Nabokov

2/8/79

The aura around each thing.
Respect it—pause a moment—before you grasp something

Aesthetic space: [*the eighteenth-century French painter Jean-Baptiste-Simeon*] Chardin, [*the American experimental film-maker*] Jack Smith

America + Western Europe are growing apart—becoming as different as they were in the 1950s. Western Europe has chosen Social Democracy (whatever the party in power calls itself), America has rejected it. Events of the 70s: 1) the discrediting of utopian communism as a plausible anchor-belief for intellectuals + artists; 2) the Euro-ization of the Western European countries; 3) the collapse of American imperialist ideology + growing cultural / political isolationism of the U.S.

2/11/79

Conversation with Enzensberger (lunch in Chinatown): Darwin as an alternative to Hegel. Hegelianism assumes the biological + the historical are two different processes. But maybe the historical proceeds naturally. An evolution, but one that can't be predicted. (What was attractive about Hegelianism was its notion of the *irony* of history.) Nobody has thought about Darwin['s] implications for 50 years in Germany, E. says. Survival of the fittest is mistrusted as survival of the strongest.

Wants to write a free kind of essay. Cites Heine as a model. I mention Lucretius—he agrees.

Canetti:

> biologistic model (*Crowds + Power*). No "history" in the Hegelian sense
> one of the great death-haters of the 20th century
> not Eurocentric. Cites Chinese or Arab thought— not as something from another culture to be "understood," but because it's true
> not a reductionist—never asks what makes an idea possible, but: "is it true?"

The strength, independence—+ marginality of Canetti's work. Was supported in the late 1930s + '40s by the Guggenheim Foundation (E. says. True?) Knew—had affair with Iris Murdoch. E. was introduced to Canetti in London by Ingeborg Bachmann . . .

Canetti: Avidity, appetite, craving, longing, yearning, insatiability, rapture, inclination. Is this the life of the mind?

2/13/79

Watching Nureyev rehearse for two hours this afternoon.

2/18/79

M[other] called in the late afternoon to say that she had received a letter from Mary Penders that Rosie died of a "massive heart attack" last Sept. 30 . . . I was surprised, and touched, by how moved she was; I didn't think she could feel much of anything . . .

2/20/79

Joseph [Brodsky]: "There is nothing more important for a narcissist than a smooth surface"
"If there is an Olympic record for tyranny, both in terms of the degree + duration, then the USSR has the gold."

2/25/79

[*The American choreographer*] Twyla Tharp reconciles me to being a woman + to being an American . . . Non-sexist dancing—strong women with their own energy, subjects not objects, playful with men—not afraid of them . . . Use of American vernacular movement (from Mack Sennett comedy, Fred Astaire, black disco dancers), of American energy. Constant contact with the floor, which is not just something to leave—as in [*the work of the choreographer George*] Balanchine. Slapping the floor—falling on it flat out, trying to get up, *hugging* it.

The account of Philip's Trilling lecture [*at Columbia University*], first by Bob, this afternoon on the phone by Diana [Trilling].

"Homage to Mr. Casaubon." Why not write a story about Philip? Do I dare? I'm afraid of my anger. Lizzie can't write about Cal—but what do I have to protect?

Write about a man who hates women—hates sex—hates love.

I'll find all the energy I need—as in "Baby."

How much damage did those eight years w[ith] Philip do?

Isn't it time I can write the truth? I'm still protecting him—Cranston in [*SS's story*] "Old Complaints Revisited"—still eager to take the responsibility on myself.

Dream: I'm a nun (?) Sexually happy, with a young adoring shy girl. Another couple? I'm convened to be reprimanded—an old gothic building—think I have gotten off—leave, accompanied throughout by a friend— In the courtyard am told I've forgotten to fill out a form—do it with some difficulty (I have to borrow pencil from friend)—go in other building with friend—am kidnapped—sexually mutilated—will bleed ("estrous vagina")—told I won't be able to have sex again.

Sources: reading [*the Indian novelist R. K.*] Narayan today; Diana about Philip ([*his lecture was on Gustave*] Courbet painting + [Andrea] Mantegna [*Lamentation over the Dead Christ*]—woman as castrated man); Philip as Grand Inquisitor

. . .

Venice > Ruskin

Artist as oracle, public figure [—Gabriele] D'Annunzio, Ruskin, Wagner

. . .

Writer as Penelope—write during the day, undo it at night

Writer as Sisyphus

In *I, etcetera*, the best stories: my "Cubist" method, telling story from different angles

Max Ernst litho[graph] (?)—1919 "Art is Dead, Let There Be Fashion"

[Undated: A reminiscence of SS's encounter with William Phillips, the editor of Partisan Review. *It must have taken place in 1960 or early in 1961.]*

At PR office in Union Square—Wm. Phillips opens metal locker + takes out Elémire Zolla's *The Eclipse of the Intellectual*
Me (thumbing through book): "It doesn't look very good, but one could review the title."
WP: "Oh. You're smart."

Lenny [Leonard] Michaels is a sprinter, Pynchon is a marathon runner.

Wordsworth's "wise passiveness"

. . .

There is no word for hypocrisy in Japanese

[*The nineteenth-century Italian writer Giacomo*] Leopardi—
anguish of solitude, obsession with transience + mortality, life-
time obsession with "noia" (metaphysical tedium, boredom)

. . .

[Undated, March]

. . . In 19th C. novelists knew about science:
—George Eliot . . . cf. medical ideas in *Middlemarch*
—Balzac: cf. preface to *Human Comedy*—theory of types: see
macrocosm (society) in micro (individual)—indiv[idual] adapts
Balzac, *Les Chouans*

Last novelist to be influenced by, knowledgeable about science was [Aldous] Huxley

One reason [there are] no more novels— There are no exciting theories of relation of society to self (soc[iological], historical, philosophical)

Not SO—no one is doing it, that's all

Series of phenomenological essays:

    —crying
    —swoonng
    —blushing

[*The nineteeth-century French scientist*] Claude Bernard: theory of internal milieu

Crying:

> Notion of "brimming"
> Body as vessel of fluids
> Tears in early 18th C. erotic literature
> Tears as proof of feeling
> Not to be able to cry = to be emotionally frigid

Swooning:

> Reaction to emotional shock (good or bad news)
> When did it stop?

. . .

"Every life is the defense of a form." Hölderlin > Nietzsche > Webern

[*In the margin:*] Europhoria

There is a great deal that either has to be given up or be taken away from you if you are going to succeed in writing a body of work

Divorce is the sign of knowledge in our time, divorce! divorce!—W. C. [*William Carlos*] Williams

3/10/79   Navarro [*in California*]

I am here to blast through my "block." One practice that might help is to try, even at the early stage of an essay, to write complete sentences. An idea in the form of a rubric often proves to be sterile.

To write one must wear blinkers. I've lost my blinkers.

Don't be afraid to be concise!

4/13/79   (plane from LA to Tokyo)

Reply to jealousy: "Don't. It (she, he) wasn't anything. I just *enjoyed* her, him."

[*The English singer and songwriter*] Graham Parker last night at the Roxy. The sarcasm of British rock.—

Spiritual aloofness. Don't encourage so much.

The arts of sarcasm.

High, pinched, monotonous voice—separating inflection from meaning

Cerebral jogging

The spavined old theory

[*Undated, April*]

Japan notes

Bowing—

The deer, begging for food in the park in Nara; someone standing with a red public phone on the street, saying good-bye over the phone; the white-gloved women operating the elevators of big department stores

    Sovereign   iconoclasm
    Skittering + dithering
    Forsworn
    Scrappy

6/1/79

To [*the American photographer*] Star Black, worrying at the beginning of their affair, D[avid] says: "Relax. There's no shortcut to tragedy."

6/14/79   Paris

"Vox Clamantis (in deserto)"—ref[erence] to St. John the Baptist—"a voice crying (in the wilderness)"

Succulent + nervous style

Wastrel

Simple words, with their little life, their magic "pop": deftly, indolent, infection, churn, dainty

The noble brigand (Robin Hood)

Moral terrorism

7/19/79   New York

A failure of nerve. About writing. (And about my life—but never mind.) I must write myself out of it.

If I am not able to write because I'm afraid of being a bad writer, then I must be a bad writer. At least I'll be writing.

Then something else will happen. It always does.

I must write every day. Anything. Everything. Carry a notebook with me at all times, etc.

I read my bad reviews. I want to go to the bottom of it—this failure of nerve.

Why I think mainly of schemas.

7/22/79

Sly, spidery 79-year-old

To have a project: to create a world.

I've become passive. I don't invent, I don't yearn. I manage, I cope.

7/25/79

Story about [the twentieth-century English writer J. R.] Ackerley-figure—see Spender essay [in] NYRB [The New York Review of Books].

God may forgive, but He rarely exonerates.

New "revolutionary" regimes replacing the old dictatorships (Shah [of Iran] > Khomeini . . .)—new blends of cruelty and hypocrisy

[Marina] Tsvetayeva, Mandelstam—accelerated poets.

Someone said to condemn Lizzie's prose: "It's as if she left out every other line."
A good idea.

Joseph told me yesterday that he was trying to beat Vergil (the *Bucolics*). Also that [*the Russian writer Vladimir*] Bukovsky told him in Cambridge recently that there are CIA agents in Amnesty [International]. (Not Whitney Ellsworth, new president of American Amnesty.) If it's infiltrated by the CIA, then there are also KGB agents, too.

Joseph's image for the Coliseum: Argus's skull

. . .

"To discuss one's spiritual life journalistically is impossible."

Re-read [*Broch's*] *The Death of Virgil*

Donald Carne-Ross, "Classics + the Intellectual Community," *Arion*," spring, 1973

. . .

Maritime traditions: punctuality and candor

. . .

11/2/79   NYC

Two good days of work on the story, much material, vivid associations, crowds of details. But the writing doesn't pour. It's too laborious, too constructed.

Who is talking? Is the problem (for me) that I'm writing in the third person—with interspersed scraps of dialogue?

Wring the naïveté out of it. Go faster.

Lizzie: "Well, it's curtains for him, or, as my students would say, drapes."
Resigning from Barnard: "I can't stand it another minute, those horrible little girls coming in with their horrible little stories, and I say to them, 'The word you're looking for is curtains, not drapes.' "

Plus ça change:

1728: Robert Walpole, Prime Minister, applauded John Gay's *The Beggar's Opera* from his theatre box when they sang lyrics accusing him of bribery + vice. He even called for an encore, after which the audience applauded *him*.

[Plato's] *Republic*: "[*In a democracy, the father*] accustoms himself to become like his child and to fear his sons ... Metic [*resident alien*] is like citizen and citizen like metic, and stranger like both [*in the margin:* (Ernst) Rhys] ... The schoolmasters fears and flatters his pupils . . . The young act like their seniors, and compete with them in speech and action, while the old men condescend to the young and become triumphs of versatility and wit, imitating their juniors in order to avoid the appearance of being sour or despotic."

. . .

Old project: Story about the Female Messiah ([*the French philosopher Charles*] Fourier, [*the French social reformer Barthélemy-Prosper*] Enfantin, etc.)

The visual supermarket

The Puritan concern with fashion

. . .

West Coast slang: "clones" (homo[sexual] men) and breeders (hetero[exual]s)

. . .

11/28/79

I am mad, quite mad—and perhaps one can write about that. No one has noticed. My prowess in disguising it. I wander about the apartment, slyly rummaging . . . No place is the right place for my feet. Time is speeded-up. I lie down, I get up, I pace, I lie down, I sleep, I get up, and so on.

Movies seen in Berkeley (Pacific Film Archive, No. 29 + 30)

**** Bruce Conner, *A Movie*
Kidlat Tahimik, *Perfumed Nightmare*

**** Rossellini, *Europa 51*
Bruce Conner, *Cosmic Ray*
Yves Allégret, *Une si jolie petite plage*
    (1949—Gérard Philipe, Jean Servais . . .)
Boris Barnet, *Okraina* (1933)
[Andrei] Konchalovsky, *Uncle Vanya*
Bruce Conner, *Report*
* Douglas Sirk, *Written on the Wind* (Rock Hudson . . .)
       "   ", *Tarnished Angels*
       "   ", *There's Always Tomorrow*
    (starring Fred MacMurray)
Syberberg, *Die Grafen Pocci*

12/4/79

God had to shrink Himself, as they say, in order to create.
The writer?

Contemporary distrust of the masterpiece, that is distrust of
the afterlife of great art . . .

The difficulty of writing the Syberberg essay: every item of
description must have an idea between its teeth

. . .

Art is the production of mental events in / as a concrete sensuous form.

The ands implore

Drivel   "at miser's full tilt" (Pasternak)
Aghast

What is not talked about: the small pathological impulse(s) behind many of the dogmas of modernism (modernist aesthetics). For example: the fascination with grids and repression, rigidification. [—]Mondrian

12/14/79

Struggling through the Syberberg labyrinth, I have an idea for a novel. A great idea—I mean an idea for an ambitious, big book

[*In the margin:*] *novel about melancholy.* It is, after all, my subject. So I am being coherent. And something about which I can be lyrical + passionate.

Fresco, picaresque, Everything.
Re-read Panofsky—and [Günter] Grass.

Reading [*Döblin's novel*] *Berlin Alexanderplatz*—it's wonderful. He was a Jew. Sirk directed his only play around 1936— got in trouble for it

Sirk [*whom SS had met; this is presumably a reference to something he told her*] spoke of a poem from Goethe's West–East Divan that Kafka liked to recite.

. . .

12/15/79

My first novel is a portrait of Melancholy. I discover re-reading Panofsky's essay "Symbolism + Dürer's 'Melencolia' "

"The melancholy humor . . . was supposed to be coessential with earth + to be dry and cold; it was related to the rough Boreas, to autumn, evening, and an age of about sixty."

Not for nothing was I born under The Sign of Saturn: without knowing, I knew. At 27, I was drawn to describe someone of sixty + to pick for an epigraph: "Maintenant, j'ai touché l'automne des idées" [*"Now I have arrived at the autumn of ideas / thought."* —*Baudelaire*]

Now?

From grandmother's gefilte fish + glass of tea to granddaughter's menu of recreational chemicals.

•

Abdul Hamid—deposed 1909; last powerful Sultan of Turkey; paranoid—built fantasy city

1980

1/24/80

A story called "Fear of War"

Lunch with [*the American writer*] Joyce Carol Oates, her husband Ray Smith, + Stephen K[och]. Stephen speaks of his psychological weather—there's always the weather, he says. Not true, say I. But there's always the sky, says Stephen. Who goes out? I reply. Not I. I don't have weather. I have central heating. My central heating is Western civilization—my books + pictures + records.

Joyce writes all the time. She can meditate while writing. She says she has no feelings. What's the point of feeling anxiety? "I'll probably go to my death as on a conveyor belt," she said. Stephen said she had a mystical experience at 30—in London: it lasted twenty minutes . . .

One could write about her.

Interview w[ith] Oates in [Joe David] Bellamy book [The New Fiction: Interviews with Innovative American Writers, *including SS*].
Her humility.

Dinner last night with Wm. Burroughs (+ [*the British writer*] Victor Bokris, [*the American poet, photographer, and filmmaker*] Gerard Malanga). Bokris asked us, Burroughs and me, about our "legendary" meeting with Beckett two years ago in Berlin. "Very decorous," Burroughs said. Later he said: "Beckett doesn't need any input. It's all inside."

J. C. Oates' method of composing:—sentences or paragraphs. Then cut them out—then number the scraps + lay them out . . .

Joseph said: if it moves, it can't be art. Ballet? Superior entertainment. Take that Misha [*Brodksy's friend and patron, the dancer Mikhail Baryshnikov*]

I am a militant feminist but not a feminist militant. (D[avid])

. . .

[*In the margin:*] *Aesthetic: can be many spaces + many times simultaneously*

. . .

2/3/80

Syberberg—

. . . From *Caligari* to Hitler to [Syberberg's] *Hitler*—what S. aspires to. (Hyperbolic cinephilia: he starts as a film—now he ends as a film.)

S. thinks he has rescued Wagner from Hitler. True?

S. takes the eschatology of Nazism seriously.

Events have spiritual weight that has nothing to do with the weight of history

2/14/80

D[avid]'s idea: a *Tristram Shandy*–like story about a pathological liar. Confidential tone— Changes the story of his life in each chapter

2/28/80

Raimonda says of C[arlotta]: "She has a very detached relation to life. The good result of this is that she's never vulgar, never cheap. The bad part is her connection w[ith] the others."

Theme in 19th c Am[erican] lit. (Melville, James): the innocent who causes destructive impulses to be unleashed—by being innocent.

(Culture as crisis)

3/10/80

Döblin's wonderful essay on photography + death—written as preface to Sander's book: Benjamin + a poet's sensibility.

Symbolist works: [Roussel's] *Locus Solus*, [Duchamp's] *The Large Glass*, [Buñuel's] *L'Age d'Or*

I've listened to [*Leoš Janáček's opera*] *The Makropulos Case* ten times in the last three days. I want to direct it, I know how—like *Come tu mi vuoi* [*Pirandello's play* As You Desire Me, *which SS had directed at the Teatro Stabile di Torino*].

The reading is getting out of hand. I'm an addict—I need to be disintoxicated . . . It's a substitute for writing. No wonder I'm so anxious these days.

. . . The writer does not have to write. She must imagine that she *must*. A great book: no one is addressed, it counts as cultural surplus, it comes from the will.

3/15/80

Lacanianism: It gives you a heavy language to walk around in.

. . .

insipid certainties

Blind man who took up sky-diving—microphone in ear, receiving instructions from someone on the ground (woman instructor)—he broke his leg. The second time he fell holding a lead weight at the end of a 20-foot string so he'd know 2 seconds before he hit ground. He said he w[oul]d never have dared to sky-dive sighted.

. . .

Mesmerism = restructuring of the will

English artist—Edward Ardizzone (he just died)

. . .

The blind man didn't want to hear about colors, he didn't want things described to him. He often went to the movies. "You did?" "Why not," he answered. "But I didn't go to the ballet. I wouldn't, unless the music was very good." He got his sight back after two years. Micro-neurosurgery at NIH [*the National Institutes of Health in Bethesda, Maryland*]. Now he's the curator of a gallery in Soho [*New York*]. "Of course, I have no taste at all. I don't know anything about art. But I know what'll sell, what the public likes."

Wallace Stevens said of a poem that it is the cry of its occasion

. . .

The past as a chamber of horrors—and a grand school of persona and social liberty.

Ordinary language is an accretion of lies. The language of literature must be, therefore, the language of transgression, a rupture of individual systems, a shattering of psychic oppression. The only function of literature lies in the uncovering of the self in history.

. . .

Tsvetaeva said of Pasternak that he looked like an Arab *and* his horse

. . .

. . . "You're walking on my story" (to someone interrupting)

Rhythm of sexual excess (male homosexual world)

. . .

kenosis > emptying out

. . .

The child must leave paradise. Is he / she nostalgic? Not really. Describe depression (using [*the contemporary Swiss critic Jean*] Starobinski essay) then say: they called it nostalgia. End with contrast between melancholy and euphoria.

3/26/80

Barthes died.

And David is in love. "She's being Greta Garbo today." When one is romantically in love, the other usually is Garbo.

3/27/80

(on the phone; he's in S[an] F[rancisco]) Syberberg wants now to make a super-*Parsifal*, in the head of Richard Wagner.

Utopia = death

Film a system of thinking, a cosmos
Problem of utopia

Giving up life (women, love) for utopia—is it worth it? No. And yet the only . . .

My technical system: walk through Western civilization (paradise, hell)—can never do this on stage

Symbolist notion / concept of "analogies"

Basis of the one scene that Syberberg didn't shoot: Heine ballads, *Die Zwei Grenadiere* [*The Two Grenadiers*] [*—in the ballad*] two soldiers [*reminisce*] about Napoleon (Hitler)

Dietrich Eckhart's "Glacial Cosmology" . . .

3/28/80

"It's our destiny. Our computer is made like that." (Syberberg)

A one-act play. "Two Socrates"—both Socrates are on stage at the same time. Two adjoining cells. Each with their disciples. One takes the hemlock, the other leaves.

3/29/80

. . . She can't be disturbed. She's having a sentence . . .

An apartment is a drawing of one's self. My apartment(s) is [are] about exclusion—what has been conquered.

A theatre set is allusive or illusive.

Giotto is allusive.
Most famous theatre set ever—[*the Italian Renaissance architect Andrea*] Palladio's Teatro Olimpico in Vicenza is allusive (can be a temple, a church, whatever)

19th c[entury] sets are illusive

An essay on historical periodizing

Century > generation > decade

. . .

3/30/80

. . . The unit of the poet is the word, the unit of the prose writer is the sentence.

. . .

When what we hoped for came to nothing, we revived. —[*the twentieth-century American poet*] Marianne Moore

Sexually alert . . .

4/3/80

Barthes
People called him a critic, for want of a better label; and I myself said he was "the greatest critic to have emerged anywhere . . ." But he deserves the more glorious name of writer.

His body of work is an immense, complex, extremely discreet effort at self-description.

Eventually he became a real writer. But he couldn't purge himself of his ideas.

4/7/80

Art(ists) invents the ideology of modernity—

The ideology of modernity denies the fact (continuing existence) of class. It puts spectacle in the place of a more complex totality

Art pictures ideology—can show (through examining art)— its incoherence

In the 1860s, [*the French diarists, Edmond and Jules de*] Goncourt mourned the death of Paris (their Paris—of the 1830s, 1840s)

Pleasure: a commodity, a (sub-)culture

New, spectacular, artificial spaces—highly capitalized—day at the races, soccer game, picnic, boating party, bicycling in country.

Space of pleasure now institutionalized

. . .

4/12/80

An essay w[ith]o[ut] ideas: description, + modulations of description

The masculinization of homosexuality—h's no longer alienated; no longer identify with culture (against nature). Being h. no longer facilitates a critical attitude to society. Now h's affirm some of the worst, + most conventional, tastes of this society: sexism (hatred of women), consumerism, brutality, promiscuity, emotional dissociation. Not alienated but (self-ghettoized). The notion that good experience is extreme experience. Hence, drugs are *necessary*. How else could one disco for 8 hours or practice sexual abominations which are so painful.

Woolf, *Diary* (April 19, 1925): "The pale star of the Bugger has been in the ascendant too long."

And Sartre! [*He had died on April 15.*]

. . .

4/25/80

. . .

Photography as enlightenment, de-mystification, hallucination. Both.

Joseph:
Under Stalin: not censorship but blackout.
The boot of the state on the brake, slowing the "progress" of literature—to decorate this break.
Count von Metternich on reading a poem of Heine: "Excellent. Confiscate all copies immediately."
Traditional choice—setting your mnemonic apparatus in motion—+ you can never shut it down again.

•

[The following entries are undated but were clearly written in April or May of 1980, when SS was working on her Canetti essay.]

[*A box is drawn around this:*] Strippings

(In a notebook, save the strippings from stories + essays)

He was an architect, now he's a "store planner."

. . .

"I'm not brave. It's just that I don't let being afraid keep me from doing the things I wasn't afraid to do."

•

[The following is titled "A Marriage" and SS drew a box around the title. It appears to be an undated account of her marriage to Philip Rieff.]

Madness is his legacy. Of course I didn't know that when I married him. He was pitched high in my expectations. A hundred archaic longings stupefied me. I was young. The oily aromatic atoms of youth hid his bony face.

When you took your shirt off, I was shocked at [*SS wrote the alternative words "upset by"*] the roll of fat at your waist. Trembling as I put my arms around you. It was like hugging the floor.

The temptation of the spirit is a terrible thing. Pride, lust repressed. The contempt for instinct. Easy to feel superior to the others. They're not as pure as we.

Our marriage, our holy marriage. Everyone is unfaithful. So we won't be.

But we *were* pure.

You looked so much older than me. I was embarrassed by that.

Acidly observing the decline of everything—manners, language. Vulgar TV programs. Children who talk back to [*alternative: "sass"*] their parents. Students who write "it's" for "its."

•

The sexual sordidness + cynicism of French in the 19th century (Flaubert, Goncourt Bro[ther]s)—the stupidity + provinciality of English—the savagery + sufferings of Russia

. . .

German culture is the highest expression of Western culture . . . (so they didn't have liberal political institutions)

The task of art is formulated by *philosophy* in Germany. That's why all German art leads to Wagner. Nothing is *big enough* >>> They were the most advanced, the deepest culture in Europe (philosophy, scholarship + music)

Moral felon
Emotional felon

•

The aphorist's favorite subject: himself
Notebook writer's

Lichtenberg not actively misogynistic

•

. . .

[*On Canetti:*] Pre-War: Three Upton Sinclair translations (1930 & 1932—age 25 and 27); then *Auto-da-Fé* (1935); he was thirty!—then an essay on Broch (1936), he was 31; it was delivered as a speech. Says that writer is (1) original; (2) sums up age; (3) stands against his time. Ends: writer wants to breathe.

Canetti is both the writer who denies the last 150 years of thinking—as he denies history—the prototypical European intellectual of the old school. Within this curious body of work lie—both hidden + exposed—all the problems of consciousness.

"Le grand absent" is history

[*A box is drawn around this:*] Mind as Passion: Notes on Canetti Each section has equal weight therefore note form is logical

. . .

When asked, Duchamp used to say that he did nothing, that he was just a breather.

C[anetti] is a survivor,

Duchamp's idea: totally liberated man—he no longer needed to have a career, to build a reputation, to gather power . . .

The ultimate crowd is the crowd of one's thoughts. As there are fast + slow crowds, there are fast + slow thoughts.

4/26/80

The Canetti essay is about admiration . . .

The love of books. My library is an archive of longings.

Watch out for incorrect use of "presently" + "hopefully"

Two ideas—"the idea of the artistic vocation, of the artist who has renounced worldly ambitions in order to dedicate himself / herself to values that cannot be realized by commercial society" and the idea of cultural or artistic iconoclasm, the artist's alienation from society, art as transgression, adversary art, avant-garde—these have been conflated. Both seem irrelevant or unreal to most artists now.
But are scorned by art critics. But they're not the same.

Old notes (1960s) I just found:
California is the America of America
Morality = reliability

. . .

Essay: (?)
The Aphorism. The Fragment—all of these are "notebookthinking"; are produced by the idea of keeping a notebook.

One could trace history of thought / art in relation to the forms of transcription: letter manuscript notebook.

The notebook has become an art form (Rilke, Lizzie's book [*Sleepless Nights*]), a thought-form (Barthes), even a philosophical form (Lichtenberg, Nietzsche, Wittgenstein, Cioran, Canetti).

Decline of the letter, the rise of the notebook! One doesn't write to others any more; one writes to oneself.

Why? Parsimony? Don't squander one's pretty phrases, one's wisdom on someone else—a distant recipient who may not have the courtesy to save the letter.

Save it for yourself!

Hoarding ideas.

The *persona* of a notebook is different. More insolent (let's not think about the whiners!)

Aphorism. Aphorism features aristocratic pessimism [*In the margin:*] scorn, cool. Alt[ernative]: Aphorism features pessimism and rapidity.

[Canetti's] aphorisms are concentrated thought.

[*In the margin:*] Reading Canetti recalls Montaigne, Gracian, Chamfort, Lichtenberg, and (among contemporaries) Cioran—the same wisdom, essentially: a wisdom of pessimism.

Aphorisms are rogue ideas.

Aphorism is aristocratic thinking: this is all the aristocrat is willing to tell you; he thinks you should get it fast, without spelling out all the details. Aphoristic thinking constructs thinking as an obstacle race: the reader is expected to get it fast, and move on. An aphorism is not an argument; it is too well-bred for that.

To write aphorisms is to assume a mask—a mask of scorn, of superiority. Which, in one great tradition, conceals (shapes) the aphorist's secret pursuit of spiritual salvation. The *para-*

doxes of salvation. We know at the end, when the aphorist's amoral, light point-of-view self-destructs.

Example: Gracian, who concludes his book on the courtier by observing that the courtier must, logically, be a saint; or Wilde, whose brilliance seems much of the time to be Nietzsche minus the tragic sense, ends with the wretched mortifying wisdom of *De Profundis*.

4/29/80

The quotation < > the trip
Silence
The three ideas with which I have the world.
Each one needs the other two.
I can't replace one without changing the other two.

[*In the margin:*] *Trip to Hanoi*, "Unguided Tour," "Project for a Trip to China," "Debriefing"

Fictions constructed out of quotations—

The world perceived as an anthology of quotations (the essays on photography)

Stories that end with an affirmation of silence [—] "Dr. Jekyll," and *The Benefactor*

[*In the margin:*] *Death Kit* ends with a vision of death as a museum of quotations. Theme of quotation in the essays on Godard + Benjamin, + in "Project for a Trip to China"

Quotation, for me, is my continuation of the idea of "the fragment"—the first discovery of the modernist sensibility {Schlegel brothers [*August and Friedrich*], Novalis}

In Russia, people wait for the poet to have the last word. (Nowhere does literature matter so much.)

"No, tell me first," said the Hungarian exile, "between truth
    and justice which would you choose?"
"Truth."
"Right," he said.
Tout est là ["*It's all there*"]

One *must* oppose communism: it asks us to lie—the sacrifice of the intellect (and the freedom to create) in the name of justice. (And, finally, order.) Think of [*the Russian novelist and, having become an apologist for Stalin, publicist Ilya*] Ehrenburg, who knowingly sacrificed his talent.

Communism means the creation of a much more oppressive bureaucracy than capitalism.

There is no such thing as communism. Only national socialism.— That's what won. (Nationalism the most imp[ressive] political force of the 20th C.). The fascist language was defeated—the communist language survived, + became the rhetoric (+ the flag of convenience) of most new nationalisms, ex-colonialized peoples.

Hitler lost. But national socialism—small n, small s—won.

You can't become English, French, German; you are . . . But you become an American.
An invented, not a natural country.

A country in which every relation is a contract, including familyship, and may, at the displeasure of either of the participants, be broken. Indeed, should be.

[*The contemporary American satiric essayist*] Fran Lebowitz's mother: "But everything you say is a promise." The Jewish-Protestant view.

In Italy, a promise is no more than a plan, a statement of intention. It's understood that one can change one's mind.

4/30/80

An enthusiast modernist? An involuntary modernist?

Symbolist novel: examination of the inside of a fantasy

The first thing to understand is that Americans have never suffered. That they don't know about suffering. (Me last night at dinner [with] Heberto + Belkis Padilla [*the exiled Cuban poet and his wife*].

Making lists of words, to thicken my active vocabulary. To have puny, not just little, hoax, not just trick, mortifying, not just embarrassing, bogus, not just fake.

I could make a story out of puny, hoax, mortifying, bogus. They *are* a story.

5/2/80

Story about a poet (Joseph!) so much less, morally, than his work

Joseph defending the Shah [of Iran], and torture, yesterday at lunch (The Silver Palace [*a New York Chinese restaurant where SS and Brodsky ate often*]) w[ith] Stephen + Natasha [Spender], and David. And now I re-read [*Brodsky's poem*] "Lullaby of Cape Cod."

. . .

5/6/80

Yes, an essay on aphoristic thinking! Another ending, wrapping up. "Notes on Notes."

With the (1943) epigraph of Canetti. "The great writers of aphorisms read as if they had all known each other very well."

One wonders why. Can it be that the literature of aphorisms teaches us the sameness of wisdom (as anthropology teaches us the diversity of culture)? The wisdom of pessimism. Or should we rather conclude that the form of the aphorism, of abbreviated or condensed or rogue thought, is a historically-colored voice which, when adopted, inevitably suggests certain attitudes; is the vehicle of a common thematics?

The traditional thematics of the aphorist: the hypocrises of societies, the vanities of human wishes, the shallowness + deviousness of women; the sham of love; the pleasures (and necessity) of solitude; + the intricacies of one's own thought processes.

All the great aphorists struggle to assume the burden of pessimism, of disillusionment—some with more mildness (less ferocity) than others.

All note the mendacities + hypocrises of social life. And many of the great aphorists (Chamfort, Kraus) are not just condescending to but contemptuous of women; many are fascinated by their own mental processes + mental process in general (Lichtenberg, Wittgenstein).

[*In the margin:*] Taste for paradox, hyperbole

Aphoristic thinking is impatient thinking: by its very brevity or concentratedness, it presupposes a superior standard ...

The characteristic arrogance of aphoristic thinking. A pose? A spur?

. . .

... The most notable exception (to the fact that most of the great aphorists have been pessimists), Lichtenberg, [who] followed English rather than European models of scorn for human folly: he regarded himself as an adopted Englishman, and declared common sense, which he considered characteristically English, as the mind's greatest virtue.

[*In the margin:*] The English are cooler (Wilde, Auden)

[*In the margin:*] The aphorist's favorite subject: himself; Lichtenberg not actively misogynistic.

Another exception among the great aphorists is [*the Mauritian writer and painter* Malcolm de] Chazal—neither optimistic not pessimistic. Because he is a naturalist.

Canetti shares in the scorn for human folly of the main European tradition—the misanthropy, and misogyny, endemic to the aphoristic tradition.

Aphorism is generally regarded as a product of detachment, a kind of superciliousness of the mind. In Canetti, as in Cioran, aphorism is the skill (product) appropriate to the over-passionate mind of the eternal student.

Montaigne, who created the modern essay—also an aphorist?

. . .

The writing doctors . . .

5/9/80

Nijinsky was not an intellectual. He was an idea. ([*The American ballet critic*] A. [*Arlene*] Croce)
Canetti essay—it's a piece of fiction about "Canetti"—my Kien [*the tragic hero of Canetti's* Auto-da-Fé]. In *that* sense, about me.

The only review of *Under the Sign of Saturn* would be the eighth essay—an essay describing me as I have described them. The pathos of intellectual avidity, the collector (mind as every-thing), melancholy & history, arbitrating the moral claim versus aestheticism, and so forth. The intellectual as an impossible project.

If there is a unifying theme of my work it is naïve. The theme of moral seriousness, of passionateness. A mood, a tone.

I must give up writing essays because that inevitably becomes a demagogic activity. I seem to be the bearer of certainties that I *don't* possess—am not near to possessing.

5/18/80

Warsaw smells like an English city in the 50s. Coal—

Jarek [*Anders—SS's Polish translator, friend, and, during this trip to Poland, guide to the city*]: "The rule in a country like Poland is, 'Never trust someone who has power' "—

"The USSR is not the case of a revolution that failed, but of a totalitarian revolution that succeeded."

Two of the richest men in Poland—millionaires—are [*the filmmaker Andrzej*] Wajda + [*the conductor and composer Krzysztof*] Penderecki. (And [Stanisław] Lem.)

[*The Polish poet Zbigniew*] Herbert lives in W. Berlin / [*the Polish poet Czesław*] Miłosz in Berkeley

Jarek's defense of the Catholic Church. "Don't you think it stands for something universal? For moral values?"

The Soviet-built "Palace of Culture + Science"—built 1956—wedding-cake—Stalin's name incised on top is blocked-out by a sign that repeats "Palace of Culture + Science."

[*In the margin:*] A version: misunderstanding of the Empire State Building. (Another one: Moscow University.)

Jarek: "Don't you think America is the only hope of the world?"

Book illustrations + paintings of Edward Okun (1872–1945), Beardsley-ite

There are no Communists in Poland, but there are lots of policemen. No one argues about Marxist revisionism any more.

. . .

There was a pogrom in Kielce in Poland in 1946.

Jarek speaks unaffectedly of "Poland the Brave"

Pyotr talking about [*the literary critic Artur*] Sandauer, "the official Jew" in the government—who takes credit for the rediscovery of [Bruno] Schulz, but it's not true.

5/20/80   Casimierez [*Kazimierz, a district in Kraków*]

. . . The absolute absence of paradox in Tolstoy. (I am rereading *War and Peace*.)

Ashbery [*the American poet John Ashbery, who was part of the group of writers with whom SS traveled to Poland*]: "The privacy of my poetry is not a personal privacy. It is an exemplary privacy."
". . . Poems going in and out of focus."

An essay on Poland: begin with description of Polish plain, a country lacking natural boundaries. Then quote [Witold] Gombrowicz (*Testament*): a country (people) destined to inferiority.

Kraków: trams, avant-garde theatre, pollution, old city, tourists—More "conservative" than Warsaw. Wojtyła's [Pope John Paul II] seat for 25 years.

Talk on my work . . .

Literary Cubism > being in many times + many places, voices
Principle of inventory [/] quotation

. . .

It is Flaubert who (first?) said: "Nothing is boring if you look at it long enough." A century before Cage.

6/29/80   Paris

Dinner with Cioran: "I discovered that among leftists one was not allowed to be cynical." Explaining why, even when he was young—in the 1930s—he was not tempted by Communism.

On Italy: "It's paradise there. One can assassinate. One can leave the country."

. . .

If this society didn't furnish so many fantasies of violence, so many wouldn't be so interested in s-m. True??

Novel as freedom: the only rules it can violate are internal—rules of its own making.

. . .

[In the margin:] Sex instinct subject to idiosyncratic linkages (fetishisms, etc.) because not policed—no instruction, no rules. Think how extensively gender roles are policed.

. . .

Surrealism: antipathy to everyday life + sentimental ideas about love + solitude

Meta-lesbianism of mid-19th century, cultivated Boston spinsters. Olive Chancellor [*character in Henry James's* The Bostonians], etc.

. . .

Story about Joseph: "Vox Clamantis"

"What is the ethical import of all this elegant prancing?" asks Irving Howe, recent convert to Balanchine— + then replies, "there are kinds of beauty before which the moral imagination ought to withdraw."
     Bravo.
     Compare another Jew's moralism. [*The American ballet impresario and writer*] Lincoln Kirstein: "Ballet is about how to behave."

. . .

7/23/80

Life of art > the after-life of art (e.g. Venus de Milo, broken)

7/30/80

Derision, not piety

. . .

[*Highlighted:*] Great subject the West falling out of love with Communism. End of a 200-year-passion.